U.S. POLICY AND THE FUTURE OF THE UNITED NATIONS

A TWENTIETH CENTURY FUND BOOK

U.S. POLICY AND THE FUTURE OF THE UNITED NATIONS

Edited by
Roger A. Coate

The Twentieth Century Fund Press ◆ New York ◆ 1994

The Twentieth Century Fund sponsors and supervises timely analyses of economic policy, foreign affairs, and domestic political issues. Not-for-profit and nonpartisan, the Fund was founded in 1919 and endowed by Edward A. Filene.

Library of Congress Cataloging-in-Publication Data

U.S. Policy and the future of the United Nations / edited by Roger A. Coate.
        p.   cm.
    Includes bibliographical references and index.
    ISBN 0–87078–175–8 : $14.95
    1. United Nations. 2. United Nations--United States. I. Coate, Roger A.
II. Title: U.S. policy and the future of the United Nations.
JX1977.U13   1994
341.23--dc20   94–2843
                                                               CIP

Cover Design and Illustration: Claude Goodwin
Manufactured in the United States of America.

FOREWORD

*I*t would not be altogether fanciful, even though it might seem somewhat cruel, to assert that for several decades the manifest weaknesses of the United Nations were tolerated because the organization was considered somewhat irrelevant to the central struggles of the cold war. Given the restraints imposed by the rigidities of a bipolar world, the UN was shielded from responsibility for dealing with many vexing and dangerous situations. The consequences of this exemption from political accountability were most obvious in the uneven performance of the so-called specialized agencies, including, most visibly, the United Nations Educational, Scientific and Cultural Organization and the Food and Agriculture Organization.

Today, of course, the United Nations and other international organizations have a place center stage. As the shadow cast by the threat of thermonuclear war has receded, other dangers have been revealed, such as ugly patches of sectarian violence and arms proliferation. In the new environment, the United Nations has taken on fresh responsibilities. In the fall of 1993, for example, 75,105 UN peacekeepers were deployed in seventy-two countries. There also are intensified pressures on the United Nations to work on solutions to the social and economic problems that underlie conflicts. The specialized agencies have come under growing pressure from member states to reform their operations and improve their performance. It is hard to imagine, however, that the United Nations can fulfill these demanding missions without significant reform of its structure and organization.

With these issues in mind, in late May 1993, the Twentieth Century Fund and Wilton Park cosponsored a weeklong conference on the United Nations. A year earlier, we collaborated on a successful session exploring the process of building free economies and free societies in East-Central Europe. The May meeting, entitled "The United Nations: A New Role in a New World Order?" was hosted by Wilton Park at their Wiston House conference center in West Sussex, England. Some eighty scholars, diplomats, and UN officials from around the world attended. The essays in this volume were first presented at that conference. They address such issues as the problems and unfulfilled promise of the specialized and functional agencies, focusing on the potential for reforming their staffing, management, financing, program integration, and organization.

The Fund has sponsored several recent works examining multilateral politics and institutions, including Max Jakobson's *The United Nations in the 1990s: A Second Chance?* and Viron P. Vaky's and Heraldo Muñoz's essays in *The Future of the Organization of American States*. Gil Loescher's *Beyond Charity*, published this year, analyzes the global refugee crisis, and Rosemary Righter is completing a study of the United Nations' problems during and beyond the cold war.

The authors whose essays appear in this volume believe that the United Nations is vital to the maintenance of global peace and security. Furthermore, they agree that the world body cannot fulfill its promise without substantial reform and certainly not without dynamic U.S. leadership. The prescriptions that they offer merit serious attention from those who must lead the search for multilateral solutions to global problems. On behalf of the Trustees of the Twentieth Century Fund, I thank them for their contribution to the debate about how to improve the performance and the effectiveness of the United Nations. I also express the Fund's continuing appreciation to the staff and management of Wilton Park for hosting the conference and leading the sessions. Like the authors of this volume, they have been excellent partners.

Richard C. Leone, *President*
The Twentieth Century Fund
January 1994

PREFACE AND ACKNOWLEDGMENTS

The United Nations project of which this volume is a part had its genesis in early spring 1991 when Morris B. Abram, a member of the Twentieth Century Fund Board of Trustees who was then serving as U.S. permanent representative to the United Nations in Geneva, proposed the idea to the Fund. Ambassador Abram pointed out that in the wake of the collapse of the Soviet empire a unique opportunity existed for making the United Nations system work as its founders had originally envisioned. He suggested that key to capitalizing on this opportunity, however, was the reassertion of U.S. leadership in multilateral affairs with a view to strengthening and protecting liberal economic and democratic values and institutions. The Board of Trustees and Fund president Richard C. Leone recognized the need for a reexamination of the United Nations, and so this project was born.

The essays presented here are all original and represent a collective enterprise that took definite form during the weeklong conference "The United Nations: A New Role in a New World Order?" cosponsored by the Fund and Wilton Park. In this context, the authors would like to thank Richard Leone, Morris Abram, and the Board of Trustees of the Twentieth Century Fund, especially its chairman, as well as Geoffrey Denton, Nicholas Hopkinson, and Ray Raymond of Wilton Park for providing this exceptional opportunity. Also, special thanks are due Fund vice president Beverly Goldberg, assistant vice president Jason Renker, and associate program officer Matthew Leish for their assistance during the editorial process. Finally, and perhaps most importantly, we would like to thank Harry Ozeroff, program officer at the Fund, who worked tirelessly throughout the planning, editorial, and production stages of the project. His efforts were instrumental in producing this volume.

Roger A. Coate
January 1994

CONTENTS

PART I

CHALLENGES FOR THE
TWENTY-FIRST CENTURY

≈1≈

THE FUTURE OF THE UNITED NATIONS

ROGER A. COATE

*T*he United Nations has been given a second chance. The organization, frequently paralyzed by cold war rivalry, has been granted another opportunity to rise to the challenge of saving "succeeding generations from the scourge of war." Events in Bosnia and Somalia make it clear that someone must take on the role of "maintaining international peace and security." The increasing reluctance of the United States, the world's remaining superpower, to play world policeman underscores the need for collective action to solve global problems. The question is, Can the United Nations fulfill its original promise? The contributors to this volume argue that it can—but not without reform, and certainly not without U.S. leadership.

The need for an effective United Nations is real. Many of the most pressing threats to peace and prosperity are problems that national governments are ill-equipped to deal with on their own. Multilateral policies, requiring the participation and the resources of the international community of states as well as, increasingly, the global community of nongovernmental actors, offer the best possible response to these threats. If the United Nations is to serve effectively as the international community's tool for solving these problems, it will have to become a stronger and more efficient body, and that will require, in turn, a greater level of consensus among member states about the threats to global security and a greater willingness to commit the resources needed to meet those threats.

This volume is a guidebook for those who want to understand the complexities of a world that has been transformed over the past decade, a world in which the interests of the United States often are indistinct, and where the United Nations is playing an increasingly important but rather ambiguous role. In the following pages, nine leading experts on the United Nations from the worlds of academia, policy analysis, and diplomacy examine various areas of UN activity. Their essays revolve around three common themes: the challenges faced by the United Nations in the emerging post-cold war world; the constraints that the United Nations must overcome to meet those challenges and achieve its diverse mandates; and the major issues that will confront U.S. policymakers in the years ahead. They also provide recommendations for future U.S. policies toward the United Nations.

HISTORIC PERSPECTIVE

Nearly half a century ago, the vision and leadership of the United States were instrumental in forging a new world order premised on democratic values and liberal economic institutions. The United Nations was created to serve as a building block of that order, one that sought to end war and ensure global peace and security. Unfortunately, the United Nations fell victim to several problems that have frustrated its efforts to fulfill that mandate. The rapid onset of the cold war and the obstructionism of the superpowers combined to limit the UN's effectiveness. At the same time, the decolonization that followed World War II brought a swift expansion of the organization's membership. In 1945, fifty-one states signed the UN Charter; today, there are more than three times that number of members. The introduction of the cold war into the Third World, with superpower competition for allies among the new states and the unprincipled manipulation of the Third World majority by the USSR, further eroded the UN's effectiveness. When the internal weaknesses that have beset the United Nations since its establishment are added to these problems, the reasons for the organization's failure to fulfill its mandate become clearer. Now, as we approach the fiftieth anniversary of the United Nations in 1995, the international community has been presented with an opportunity to reform the United Nations to eliminate the systemic weaknesses that have kept it from achieving its goals.

The United States has provided leadership in building collective solutions to common global problems for the past seventy-five years. Nevertheless, the history of U.S. leadership in this area is not without some blemishes. The United States was the guiding force behind the creation of the League of Nations, but the isolationist sentiments of the

1920s and 1930s led it to refuse membership in the League. After World War II, U.S. leadership was indispensable for the construction of the United Nations, and throughout its formative years the United States nurtured the immature and untested organization. However, faced with a Third World majority in the General Assembly that had grown increasingly hostile since the 1960s, the United States began to retreat from active engagement in the United Nations during the 1980s. During this period, the rhetoric and actions of the United States repudiated the internationalist traditions of American diplomacy.

The gaps in U.S. leadership stem from the traditional disagreements that exist within U.S. foreign policy circles between nationalists and internationalists over the utility of multilateralism and the United Nations. These contending viewpoints were echoed recently in the report of the United States Commission on Improving the Effectiveness of the United Nations.[1] In the report, *Defining Purpose: The U.N. and the Health of Nations*, the commission's conservative members favor a more nationalist U.S. foreign policy, arguing that the United Nations is controlled by a dictatorial, authoritarian, and statist majority, and therefore can only rarely become a useful part of U.S. foreign policy. On the other hand, the commission's liberal members call for an internationalist foreign policy, arguing that the limits of American power and the reach of U.S. interests make collective problem-solving through the United Nations an indispensable instrument of U.S. policy. Since U.S. leadership will be required to revitalize the United Nations, the United States cannot return to its isolationist past. Unfortunately, the legacy of the Reagan era and the eternal contention between the proponents and the opponents of multilateralism have bequeathed to the current administration a weak foundation on which to rebuild U.S. leadership. The question that emerges is, Is Washington up to the challenge?

THE CHALLENGES FACING THE UNITED NATIONS

The maintenance of international peace and security is the principal mandate of the United Nations—and its greatest challenge. The United Nations will be judged by how well it fulfills this goal. It is, however, important to remember that the organization was created to maintain peace not only by preventing and resolving military conflict, but also by promoting "economic and social progress and development." With the end of the cold war, the principal long-term threats to global peace are more likely to arise from economic and social distress than from strategic rivalry.

Today, although the liberal democratic and economic values of the West have prevailed over fascism and communism, long-repressed forces of ethnic identity, religious fundamentalism, and militant nationalism threaten to destroy peace at flashpoints around the world. As illustrated by instances of communal violence in the Balkans, Africa, and the republics of the former Soviet Union, these forces have an enormous potential to foster civil and international conflict. Indeed, direct military confrontation remains the most immediate threat to global peace and security.

PEACEKEEPING

Not surprisingly, the peacekeeping activities of the United Nations have grown considerably in response to the recent immediate threats. Over the past five years, for instance, the Security Council has authorized as many peacekeeping missions as it did throughout the previous forty years. The yearly number of UN peacekeeping operations has doubled to eighteen since 1991, placing just over 75,000 peacekeepers under the blue flag of the United Nations. And the costs of peacekeeping have risen with the commitments: while a year's peacekeeping expenditures amounted to $700 million in 1991, they approached the $4 billion mark in 1993.[2]

It is important to remember that, in addition to the change in magnitude, the nature of UN peacekeeping activities also has changed substantially in the post-cold war era. Entirely new challenges, such as providing humanitarian assistance during internal wars, have forced the organization to assume a "peacemaking" role. However, rather than establishing the principles behind this new peacemaking role, the United Nations has merely expanded its traditional "peacekeeping" operations. Traditional UN peacekeeping missions, such as those in Lebanon, Cyprus, or the recent Cambodian operation, consist of unarmed or lightly armed blue helmets patrolling demilitarized zones in regions where, due to the agreement of all sides, there is a genuine peace to be kept. Between 1948 and 1988, the UN launched thirteen such missions.

The successful UN response to Iraqi aggression in the Persian Gulf War illustrates the "warmaking" role of the United Nations, also exemplified by the Korean War, rather than the typical conflict that confronts the organization today. In its warmaking role, the United Nations collectively backs the victim or victims of an aggressor state. Like peacekeeping, the principles behind the UN's warmaking role have been established and are clearly understood. Unfortunately, the principals underlying the UN's peacemaking role have yet to be clearly defined. The failure of several current UN operations, such as those in Bosnia and Somalia, reveals that the peacekeeping and warmaking methods devised during the cold war are grossly inadequate for the peacemaking role that has been thrust upon the organization. In response to wholly new security challenges, such as providing humanitarian assistance during internal conflicts, the United Nations has merely expanded its traditional peacekeeping operations. While the successful UN response to Iraqi aggression in the Persian Gulf War raised the organization's credibility, that conflict exemplifies the traditional UN collective security function epitomized by the Korean War rather than the typical situations that confront the United Nations today. The failure of several current UN operations reveals that the peacekeeping apparatus constructed during the cold war is now grossly inadequate.

For the United Nations to respond effectively to the collective security challenges of the emerging era, the organization will need to outline clearly the conditions under which it would initiate new peacekeeping operations. The United Nations cannot resolve every conflict, and therefore it cannot afford—either politically or financially—to undertake missions that have only a limited chance for success.

A number of recent operations illustrate both the challenges and the limits of UN peacekeeping activities. The case of Cambodia is an illustration of the continuing relevance of traditional peacekeeping operations. In Cambodia, traditional peacekeeping fostered the process of national reconciliation by deterring a resumption of conflict. However, the Cambodian case also illustrates the substantial challenges facing the organization in the area of nation-building. While the UN operation in Cambodia was able successfully to monitor and enforce a cease-fire, repatriate significant numbers of refugees, and hold national elections, it was less successful in creating new governing institutions in that country.

The United Nations has had rather limited success in dealing with ethnic, religious, and nationalist conflicts, such as those in the former Yugoslavia. UN peacekeeping forces in Bosnia have been left to provide humanitarian assistance rather than attempting to restrain the combatants, and therefore the organization has been unjustly criticized for policies that are perceived as sanctioning "ethnic cleansing" and aiding in the slaughter of civilians. However, the failure to stop the bloodshed is due not to the United Nations, but to the fact that governments, and especially European governments, are unwilling to pay the price in lives and treasure required to end those conflicts.

The UN intervention in Somalia provides yet another example of the challenges that the United Nations confronts when dealing with internal conflict. In that country, the efforts of the United Nations to separate warring clans and to build new civil institutions have illuminated the organization's weaknesses in this area. Likewise, attempts to resolve the civil war in Angola and the strife in Haiti have broken down during the past year; Angolans have resumed the bloody conflict that has devastated their country, and the Haitian military and the police have returned to their former defiance of the United Nations and the Organization of American States, making a peaceful settlement of that nation's troubles only a remote possibility.

The difficulties encountered by the United Nations in dealing with conflicts such as those in the former Yugoslavia and in Somalia illustrate a significant challenge facing the organization. The United Nations and the permanent members of the Security Council must redefine the role of the major powers in UN peacekeeping operations. The Clinton administration recently completed a comprehensive review of U.S. peacekeeping policy (Policy Review Document 13) that called for a new commitment from the United States to UN peacekeeping operations and went as far as endorsing the placement of American troops under UN command.[3] In his September 1993 speech to the General Assembly, however, President Clinton sounded a more cautious note when he called on the United Nations to recognize its own limitations and use more discretion when responding to new conflicts.

The United Nations, now involved in more peacekeeping operations than ever before, also must create an effective institutional capacity to plan, organize, carry out, and lead complex military operations. Currently, the organization continues to manage its peacekeeping activities as if they were infrequent responses to exceptional situations; indeed, it was only recently that the United Nations established a full-time peacekeeping operations center within the Secretariat in New York City. While it has begun to make minor improvements in this area, more sweeping changes will be necessary before it can adequately manage its peacekeeping operations.

PREVENTIVE DIPLOMACY

As with any other disease, the best way to lessen the death and destruction caused by war is through prevention. Consequently, the United Nations must confront the challenge of anticipating and reacting to potential conflicts before they turn violent. This primarily involves enhancing UN capacities and effectiveness in early warning and preventive diplomacy, in controlling the sale of conventional military hardware, and in stopping the spread of chemical, biological, and nuclear weapons.

Conventional armaments pose an ever greater threat to regional peace and security as they become more and more destructive and easier to obtain, operate, and maintain. Institutions like the UN Disarmament Committee in Geneva will play an increasingly indispensable role in global efforts to reduce the threat from conventional warfare. In addition, the clandestine attempts of North Korea, Iran, and Saddam Hussein's Iraq to develop nuclear weapons illustrate the long-term threat posed by nuclear proliferation. The International Atomic Energy Agency (IAEA) has, particularly following the Persian Gulf War, begun to play an assertive linchpin role in global efforts to protect against the proliferation of nuclear weapons. But perhaps most important is the UN role in negotiating and legitimizing arms control initiatives such as the Non-Proliferation Treaty, the Biological and the Chemical Weapons Convention, or a future Comprehensive Test Ban treaty as endorsed by President Clinton in his September 1993 speech to the General Assembly.

MEETING SOCIAL AND ECONOMIC NEEDS

Enduring global security requires social and economic conditions that can be a basis for peace. Today, the conditions needed to sustain democracy and market economies are endangered by a growing multitude of interdependent and seemingly unsolvable social and economic problems that stem from the human suffering caused by poverty, hunger, disease, and the denial of basic human rights.

The development of impoverished regions and the sustained prosperity of the industrialized countries are fundamental prerequisites for global peace and security. Three decades of economic aid, however, have done relatively little to improve standards of living in the world's poorest countries. As a result, the conflict between the industrialized and the developing worlds, which subsided during the 1980s after the diplomatic strife of the previous decade, is reemerging as the poverty and inequality that gave birth to that conflict continue to grow. The revival of the North-South conflict in the United Nations will increasingly challenge the capacity of member states to forge effective responses to the problem of underdevelopment.

The long-term sustainability of economic prosperity in the advanced industrialized world and the creation of growth in the underdeveloped world are dependent on a sound global economy. Building the basic social and economic infrastructures that are an integral part of development therefore will continue to be an important component of UN activities. To achieve these goals, the institutions comprising the

UN system will have to become more effective, the work of those organizations will need to be integrated and rationalized, and the massive
waste and inefficiency that characterize the system will have to be
reduced. In addition, UN organizations will need to work in greater
harmony with the International Monetary Fund, the World Bank, and
other multilateral financial institutions to ensure that international economic policies do not adversely impact the infrastructures that are a
prerequisite for development.

Within the exceedingly complex, dynamic, and continuously evolving global economy, the developed countries are encountering the difficult transition from highly centralized, manufacturing-based economies
to more decentralized service economies based on the processing of
information. While the United States and other advanced industrial societies undergo the transition to this "information age," the vast majority
of the world's people will continue to struggle through quite different
transitions to new economic and political structures. The programs of the
UN system must address not only these two widely divergent worlds, but,
more importantly, they must endeavor to bridge the gap between them.

The United Nations also faces the challenges posed by a broad
range of serious and expanding humanitarian concerns that result from
war, famine, disease, natural disasters, and the violation of civil and
political rights. The United Nations has encountered substantial problems in attempting to respond to emergencies such as refugee flows,
disaster relief, the preservation of human rights, and the global AIDS
epidemic. During his first year in office, Secretary-General Boutros-
Ghali created a new Department of Humanitarian Affairs (DHA) to
overcome the fragmented nature of the organization's previous responses to these crises. Unfortunately, the new department, which was
charged with undertaking system-wide planning for UN responses to
major emergencies, has not yet lived up to its mandate, severely limiting the organization's effectiveness.

The civil conflicts produced by social and economic distress present
vital security problems. The communal conflicts in Bosnia, Somalia,
and parts of the former Soviet Union are, at their core, outrageous violations of human rights. These situations illustrate how the forced displacement of peoples, the environmental damage caused by refugee
flows, and the famines induced by civil war impact the international
community, and they have forced the members of the United Nations to
rethink the entire notion of humanitarian assistance.

The United Nations has intervened in the internal affairs of member states to provide aid to civilian populations in Somalia and Iraq.
The difficulties it encountered in these cases illustrate the problems

inherent in dealing with internal conflicts. For example, UN institutions such as the High Commissioner for Refugees have proved ill-equipped to respond to the internal displacement of peoples. More importantly, as demonstrated in Somalia, the United Nations has a limited capacity to rebuild nations and create the foundations of civil society.

Since its inception, the United Nations has done much to establish international human rights standards, but it has largely failed to implement them. The United Nations must seek to strengthen the observance of these standards by expanding and improving its machinery for monitoring and bringing pressure to bear on those states that violate them.

Any new world order also must provide for the health of the earth's people and its ecosystems. Since health remains the essential foundation of economic growth, development, and international peace, providing decent and humane medical care to the people of the world, and especially the less fortunate, is yet another critical challenge. Moreover, both the developed and the developing countries have done irreversible damage to the environment through economic development. The challenge for the future is immense: we must find ways to provide both a cleaner environment and a sustainable level of economic growth. The 1992 UN Conference on Environment and Development, which was asked to integrate these two aims, was more of a rhetorical than a substantive success, in part due to the obstructionism of the Bush administration. The new UN Commission on Sustainable Development provides some hope of overcoming earlier obstacles in the path of sustainable development. As several authors in this volume assert, the greatest challenges in this area will be to incorporate nongovernmental players into the process of finding solutions.

THE CONSTRAINTS ON UN EFFECTIVENESS

The international community is turning to the United Nations to solve a mounting number of crises, but serious constraints continue to frustrate the efforts of member states to make the UN a more effective tool for solving the world's problems. One theme running through this volume is that the most immediate and significant constraint faced by the United Nations is a lack of adequate financing. The United Nations is being called on to play an increased role in meeting the challenges faced by the international community. As a result, the operational activities of the United Nations have multiplied substantially over the past few years while its regular budget has remained stable. A recent Ford Foundation report noted that the manner in which the United Nations is financed "does not provide the capacity or the flexibility to respond effectively and expeditiously to the many challenges that now confront it." As the report points out, these financing mechanisms "jeopardize the very purposes that the world community asks the U.N. to serve."[4]

The current cost of financing the United Nations is relatively minor when compared with the national budgets of the vast majority of member states. The 1992 UN budget amounted to roughly $5.2 billion,[5] which is less than the budget of New York City. In addition, the UN spent approximately $1.4 billion on peacekeeping in 1992, while the previous year's military budget of the United States was over $300 billion. In 1991, member states invested an average of $1.40 in UN peacekeeping activities for every $1,000 that they spent on their own armed forces, and the United States spent over $2,000 on its own military for every dollar that it invested in UN peacekeeping.[6]

The most pressing and important financial issue facing the United Nations involves the failure of many member states and, most importantly, the United States, to pay their legally binding obligations to the organization. As the Ford Foundation report noted, "If all governments paid their assessed contributions in full and on time there would be no serious U.N. financial problem, at least at its present level of operations. Late payments, and failures to pay, gravely debilitate an organization that is not permitted to go into debt. . . ."[7]

The cost of financing the United Nations will almost certainly increase substantially in the future. Faced with many problems that they cannot handle alone, the members of the United Nations have directed the organization to take on new responsibilities. The organization is increasingly in demand for responding to refugee flows and other humanitarian emergencies. And, the requirements of building sustainable development, improving human health, and preserving human rights will lead to additional demands on the United Nations in the years ahead. As the authors in this volume repeatedly stress, these are tasks that can only be undertaken through a global organization such as the United Nations. Over the short term, the effectiveness of the United Nations will be severely constrained if member states continue forcing the organization to spread its inadequate resources across a multitude of assignments.

Adequate financing will not, however, solve all the problems of the United Nations. The organization also is constrained by severe management problems that foster bureaucratic waste, ineptitude, and inertia. A compelling case for reforming UN management was recently made in a report by Richard Thornburgh, the former U.S. Attorney General who briefly served as UN Under Secretary-General for Administration and Management.[8] That report pointed out that pervasive wastefulness and inefficiency, as well as the nonfunctional procedures, positions, and bureaus of the United Nations, undermine confidence in its abilities across the entire range of its activities. Thornburgh has helped to create the impetus for reform, but reform will not be easy. Public and governmental support for increased financing of the United Nations will hinge on a more positive view of the organization and, conversely, the future credibility of the United Nations depends to a large degree on improving the effectiveness of its management, the quality of its staff, and the efficiency of its administration.

The most significant long-term constraint on the effectiveness of the United Nations is the lack of coordination in the UN system. Coordination problems are primarily the result of the ad hoc construction of the UN system around functional areas such as health, agriculture, and telecommunications, which has yielded a decentralized and legally autonomous constellation of organizations. Consequently, the United Nations system is handicapped by a lack of coordination among the many overlapping and competing agencies, committees, and programs that have proliferated over the years.

The Economic and Social Council's (ECOSOC) responsibilities to promote coordination are defined in the UN Charter, and specific bodies such as the Advisory Committee on Administrative and Budgetary Questions, the Administrative Committee on Coordination, and the Committee for Program and Coordination have been created to improve cooperation throughout the UN system. Nevertheless, because of organizational turf battles or a lack of resources, the existing machinery simply has not worked and very little effective coordination actually occurs within the UN system.

The bloated organizational structure of the United Nations has been the target of many efforts at restructuring. There is currently much discussion about reforming the Security Council, the Secretariat, and ECOSOC. When he assumed the leadership of the United Nations at the beginning of 1992, Secretary-General Boutros-Ghali sought to streamline the Secretariat by reducing the number of under and assistant secretaries. These reforms cut the number of under secretary positions from thirty-eight to ten, and reduced the number of assistant secretaries to twenty-six. Unfortunately, these reforms did not go far enough, and some of the benefits derived from them have been nullified by the subsequent creation of additional positions within the Secretariat.

Efforts to reform the United Nations have highlighted the thorny and deeply contested question of what the member states actually want from the UN system. Member governments must arrive at a consensus about their commitment to multilateralism and the resources they will contribute toward providing the United Nations with adequate capabilities. Moreover, a greater consensus is needed among member states over the goals of the United Nations to give UN agencies the signals that will enable them to function efficiently. As long as there is a lack of consensus on these fundamental questions, efforts to reform the UN system are likely to be of little benefit. It is here that clear, coherent, and persistent U.S. leadership in pursuit of a concise reform agenda will be most indispensable.

U.S. POLICY TOWARD THE UNITED NATIONS

The end of the cold war has presented the U.S. government and the American people with a unique opportunity to lead a reform of the UN system. Global peace and security and the vital interests of the American people are inherently linked to building a democratic world order and a liberal global political economy. Multilateral cooperation and burden-sharing represent the most effective way to deal with many of the challenges that threaten domestic security, international stability, and human well-being around the globe.

The history of the U.S. relationship with the United Nations has, however, left a legacy that needs to be carefully considered when promoting U.S. leadership of the United Nations. Leadership means building a following, and leadership within the United Nations requires gaining the support of important member states. In multilateral diplomacy, support is assembled primarily through tolerance for the views and interests of other states, rather than through the promotion of narrow special interests. Support is earned through an acceptance of diversity, rather than by a reliance on ideologically driven parochialism.

The policies that dominated U.S. multilateral diplomacy throughout the 1980s often were ideologically charged or driven by special interests. Those policies left a legacy that cannot be ignored by U.S. policymakers because it will profoundly impact America's future efforts to assume a stronger leadership role in the United Nations. Perhaps most importantly, U.S. officials will have to convince other influential UN member states that they are committed to multilateralism.

When we move beyond general discourse, what becomes clear is the lack of a coherent understanding or consensus about the foreign policy objectives of the United States within the United Nations. There is no agreement over what the United States needs, wants, or should expect to gain from the United Nations. For some time now, the multilateral policies of the United States have been proceeding without coherence or direction, and there is now a real crisis in this area of U.S. foreign policy. Scattered mandates and diverse bureaucratic interests have resulted in fragmented U.S. policies toward the UN system. Thus, while the environment of world politics provides a profusion of challenges to U.S. policy, the internal environment of U.S. policymaking presents yet another challenge in its own right.

ORGANIZATION OF THE BOOK

With local and regional conflicts persisting in many parts of the globe, world attention has been focused in recent years on the peacekeeping activities of the United Nations. As natural disasters, economic decline, and human rights abuses attract more public interest, however, we are beginning to see a greater emphasis on the economic and social dimensions of peace. This volume provides a platform for examining U.S. policy in both of these realms. Because the military aspects of collective security have been addressed in detail by many commentators over the past few years, the volume places somewhat greater emphasis on social and economic issues. Unifying themes are provided by the focus on increasing the effectiveness of the United Nations as well as by an emphasis on the vital role that must be played by the United States.

The chapters in Part I examine the issue of reforming the United Nations system from very different perspectives. In chapter 2, the first of these chapters, Ambassador Ronald I. Spiers, a long-time U.S. diplomat and high-ranking UN civil servant, examines organizational reform from the statesman's perspective, focusing on practical reforms of the United Nations that can be accomplished over the short term. His discussion focuses on four major issue-areas that have been the center of current reform discussions at the United Nations: administrative and management reform of the Secretariat: structural reform of central UN institutions such as the Security Council; reform of the peacekeeping and peacemaking capabilities of the United Nations; and, finally, financial reform.

In chapter 3, Roger A. Coate expands the reform focus to encompass structural changes in the broader system of UN organizations. The chapter takes a more theoretical approach than its predecessor, examining the fundamental requirements for increasing the effectiveness of the UN system through improved interagency coordination. Consequently, the chapter focuses on the need for consensus, commitment, and organizational capacity to enhance effectiveness throughout the UN system. Coate stresses the need for greater coordination at the level of national policymaking institutions, processes, and procedures because

the conflicting goals of different departments within member governments have hampered the effectiveness of the United Nations. The
improved coordination of U.S. policies toward the United Nations and
a commitment to multilateral diplomacy are crucial to improving the
effectiveness of the UN system because of the pivotal role played by
the United States within the organization.

Part II focuses on three clusters of interrelated issue-areas. Military
security issues and institutions are the focus of chapters 4 and 5. In
chapter 4, Barry M. Blechman asks the important question, Has the UN
already failed in its third chance at establishing an effective collective
security system? A former assistant director of the U.S. Arms Control
and Disarmament Agency, Blechman adroitly exposes the internal
workings of the UN collective security system. He brings to light the
strengths and weaknesses of a system that was established during the
cold war to address a relatively small number of international conflicts,
and lucidly explains the challenges that the growing number of quickly developing, often primarily internal conflicts exert on the UN security
system. Basing his arguments on the adage that an ounce of prevention is worth a pound of cure, Blechman offers carefully weighed and
reasoned recommendations for enhancing both the collective security
system itself and Washington's role in international collective security.

In chapter 5, Thomas W. Graham, senior program advisor on international security at the Rockefeller Foundation, examines the role of
the International Atomic Energy Agency (IAEA) in halting the spread of
nuclear weapons. Graham explores the three challenges that face the
IAEA: enforcing measures to ensure that there is no proliferation of
nuclear materials and technologies among the states that are parties to
the Nuclear Non-Proliferation Treaty (NPT); dealing with problem
countries such as Iraq, Iran, and North Korea that seek to gain nuclear
weapons capabilities despite their membership in the NPT; and, making itself a more important part of the post-cold war search for collective
solutions to the broader problem of nuclear proliferation.

Graham argues that the recent refinements in IAEA enforcement
measures have improved its capacity to monitor the activities of NPT
states. More importantly, the IAEA has increased its effectiveness in
dealing with problem states, which is particularly evident in the case of
Iraq. Graham concludes by arguing that the developed and the developing countries should reassess their expectations concerning the IAEA,
as well as the costs and benefits of nuclear technology.

Chapters 6 and 7 focus on human rights and the humanitarian
aspects of global security. In chapter 6, Ambassador Morris B. Abram
draws on his thirty years of involvement with UN human rights

institutions to analyze and make recommendations about future U.S. policy in this critical area. Maintaining the style that won him respect as the Permanent Representative of the United States to the UN Office in Geneva, Abram calls for the United States to stand firm in its unswerving commitment to a universal definition of fundamental human rights that is applicable to all cultures. He asserts that the best approach to this is the improved enforcement of already existing international law with the help of a strengthened Commission on Human Rights. Abram further calls on the U.S. government to use its power boldly to lead efforts to enhance the capacity of the United Nations to promote basic individual rights.

Chapter 7 tackles one of the most complex and volatile issues on the global agenda—refugees. Gil Loescher, a leading academic expert on UN refugee activities, examines the problems that continue to plague UN efforts in this politically sensitive realm. In recent years, refugee movements have severely strained the capabilities of the UN High Commissioner for Refugees (UNHCR). The internal nature of many contemporary conflicts and the particularly challenging issue of protecting persons displaced within their own countries have complicated the provision of humanitarian assistance to refugees. Calling for preventive solutions that address the underlying causes of refugee flows, Loescher emphasizes the interrelationship of refugee problems with other issues on the UN agenda such as collective security and development.

Chapters 8 and 9 focus on selected institutional issues in the social and economic area. Leon Gordenker, a leading scholar of international organizations, closely analyzes the vitality of the World Health Organization (WHO) in chapter 8. Gordenker emphasizes the influence of individuals in specific roles within the agency and challenges readers to consider the impact of leadership as well as the ideological orientation of large donor governments on the effectiveness of WHO. He also considers how the organizational ideology of WHO has molded its programs and led to substantial controversy. Gordenker uncovers fundamental problems with the manner in which WHO responds to global health problems and makes policy recommendations for dealing with deficiencies that have been eroding the effectiveness of this indispensable agency.

Chapter 9 explores the challenges and the constraints facing the new UN Commission on Sustainable Development. Kathryn G. Sessions, a leading analyst of UN affairs, and E. Zell Steever, a former adviser to the U.S. delegation to the Earth Summit, provide the context for building effective U.S. policies in this critical issue-area. Sessions and Steever argue that the traditional conflict between the environment and economic growth is a false dichotomy that has hampered progress on sustainable development by blinding us to the absolute necessity of cooperation in this field. The intense activity surrounding the Earth Summit has given broader acceptance and impetus to the concept of sustainable development. Sessions and Steever discuss the constraints on such a far-reaching reorientation of priorities and offer substantive policy suggestions for U.S. leadership in this area.

In the final chapter of the volume, Ambassador James F. Leonard, the deputy permanent representative of the United States to the United Nations during the Carter administration, provides an overview of U.S. policy toward the United Nations. Seeking to specify priority areas for future U.S. policies toward the organization, Leonard addresses three interrelated questions: What issues *must* be dealt with through the UN? What issues *cannot* be managed effectively through the UN? And, On what issues does the United States have options? To answer these questions, he presents an analysis of possible priorities for U.S. policies and makes recommendations for the exercise of U.S. leadership. Leonard argues that five issue-areas should be of primary U.S. interest: international security, the global economy, the global environment, humanitarian assistance, and human rights.

Drawing on his experience as a diplomat and a policymaker, Leonard argues that international security, narrowly defined, should remain foremost among these priorities and that U.S. leadership is especially required in this area. While pointing out that many issues do not require the leadership of the United States, Leonard also argues that it is nonetheless very important for the United States to participate actively in the development of collective solutions to common global problems. The United States will certainly not get its way on every item on the UN agenda, but it can positively influence the activities of UN organizations and the solutions that they employ to overcome global problems. Moreover, by setting an example of measured concern and effort, U.S. officials can broaden the legitimacy of the United States as a world leader.

$\approx 2 \approx$

REFORMING THE UNITED NATIONS

RONALD I. SPIERS

*T*he United Nations was the "new world order" vision of the victorious powers of the Second World War. Those drafting the UN Charter believed that the alliance that produced victory could continue into the postwar era, thereby ensuring world peace. This was not an unreasonable assumption, but we now know that the cold war and the United Nations were born together as Siamese twins. Happily, the United Nations did not go the way of the League of Nations, but neither did it become the central element of world affairs envisioned by its founders.

Throughout the cold war years, the United Nations was of essentially marginal importance for dealing with the core international issues of war and peace. Issues affecting the security of the major powers were dealt with either bilaterally or through other international institutions—such as NATO, the Warsaw Pact, the G–7, the Bretton Woods institutions, or limited arrangements like arms control agreements that were designed to moderate competition and enhance strategic stability—rather than through the United Nations. During the cold war era, questions about the organization's efficiency, capabilities, and cost-effectiveness were either ignored or considered of little significance by senior foreign policy decisionmakers in the United States. Since the end of the cold war, events in Iraq, Somalia, Cambodia, and Angola demonstrate that our foreign policy can no longer fail to take account of the United Nations.

The United Nations has moved closer to center stage with the end of the cold war and the emergence of new "global issues." These new types of global issues, which include drugs, the environment, refugee flows, and the management of the global commons, are being assigned to the world body. Most importantly, they have as their common element the need for a high level of international collaboration. In addition, the traditional international problems involving issues of peace and security in all quarters of the globe, economic development, human rights, and the many types of political crises, which were previously dealt with through other channels and institutions, are being put before the organization every day. As a result, the structures of the UN system are being stretched to the limit of their capacity and beyond.

The increased attention paid to the strengths and limitations of the United Nations has been a direct result of the increased utilization of the organization and the rapidly rising expectations regarding its role in world affairs. Accordingly, the reform of the United Nations has begun to receive increased attention in member state capitals, among UN delegations, in the press, within the academic community, and among public support groups. There is a growing recognition that the organization is neither as efficient nor as effective as it needs to be—or as it can be—to meet the challenges ahead.

Discussions of UN reform are appropriately centered around four major areas: the Secretariat, the structures of the institutions comprising the world body, enhancement of collective security capabilities (peacekeeping and peace enforcement), and finances. Various working groups of member states have been formed over the years to restructure the Secretariat and to improve the effectiveness of the General Assembly, the Security Council, and the Economic and Social Council. Informal discussions among members of the Security Council have focused on changes in the council's membership or on giving a meaningful role to the Military Staff Committee. By and large, these discussions have resulted in only marginal changes at best.

The discussions about UN reform have not led to any major reforms up to this point, and they may never do so unless determined efforts are made to bring about real reforms of the organization. As with previous reform attempts, there is a deep-seated resistance to change within the United Nations itself, and there is little consensus among member states beyond a feeling that change and modernization are needed to enable the United Nations to meet the multifaceted challenges now being placed before it.

Leadership from the United States and other principal member states is urgent and crucial in order to bring the United Nations into the contemporary world and give it a chance to meet the rising expectations of the international community. Unless the United States exercises strong leadership and provides a clear sense of direction for reform efforts, the opportunity to achieve real and lasting changes will pass.

This chapter proposes specific recommendations for UN reform in the four areas mentioned above. It does so from the perspective of a career diplomat whose duties spanned more than forty years and several associations with the United Nations, including a junior post from 1955 to 1960 dealing with issues from the Suez crisis to atomic weapons control, five years as chief management officer of the U.S. Department of State, and a culminating three-year stint, from 1989 to 1992, as the senior U.S. diplomat in the UN Secretariat.

This combination of experiences has led to my conviction that the United Nations will be an overwhelmingly important part of any emerging world order, and that substantial change is required if the organization is going to play an effective and meaningful role within that order. It is wrong to conclude that the multicultural nature of the institution precludes reform and that therefore any reform effort is hopeless. Determined and persuasive leadership by the most influential member states can move the organization in the direction of greater coherence and effectiveness.

SECRETARIAT REFORM

Secretariat reform is the most important issue in the debate over UN reform, even though this area receives the least attention among the four areas mentioned above. This is because there are few people who have had the firsthand experience at the highest levels of the UN system that provides insight into the requirements for a more effective organization. As a result, discussions of reform tend to focus on higher-profile issues such as reconfiguring the Security Council or reinvigorating the Military Staff Committee. Yet it is the Secretariat—one of the principal "organs" of the UN Charter—on which the member states depend each day to recommend courses of action, prepare for diverse contingencies, and implement the decisions of the member states. If the Secretariat is inefficient, poorly staffed, or badly organized, the effectiveness of many UN activities will suffer accordingly.

The Secretariat is, in fact, inefficient, poorly staffed, and badly organized, and its modernization and streamlining are urgent and indispensable to the future success of the organization.

The obstacles to Secretariat reform are formidable, and to date they have forestalled any effort in this area. Although the UN Charter names the secretary-general as the "chief administrative officer" of the organization, administration has received only limited attention from the succession of secretaries-general, who without exception have come to their task overwhelmed by political issues and generally with little background in or taste for the management of a large organization. As a consequence, the Secretariat tends to be ineffective in important ways. It is characterized by confusion as to responsibility, lack of accountability, waste of resources, and low morale.

At the request of Secretary-General Javier Pérez de Cuéllar (who was probably only looking for a topic of conversation during an interview prior to my appointment as under secretary-general in 1989), I provided an assessment of the steps that might be taken to move the Secretariat into the modern era. The suggestions that I made in that assessment are essentially the same as those that I advocate today.[1]

The single most important step that could be taken is to establish the position of "Deputy Secretary-General." Large organizations, such as U.S. cabinet departments or major business enterprises, cannot function coherently without a clearly designated second-in-command. The secretary-general is currently inundated by the responsibilities—both substantive and ceremonial—of his position. The secretary-general is without an alter ego who can be assigned special or continuing responsibilities, and there is presently no one delegated to take command of the Secretariat if the secretary-general is absent or becomes incapacitated by illness, and the proposal to designate one of the under secretaries as "primus inter pares" is only a potential source of trouble. Finally, there is no one within the Secretariat above the level of under secretary-general who can look at the entire range of UN activities from the same perspective as the person at the top.

Previous proposals to create the position of deputy secretary-general have generally met with suspicion from incumbent secretaries-general, a suspicion which may be attributed to the fear that the occupant would develop a separate power base among the member states or the staff, and use this support to challenge the authority of the secretary-general. I believe this objection is without merit. This concern would be diminished if the deputy were personally selected by, and served at the pleasure of, the secretary-general. In addition, to meet the potential objections of member states, the secretary-general's choice for the position could be subject to ratification by the General Assembly, perhaps with the understanding that the deputy would be from a different geographic region than the secretary-general.

The second most important measure involving Secretariat reform is the restoration of a manageable structure of authority. In 1946, when the Secretariat was originally created by the General Assembly, it was given a structure that included eight assistant secretaries-general, a number consistent with management experience governing the "span of control." In 1991, however, more than forty officials reported directly to the secretary-general, which is a number well beyond the capacity of any person to supervise effectively. Unfortunately, the number of officials reporting directly to the secretary-general has not been seriously reduced under the current administration.

There is no justification for more than five under secretaries, with the five having portfolios for the following areas: political and security affairs (including peacekeeping operations), development and economic affairs, social and humanitarian affairs, management and finance, and secretariat, conference, and information services. In addition, there would have to be a small number of "staff" positions, such as a legal counsel, a press and public relations adviser, and the chief of an internal secretariat, reporting to the secretary-general and the deputy. Such a structure represents a manageable number of senior officials that would comprise a core team backed by fewer than twenty assistant secretaries, each directly responsible to a single under secretary (see Figure 2.1.). Moreover, the under secretaries should be given line responsibilities heavy enough to attract first-class talent.

Under this reorganization, lines of command and accountability within the Secretariat would be clarified as related areas of organizational responsibility were placed under a single under secretary. The overlap and duplication that plagues the UN bureaucracy would be eliminated, and the supervisory burden of the secretary-general and the deputy would be apportioned in a rational manner.

In addition to the basic reforms designed to simplify the organizational structure and increase the efficiency of the Secretariat, several new positions should be established within the Secretariat. First, an inspector-general is needed to uncover the waste, fraud, and abuse that occurs in any large organization. The existing Joint Inspection Unit has often done useful work, but it is generally employed as a sinecure for superannuated ambassadors seeking high pay and travel in exchange for occasional papers on marginal subjects. As a result, it is not very effective.

Second, an internal executive secretariat should be established within the Secretariat. Such an internal secretariat would be staffed on a full-time basis by international civil servants who are not answerable to their national governments, but rather are impartial with respect to the positions of member states. The internal secretariat would be responsible for ensuring the development of policy options and the implementation of high-level decisions throughout the UN system. Currently, there is no central unit to manage the flow of decisions and work, and as a result, the secretary-general's personal staff spends too much time and effort duplicating the policymaking roles of senior UN officials.

Figure 2.1
Reorganized Secretariat

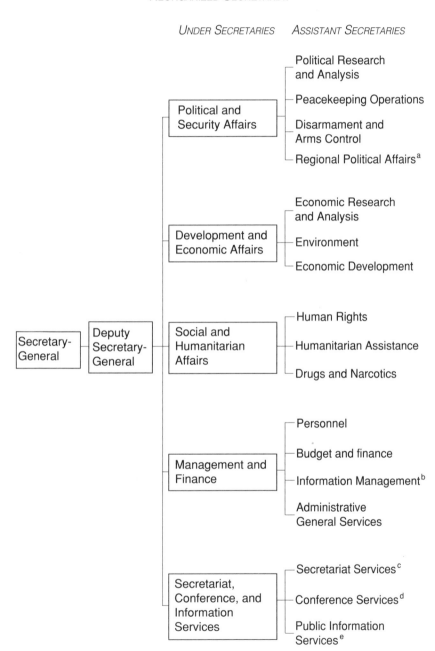

Under Secretaries   *Assistant Secretaries*

Secretary-General — Deputy Secretary-General

Political and Security Affairs
- Political Research and Analysis
- Peacekeeping Operations
- Disarmament and Arms Control
- Regional Political Affairs[a]

Development and Economic Affairs
- Economic Research and Analysis
- Environment
- Economic Development

Social and Humanitarian Affairs
- Human Rights
- Humanitarian Assistance
- Drugs and Narcotics

Management and Finance
- Personnel
- Budget and finance
- Information Management[b]
- Administrative General Services

Secretariat, Conference, and Information Services
- Secretariat Services[c]
- Conference Services[d]
- Public Information Services[e]

Third, the Secretariat needs a mechanism for the systematic review of the organization's policy priorities so that lower-priority activities can be terminated and their resources reallocated. Such a review is increasingly needed because of the growing constraints on those resources. The deputy secretary-general could be assigned the task of chairing a policy-priorities group that would consist of the under secretaries and that would be aided by a special staff of experts in management systems analysis.

Fourth, an assistant secretary subordinate to the management under secretary should be assigned to modernize the organization's information systems and establish a local area network that would connect by computer the Secretariat, the member-state delegations, and, ultimately, the overseas offices of the United Nations. This would permit a massive reduction in the flow of UN documentation, which now far exceeds the capacity of the organization to administer. It would also facilitate changes in the daily journal, the production of up-to-date telephone and delegation lists, and the distribution of UN documents, and most importantly, it could simplify the negotiation of Security Council and General Assembly resolutions.

Delegations from the less affluent countries tend to feel that computerization of the United Nations is meant to disadvantage them, although it would in fact empower them. Within the Secretariat itself, there is little readiness to adapt to new technologies. When confronted by modern technology, the senior Secretariat staff suffers from the same generational problems that are found in many other bureaucracies. But arguing that advanced computer and communications systems are too costly for the already overburdened institution is like arguing that because automobiles are more expensive than the horse and buggy we should continue to use the latter. In that direction lies irrelevance.

Fifth, there should be a complete review of the Secretariat's personnel practices, and appropriate changes should be made in the way that it recruits, promotes, evaluates, and trains its staff. The Secretariat's

---

a. Perhaps including two assistant secretaries dividing geographic-area responsibilities.

b. Including communications services.

c. Including servicing of the General Assembly, Security Council, etc.

d. Including translation and interpreting services, meeting scheduling, editing, printing, and document distribution.

e. Including the supervision of UN libraries.

current personnel procedures are inconsistent with the development of the competent meritocracy that is required to deal with the important problems faced by the United Nations. As a consequence of years of improvised, backward, and careless personnel practices, staff morale has been severely damaged.

Numerous deficiencies are apparent in the personnel practices of the Secretariat. For instance, it lacks a worthwhile staff-evaluation system, though this is admittedly a difficult job in any bureaucracy. Moreover, promotion within the Secretariat is not competitive nor is it based on merit, and staff discipline is very low in some departments. In addition, the policies for recruiting new Secretariat personnel are unclear, and professional training is almost nonexistent. Collusion between staff members and state delegations seeking to justify the continued employment of their nationals is quite common, and often leads to "requests" by the General Assembly for prolonged studies and reports that have no purpose and will never be read.

Sixth, the United Nations should rationalize the way that the organization is represented in member-state capitals. UN offices abroad should become better integrated, serving under a single official appointed by and responsible to the secretary-general rather than to the constituent organizations of the world body. Properly staffed UN offices abroad also could provide "early warning" capabilities and assist in carrying out the functions required for a more "preventive" approach to diplomacy.* UN "resident coordinators" can be more than just on-site managers overseeing the activities of their agency. As with national embassies, the resident coordinators develop personal contacts, special insights, and unique sources of information—the advantages of direct, firsthand observation that cannot be achieved through other means.

Finally, the United Nations should dispense with the practice of giving specific states an "entitlement" to certain Secretariat positions. Senior appointments within the Secretariat should be "political" only in the sense that officials serve at the pleasure of the secretary-general. Candidates for senior positions should be nominated by member governments from among their most competent citizens, and the final choice regarding appointments should be made by the secretary-general.

The permanent members of the Security Council should take the lead in doing away with the principle of entitlement for staffing senior positions in the Secretariat, rather than being the first states to demand those positions as "patronage." Any secretary-general will certainly

---

*The role of the UN High Commissioner for Refugees in a preventive approach to humanitarian diplomacy is discussed by Gil Loescher in chapter 7 of this volume.

understand the importance of maintaining geographic diversity within the Secretariat, and the number of senior positions at the levels of under secretary and assistant secretary should provide ample opportunities to create diversity, especially if a new principle is widely accepted that no national can succeed a fellow citizen in a given position.

Although there is resistance to all of the proposals discussed above, a number of national delegations have become convinced that these changes are needed. Within a multicultural environment such as the UN Secretariat, where practices like "geographic balance" have become icons, reform proposals of any kind are frequently unwelcome. It will take a strong and determined Secretary-General, backed by the support of powerful leaders and key countries, to bring about a significant reform of the Secretariat.

The current secretary-general began his tenure by substantially reducing the number of senior officials that report to him. Instead of proceeding down the reform path, however, he has backtracked by creating additional under secretary positions while eliminating the needed assistant secretary posts. The important opportunity for change and improvement that exists when a new secretary-general takes over has thus been allowed to pass. Nevertheless, member governments can press the secretary-general to go back to the path he originally intended to follow.

STRUCTURAL REFORM

Most proposals for the structural reform of the United Nations tend to concentrate on restructuring the Security Council or on enhancing the General Assembly's authority vis-à-vis the Security Council. There is clearly a growing restiveness among UN member states over the disproportionate amount of power lodged in the Security Council, particularly now that the end of the East–West conflict has removed many of the shackles that previously hampered the council's ability to act. This concern is amplified by the fact that Germany and Japan are now greater financial contributors to the United Nations than most of the current permanent members. The concern about the inordinate power of the Security Council has not, however, coalesced into practical proposals for action.

THE SECURITY COUNCIL

The present configuration of the Security Council naturally satisfies the permanent members, who are in a position to bar any change. It is certainly the case, nevertheless, that the composition of the council

freezes in place a structure which has been transcended by developments in world affairs since the UN Charter was signed in 1945. As a
result, the majority of member states are restive and dissatisfied with a
perpetuation of the existing status quo.

There is an inherent conflict between maintaining the effectiveness
of the Security Council and modernizing its structure. Expanding the
membership of the council will necessarily reduce its current level of
effectiveness. Most members of the United Nations seem to favor an
expansion of the council from its present fifteen members, but many
member states would not accept any change that simply increased the
representation of the European and developed countries by, for example, adding Japan and Germany. The majority of member states would
demand a balanced expansion of the council that included new members from other geographic regions and from the developing world.

At this time, it is clear that both Japan and Germany have a strong
case for inclusion among the permanent membership of the Security
Council, and their determination to achieve that status will certainly
intensify over time.

Despite the general skepticism that there will soon be any consensus on the specifics of change, altering the structure of the Security
Council is not an entirely academic question. Two factors are of particular importance: first, the pace of integration in the European
Community and, second, the ability of Japan to build a domestic consensus concerning the kind of world role that country should play in the
future. Whatever may be said regarding the positions of Britain and
France as preeminent world powers, each has a more global perspective
than Japan and Germany, which both seem to be suffering from lin-
gering post-Second World War traumas.

Among UN delegations in New York, the most commonly discussed proposal for the reorganization of the Security Council, and the
one which might ultimately command a consensus among member
states, involves the transfer of the British and French seats to the
European Community, the development of a new category of membership (permanent or semipermanent but without the right to veto)
for major regional powers, and the election of the remaining members
by the General Assembly from among the regional groups. The problems with this proposal are easy to discern: First, there is little chance
that the integration of the European Community will proceed far
enough in the near future to compel Britain and France to give up their
permanent seats. Second, while India, Brazil, Nigeria, Japan, and Egypt
are commonly identified as the logical candidates to hold the regional
"permanent" seats, Pakistan, Mexico, Argentina, and perhaps other

states could object to the inclusion of those states. For the time being, one must remain agnostic about the restructuring of the Security Council, but the situation could change rapidly.

THE GENERAL ASSEMBLY

One consequence of the widespread unhappiness about the current composition of the Security Council among member states is that, once again, attention is being paid to enhancing the authority and functions of the General Assembly. As with previous instances, however, the discussions about increasing the assembly's powers have yet to produce significant results. This may be due to the fact that the working groups established to examine ways to increase the effectiveness of the assembly have generally suffered from a lack of leadership.

In fact, the quality of the General Assembly's work has deteriorated in recent years. Its agenda is extremely resistant to being streamlined or rationalized, and many agenda items are trivial, overlapping, or of very narrow interest to the member states. The assembly's General Committee, which is nominally responsible for controlling the agenda, fails to exercise any discipline over the agenda, and it certainly does not function properly as a "rules" committee. In addition, the right of every member state to place any item on the agenda, no matter how parochial or trivial, continues to be sacrosanct. As a consequence, the assembly's agenda has grown to over 150 items, each of which is considered in either plenary or committee meetings during the fall session. At this point, what the General Assembly requires most is leadership to define its role and bring its potential influence to bear on the issues that count.

The General Assembly holds the purse strings of the United Nations, and its most important function is the consideration and approval of the organization's biennial budget. However, this function is essentially entrusted to the lower-level representatives in the assembly's Fifth Committee, whose meetings the ambassadors seldom attend. There is a strong inclination in that committee toward micromanagement, and as a result, little attention is paid to the big issues which should underlie discussions about the utilization of resources. In addition, the UN budget should be developed earlier in the year, rather than delaying the start of budget consideration until the opening of the fall meeting in September. The budget should be ready for final approval by the General Assembly plenary in mid-October.

A similar situation prevails in the Advisory Committee on Administrative and Budgetary Questions (ACABQ), which is supposed to consist of experts acting in a nonrepresentative capacity. The quality, expertise, and seniority of the personnel selected for membership in ACABQ leave much to be desired. The committee has an important role to perform and much more attention should be given to its staffing.

The General Assembly should recognize that it can and must operate throughout the year, and should adopt procedures to take advantage of this fact. Most of the delegations at UN headquarters in New York operate on a year-round basis, while the work of the assembly and its committees is squeezed into the three months between the third week in September and the Christmas-New Year holiday. Ironically, the General Assembly's calendar originated in a Europe-centered age when it was necessary that UN meetings correspond with the sailing dates of ocean liners to and from New York. In the contemporary world, there is no reason why the assembly cannot focus on the most significant political, social, and economic agenda items when heads of state are present at the fall meeting, and allow committee work to proceed as necessary throughout the year.

The General Assembly could also improve its efficiency by reducing the number of its committees from the present seven to four. The proposed four committees would include: Political (the current First Committee), Economic and Social (Second and Third), Administration and Finance (Fifth), and Legal (Sixth). The existing Special Political Committee tends to become mired in prolonged and unproductive discussions about disarmament resolutions, duplicating the work of other committees, and it is no longer needed. The work of the Fourth Committee has been completed with the effective end of colonialism. The few remaining colonial issues, such as East Timor, should be dealt with in plenary or in the First Committee. In addition, the reform of the Economic and Social Council (ECOSOC), which is discussed below, is of some relevance for the reorganization of the General Assembly committees.

Finally, the General Assembly has fallen into the practice of picking its president on the basis of geographic rotation, rather than seeking a knowledgeable, experienced, world-class statesman who could provide the calibre of leadership that has been dramatically lacking over the past dozen years. Under current practice, the president of the assembly is no more than a presiding officer who follows a script provided by the Secretariat while enjoying the prestige and perquisites of the office. Although the president of the General Assembly is the leader and principal representative of the nearest thing the international community has to a world parliament, most presidents have done little or nothing to use the potential of their position to mobilize world opinion and initiate UN action on important global issues.

Were the General Assembly to institute reforms that would provide it with fewer but more-important agenda items, fewer constraints on its operating schedule, and a more manageable committee structure, and were the Fifth Committee to become less bureaucratic and engage the attention and participation of senior UN officials, this would go some distance toward meeting the goals of those who seek to enhance its relevance and effectiveness.

THE ECONOMIC AND SOCIAL COUNCIL

Much of the work now undertaken by the Economic and Social Council is of questionable relevance to the larger problems that the United Nations must address. As a result, the effectiveness of ECOSOC has been another source of concern for many member governments in recent years, and this has led to proposals for structural reform. Many observers have concluded that reinvigorating ECOSOC is a hopeless enterprise, and therefore the attention this objective has received in recent years has been largely rhetorical (although the 1991 "Nordic UN Project" report did make comprehensive recommendations for change).[2]

There is a general lack of consensus among member states on the utility or practicality of reforming ECOSOC. This is illustrated by the fact that the one significant reform of ECOSOC in recent years, which resulted from Japanese pressure, was to end the annual summer meetings in Geneva. The primary effect of those summer meetings was to make ECOSOC sessions a pretext for a European vacation for the New York delegations. The fact remains that the real experts with serious national responsibilities shun ECOSOC meetings, and the truly challenging issues are not discussed at ECOSOC meetings, or are only covered briefly in passing.

One problem with ECOSOC is that its membership has been expanded from eighteen to fifty-four, and the relevance of its deliberations has diminished proportionally. This should stand as an object lesson to those who are calling for the expansion of the Security Council. A second problem with ECOSOC is that it has become increasingly irrelevant and ineffective, and as a result, it now plays only a minimal role in coordinating UN activities in the economic and social fields. It is difficult to see that there is now any real difference between the work of the General Assembly's Second and Third Committees and the mandate of ECOSOC. In addition, most economic and social programs are developed and implemented by the autonomous specialized agencies. And even though the specialized agencies are required to send annual reports to ECOSOC, the latter does not play the coordinating role that it was originally intended to perform.

To overcome ECOSOC's deficiencies, attempts have been made to give its meetings some thematic significance, but the fact remains that the member states do not attach enough importance to its deliberations to send high-level decisionmakers from their capitals. Accordingly, ECOSOC has been caught in a "Catch-22": It cannot play a more effective role overseeing UN activities without the active participation of member governments, but it also cannot interest governments in its activities without first becoming more effective. As a result of this dual problem, ECOSOC's efficiency and effectiveness continue to spiral downward.

Notwithstanding the significant problems now facing ECOSOC, it can still play an important role within the structure of the United Nations. It could, in theory, perform the important function of providing a high-level forum for the discussion of macroeconomic issues without duplicating the activities of the Bretton Woods institutions. In addition, suggestions to expand ECOSOC into a Committee of the Whole of the General Assembly or to give it the responsibilities of the Second and Third Committees have some promise, and they are very much worth pursuing.

REFORM OF COLLECTIVE SECURITY MECHANISMS*

The peacekeeping activities of the United Nations now have all the characteristics of a big-time military operation, as recent events in Somalia, Bosnia, and Cambodia, among other places, demonstrate. As of November 1993, there were 75,105 peacekeeping personnel (including over 4,000 from the United States) in the field at an annual cost of almost $3 billion. With the end of the cold war, it is natural that we should ask if the United Nations can now implement the collective security system proposed in the UN Charter.

The cold war prevented the UN collective security system from developing along the lines envisioned by those who drafted the UN Charter. A UN military force, which would have been established under Article 43, and the Military Staff Committee became dead letters during the cold war years. The existing UN peacekeeping mechanisms grew organically in response to immediate needs and as agreement among the member states became possible; as a result, peacekeeping is often referred to as "Article 6 ½" of the charter. As the most innovative aspect of the international community's search for alternative means to ensure

---

* Several of the issues dealt with in this section are also discussed by Barry M. Blechman in chapter 4 of this volume.

world order, UN peacekeeping represents the refusal of the member states to be fully paralyzed by East-West stalemate.

It is not certain that Article 43 would have been implemented even if there had been no cold war. And it is quite possible that the best course for the international community is to continue on the road of pragmatic, trial-and-error institution-building. This was the view of recent secretaries-general, who have presented only modest proposals for further development of peacekeeping and peace-enforcement capabilities. Yet even those limited reform proposals have not met with enthusiastic responses from the major powers.

In his January 1992 *Agenda for Peace* report, Secretary-General Boutros Boutros-Ghali recommended that the Security Council

> consider the utilization of peace-enforcement units in clearly defined circumstances and with their terms of reference specified in advance. Such units from Member States would be available on call and would consist of troops that have volunteered for such service. They would have to be more heavily armed than peace-keeping forces and would need to undergo extensive preparatory training within their national forces. Deployment and operation of such forces would be under the authorization of the Security Council and would, as in the case of peace-keeping forces, be under the command of the Secretary-General.

Boutros-Ghali went on to say that "such peace-enforcement units should not be confused with the forces that may eventually be constituted under Article 43."[3] He further recommended, however, that the Security Council (with the support of the Military Staff Committee) initiate negotiations in accordance with Article 43.

The response, or rather the lack of a response, to these proposals illustrates the greatest problem faced by the United Nations in creating an independent military capability. As the secretary-general observed in his *Agenda for Peace* report, "Member States were requested in 1990 to state what military personnel they were in principle prepared to make available; few replied."[4] The United States limited its public reaction to the secretary-general's proposals to President Bush's offer (in his 1992 address before the General Assembly) to make Fort Dix available to the United Nations as a training facility.

Later in the *Agenda for Peace* report, Boutros-Ghali reiterated his request for the initiation of Article 43 agreements, saying that "Stand-by arrangements should be confirmed . . . through letters between the

Secretariat and Member States concerning the kind and number of skilled personnel they will be prepared to offer the United Nations as the needs of new operations arise."[5] The secretary-general's hope is that through the negotiation of standby arrangements with member states willing to provide the United Nations with units on short notice, the organization will be able to put an advance guard on the ground within twenty-four hours of a Security Council decision to start a new operation, and to cut the force buildup time from the current three-to-four months to two months or less.

The secretary-general also drew attention to another deficiency of UN peacekeeping mechanisms, the shortage of readily available peacekeeping equipment and logistic capabilities:

> The United Nations has no standing stock of [peacekeeping] equipment. Orders must be placed with manufacturers, which creates a number of difficulties. A pre-positioned stock of basic peace-keeping equipment should be established, so that at least some vehicles, communications equipment, generators, etc., would be immediately available at the start of an operation. Alternatively, Governments should commit themselves to keeping certain equipment, specified by the Secretary-General, on stand-by for immediate sale, loan or donation to the United Nations when required.
>
> Member States in a position to do so should make air- and sea-lift capacity available to the United Nations free of cost or at lower than commercial rates, as was the practice until recently.[6]

The United States is better positioned than other UN member states to provide the kind of logistic support that the United Nations needs, and it is in this area that the United States can make the greatest contribution to collective security in this new era.

The Secretariat officials responsible for UN peacekeeping operations have done superior work with a small staff for years. They have become masters at innovation and at cobbling together ad hoc solutions to problems. It would now appear that there is an opportunity to systematize the mechanisms of UN peacekeeping by following the recommendations in the secretary-general's *Agenda for Peace* report. It is to be hoped that the Clinton administration will provide more leadership in this area than its predecessors did.

In the meantime, the United Nations has taken some actions to improve its peacekeeping operations. It is establishing an operations center with secure voice and data communications links to all UN peacekeeping missions around the world, which is a long-overdue step. It is strengthening its staff of military planners. It has initiated talks with member governments to identify the types of forces, equipment, and support that it can count on to be available. However, these steps are only the first ones on a long road.

FINANCIAL REFORM

The foregoing discussion has little relevance unless something is done to deal with the perpetual financial crisis of the United Nations. The Security Council has fallen into the unfortunate habit of blithely authorizing extensive peacekeeping operations while trusting that some member countries will provide the needed resources. The analogy used by former UN Under Secretary-General Richard Thornburgh in a March 1993 report to the secretary-general is apt: ". . . peacekeeping funding is still much like a financial 'bungee jump,' often undertaken strictly in blind faith that timely appropriations will be forthcoming."[7]

As of November 1993, UN member states were in arrears on their payments for the regular budget of the organization by almost $530 million. Of this amount, over $284 million (54 percent) was due from the United States. The Russian Federation was the second biggest delinquent with arrearages of over $48 million (13 percent). In addition to the regular budget, there are substantial arrearages of over $1 billion in the budgets for the thirteen peacekeeping missions, with over $130 million due from the United States and over $515 due from Russia.[8] It is clearly difficult to get too self-righteous about the failings of the United Nations in light of the U.S. record in this area.

The financial difficulties of the United Nations have preoccupied the last two secretaries-general, who have each advanced similar proposals to cope with this continuing problem. The Ford Foundation, in consultation with Secretary-General Boutros-Ghali, in 1992 convened an independent and international advisory group on UN financing. This group was cochaired by Shijuro Ogata, the former deputy governor of the Japan Development Bank, and Paul Volcker, the former chairman of the Board of Governors of the U.S. Federal Reserve Bank, and it included high-level people with a wide range of geographic backgrounds. The group's report[9] confirmed what is generally known: The United Nations lives on a "hand-to-mouth" basis that is totally inconsistent with its expanding responsibilities and the needs for consistency and effective planning. The responsibility for this situation lies directly at the feet of the member governments, and particularly the United States.

Most of the suggestions put forward by the Ogata-Volcker panel are similar to those that were placed before the General Assembly in 1991 by Secretary-General Pérez de Cuéllar and revisited by Secretary-General Boutros-Ghali in his *Agenda for Peace* report. The Ogata-Volcker recommendations combine general exhortations with specific proposals for reform. An example of the former is, "All countries must pay their assessed U.N. dues on time and in full." The specific proposals are sensible and more or less obvious: Dues should be paid in quarterly installments (presently they are due in full by the end of each January), interest should be charged on late payments, the Working Capital Fund should be doubled to $200 million by a one-time assessment, a revolving peacekeeping fund of $400 million should be created, there should be a unified peacekeeping budget financed by a single annual assessment, and all UN programs financed through voluntary contributions should have their administrative expenditures financed by assessed contributions. Interestingly, the panel concluded that the United Nations should not be given the authority to borrow money, as had been proposed by the secretary-general.

The responsibility for the financial problems of the United Nations resides with the member states, and especially the permanent members of the Security Council. Former Under Secretary-General Thornburgh's "bungee jumping" imagery is vividly appropriate in this respect. The member governments must decide whether they have the will and the ability to meet the obligations implicit in their decisions. The votes of member governments in UN bodies presumably are the product of instructions from political authorities in capitals who, it would seem, have little or no contact with those responsible for delivering the necessary financial resources. As the official formerly responsible for the U.S. State Department budget, I am well aware of this problem.

One frequent recommendation, which is reiterated again in the Ogata-Volcker report, is that member governments should finance UN peacekeeping operations out of their defense budgets because peacekeeping can be seen as an investment in global stability and thus national security.[10] The amounts involved in supporting peacekeeping operations would overwhelm the resources available to the Department of State, whose budget must compete at a disadvantage in the U.S. Congress with the other executive department budgets, which have the benefit of being more important to the domestic constituencies of the congressmen deciding on their requests.

The indications are that the Pentagon has little enthusiasm for being saddled with an additional competitor for limited funds. And, of course, the Department of State is loath to lose the influence over policy that it currently receives from its control over the U.S. funding for UN peacekeeping operations. It will be even more difficult to persuade the congressional subcommittees, which are highly jealous of their jurisdiction, to surrender or to share the authority that they now have over the allocation of these funds. This is a matter for presidential attention.

Finally, in addition to paying its arrearages to the United Nations, one further action is required of the United States: the Clinton administration should reverse a decision made in the Reagan administration's early years to allow the UN dues of the United States to slip by a year. Even if the United Nations adopts a quarterly payment schedule, as proposed by the Ogata-Volcker panel, it will still be important to have UN assessments appropriated in good time. The world body currently must make do without payments from the United States, which furnishes 25 percent of the organization's budget, for at least the first nine months of each fiscal year. Money due from the United States by January is not available until the U.S. fiscal year begins the following October, and then only if Congress has approved the president's budget by that time. The U.S. payment schedule is a legacy of the period when the United States was in an ideological confrontation with the United Nations, and of the "smoke-and-mirrors" approach to budgeting to which the Reagan administration was prone.

The financial elements of UN reform are crucial, and one cannot permit oneself too much optimism given the stringent financial situation confronting a majority of the member states. The "good citizens" of the UN community—such as the Nordic countries, Canada, and a few other states in Western Europe—have helped to overcome the delinquencies of some richer member states. However, the amounts involved in financing both present and prospective peacekeeping operations are of such a magnitude that it is the relatively more affluent countries like the United States, Germany, and Japan—which together contribute almost half of the UN budget—on which the organization must rely.

Perhaps the most immediate need in the area of financial reform is for the member states to stop loading additional responsibilities on the organization until some of the reforms advocated here are put in place and the United Nations is in a position to meet its present responsibilities. The United States, like the other members of the Security Council, routinely votes for new peacekeeping or enforcement operations with little consideration of how they are to be financed. Once a new operation is launched, attention is turned to other matters and the secretary-general is left to improvise or to make the rounds of member states with a begging bowl in his hands. This is irresponsible government; the members of the Security Council apparently have yet to accept that "to govern is to choose."

Member states must recognize the need to prioritize UN responsibilities in the light of the organization's limited resources and forgo action when it is clear that the necessary resources are unlikely to be available.

CONCLUSIONS

This final section seeks to highlight the most important recommendations for a reconsideration of U.S. policy toward the United Nations, a subject which the Clinton administration has yet to deal with publicly.

In summary, U.S. leadership is urgently needed in a number of areas. First, the United States should seek to bring about a restructuring and streamlining of the Secretariat, including the creation of a Deputy Secretary-General position. There should be a reduction in the number of under secretaries and a rationalization of their respective areas of responsibility and accountability. Additional important reforms include the creation of a full-time internal secretariat and an inspector-general. And there also must be a modernization of the communications and information technologies available to the organization.

Unless the structures, procedures, and equipment of the Secretariat are renovated and streamlined, the major component of the UN system that is responsible for implementing the decisions of the member states will not command the confidence and the respect that it requires to effectively perform the tasks entrusted to it.

Second, the United States should squarely confront its responsibilities in the area of UN financing. In addition to the rapid payment of its arrearages, the United States should pay its annual assessments on time rather than nine months after they are due. Most importantly, the United States should reorganize its internal policymaking procedures and structures so that it does not propose or vote for peacekeeping or enforcement operations that it has no prospect of being able to help pay for. No organization can perform effectively under the financial constraints that now face the United Nations, which is owed over $2 billion by its member states to pay for programs they have approved.

Third, while the United States now supports the addition of Japan and Germany to the Security Council, this will remain an essentially meaningless gesture until a reasonable and realistic proposal for restructuring the council—one that does not simply open the gates of expansion—has been worked out through difficult negotiations among the member states. The Security Council is an institution designed for the world of the 1940s, and it now must operate in the global environment of the 1990s. Its composition must reflect the current realities of world power if it is to function with authority.

In addition, when the Security Council is restructured, the Military Staff Committee should be reinvigorated so that it can take over the responsibilities for planning UN military operations that are now being developed within the Secretariat.

Fourth, the United States should take the process of electing the president of the General Assembly seriously, and not simply abdicate the choice of a president to the principle of rotation among the regional groups. The United States should also take the initiative in refocusing the General Assembly's procedures and organization to give it a stronger and more relevant voice in the international community's deliberations on important global issues. The General Assembly is the committee of the whole and, over the years, it has become sidelined into its present state where, for all practical purposes, it is virtually ineffective. If it is properly reorganized and allowed to play a greater role, the General Assembly can make important contributions to international peace and stability.

Fifth, the United States should be a more forthcoming contributor to UN peacekeeping operations. The U.S. government should reconsider its reluctance to invigorate the Military Staff Committee, to earmark specific U.S. forces and logistic support for UN military operations, and to have U.S. personnel participate in joint peacekeeping training exercises. In addition, the United States should indicate its willingness—under the appropriate circumstances—to place U.S. forces under UN command. If the concept of collective security is to have any meaning in the international order of the future, as the world's most powerful nation, the United States must play a suitable leadership role in partnership with other states.

For the leaders of the United States, the underlying reality is that neither the American public nor the citizens of other countries are prepared to see the United States assume the role and the burden of being the policeman of the "new world order," even though that role seemed completely natural during the cold war. Domestic economic and social problems preoccupy the United States, and like a family that suddenly discovers its credit-card charges have gotten frighteningly out of control, we now realize that serious life-style changes will be necessary for disaster to be averted. As a consequence, collective action must be the preferred course in all matters in which our vital national interests—and by "vital" I mean those very few issues with real life-and-death implications for the United States—are not at stake.

If the United Nations did not exist as a mechanism for collective action, the international community would have to invent such a mechanism. The great irony of the United Nations today is that agreement on the UN Charter would probably be beyond the reach of the international community. Therefore, we must think in terms of building organically on what we have already accomplished. This entails programmatic, step-by-step, undramatic, and consensual actions to improve the efficiency and effectiveness of the United Nations, as in the proposals advocated above.

The challenge for the United States is to build a common cause with all like-minded member states so that the international community can move forward in building the consensus that will be necessary to bring about a constructive reform of the UN system. We cannot wait passively for reform to happen on its own, for it is unlikely to do so. So far, the United States has not exercised the requisite leadership, nor has it articulated a vision for change which can generate support and move the United Nations into the future.

≈3≈

INCREASING THE EFFECTIVENESS OF THE UN SYSTEM

ROGER A. COATE[*]

One of the greatest challenges confronting the international community at the end of the twentieth century is increasing the capacity of the United Nations system to mount and sustain effective multilateral responses to the many global problems that threaten peace, security, and human well-being. Building and maintaining multilateral action of this kind, as we shall see, first requires consensus, organization, and commitment;[1] these comprise the foundation needed to integrate and rationalize all the activities of the United Nations. Throughout the history of the world body, however, each of these essential prerequisites of multilateral action has been lacking to varying degrees. If the organization is to realize its potential, this failure will have to be addressed in a systematic and thorough fashion.

CONSENSUS

Consensus is the most critical element for sustaining multilateral action. Whereas unilateral diplomacy—the relations of one state with other states—revolves around the efforts of individual countries to promote

* I wish to thank Morris Abram, Peter Breil, Jack Fobes, Katie Laatikainen, Gene Lyons, Jeff Morton, Harry Ozeroff, Don Puchala, Peter Soderholm, and Ray Wanner for their helpful comments and other contributions.

their particular nationally determined interests, multilateral diplomacy encompasses a broader process of defining and acting on those values, stakes, and interests that are shared with the other members of the international community. That is why creating new structures, altering old ones, or otherwise undertaking significant structural reform makes little sense until there is general agreement among memberstates regarding the basic principles that govern the activities of the UN system. Agreement is also needed regarding the goals agencies, both individually and collectively, should be seeking to achieve, what values and collective interests are to be pursued by the United Nations, and with what priorities. In order to be effective, multilateral policies need to be viewed as legitimate, and consensus provides the necessary foundation for this legitimacy.

For example, with the end of the cold war, a consensus has emerged among UN members over the need to expand and enhance the military aspects of UN peacekeeping activities. Supported by this tenuous consensus, the United Nations has doubled the number of its peacekeeping operations since 1991, and the organization now has nearly 80,000 soldiers serving under the UN flag in eighteen peacekeeping missions around the world. But a similar consensus does not yet exist among states over the principles that should underlie collective responses to the social and economic sources of conflict.

If the international community is to address adequately the long-term threats to global peace and security, however, the economic and social activities of the United Nations will have to play a large role in the efforts to construct a secure world order. Secretary-General Boutros Boutros-Ghali recognized this in his 1993 report, *An Agenda for Peace*, in which he argued that global security will require coming to grips with economic disparity, social injustice, political oppression, and the other underlying causes of conflict.[2] (Even *An Agenda for Peace* discusses these aspects of the problem in terms of dealing with the aftermath of armed conflict rather than with its prevention.) Addressing the long-term social and economic threats to global security will require agreement about the principles underlying collective action, particularly in those areas involving humanitarian assistance, refugees, human rights, and abject poverty.

Consensus-building is the very heart of multilateral diplomacy, and it is founded on what is referred to as the "forum function" of international organizations; that is, the processes of dialogue, exchange, and debate through which a consensus is worked out. The hammering out of resolutions and declarations, as well as finger pointing, name calling, and frustration venting, are all part of this forum function.

A broad international consensus on the basic values, goals, and priorities underlying collective action is not a natural or easily attainable state of affairs. The world is comprised of peoples with exceedingly diverse cultural, ethnic, religious, and ideological backgrounds. Given such diversity and the presence of many associated forces that are antithetical to Western democratic values, it is unlikely that a global consensus over basic values and goals in which the United States can join will evolve without constructive U.S. involvement. Yet, in the past, U.S. policymakers have shown little understanding of, or tolerance for, the parliamentary style of multilateral diplomacy that is produced by this diversity. All too often, the U.S. government has shown a tendency to react defensively or to withdraw from multilateral forums in favor of approaches to solving international problems that rely on unilateral diplomacy.

While policies that rely on unilateral diplomacy can be very effective for dealing with many of the problems faced by nation-states, a reliance on unilateral diplomacy may severely limit the ability of the United States to foster an international consensus. Unilateral policies are typically of little utility for addressing global problems because, as noted, many of these problems require collective action for their solution. In addition, because unilateralism is built around self-reliance on the part of states, it tends to foster an atmosphere of contention and discord. As a result, a reliance on unilateral diplomacy may reduce the ability of the United States to construct multilateral solutions to global problems. The leaders of the United States must therefore seek the appropriate balance between unilateral and multilateral policies.

Ensuring Organizational Capacity

The creation of greater consensus will not alone provide a solution to the problems that plague the UN system. There are a number of organizational constraints that must also be overcome. Just as the UN Secretariat in New York is hindered by financial austerity, poor management, and personnel difficulties, similar problems inhibit effective action throughout the UN system of organizations. While certain problems are specific to individual UN agencies, other problems, ranging from inadequate methods for performance evaluation, antiquated recruitment procedures, and inferior salary scales to sheer incompetence, are pervasive throughout the system and will require uniform system-wide responses. Given that the largest portion of UN resources has historically gone into economic and social activities, it is not surprising that the greatest effort has gone into administrative and financial reforms in this sphere.[3]

Previous efforts to reform the economic and social activities of the United Nations have been guided by an understanding that the scope of the problem goes far beyond issues of management and finance. Much broader, more pervasive, and more fundamental organizational problems have been acknowledged for decades and they continue to plague the organization. Over twenty years ago, for example, the Jackson Report commissioned by the UN Development Program (UNDP) suggested that the problems plaguing the United Nations in the economic and social fields were produced by fundamental difficulties associated with creating effective cooperation and coordination across the system of UN agencies.[4]

Part of the problem is that the United Nations system is not the coherent, cohesive, and hierarchically organized structure that the term "system" implies. States constructed the UN system of affiliated and autonomous agencies incrementally to facilitate cooperation in response to international problems. As a result, the UN system is comprised of some thirty multilateral institutions with mandates covering issue-areas from human health to telecommunications to the global environment. Several of these agencies, such as the International Telecommunications Union (ITU), the Universal Postal Union (UPU), and the International Labor Organization (ILO), predate the United Nations by many years.

Sixteen of the institutions affiliated with the United Nations have been designated "specialized agencies" according to the Charter; they are legally autonomous organizations related to the United Nations by special agreement. The remainder of the organizations affiliated with the United Nations are bodies created by and reporting to the General Assembly and/or ECOSOC. These bodies vary widely in their composition, nature of operation, and degree of autonomy. (The appendix to this volume lists the specialized agencies, affiliated organizations, and the principal subsidiary bodies of the United Nations.) Moreover, the problem is exacerbated by a lack of oversight from governing bodies and the reluctance of these organizations to place themselves within a hierarchical structure that could restrict their flexibility and independence. In addition, a complex and somewhat incoherent system of funding and program linkages greatly complicates any attempt to establish effective structures for system-wide coordination. As a result, the central coordinating role of ECOSOC that was envisioned in Article 57 of the Charter has never been realized in practice.

Subsequent inquiries into the deficiencies of the UN system have continued to build on the theme of inadequate coordination. The 1975 report of the Group of Experts on the Structure of the United Nations System (the Group of Twenty-five) and the 1977 report of the

Ad Hoc Committee on the Restructuring of the Economic and Social Sectors of the United Nations System (the Dadzie Committee) both offered recommendations for concrete, albeit relatively minor, changes aimed at improving the functioning of UN agencies. While some of those recommendations were acted upon, most have at best been only partially implemented and the functioning of ECOSOC and the other targets of reform has not improved significantly.[5]

Despite the broader perspectives inherent in several recent studies of UN reform, including the 1987 report by the United Nations Association of the United States (UNA-USA), *A Successor Vision*; David Steele's 1987 book, *The Reform of the United Nations*; the Nordic UN Project's *The United Nations in Development: Reform Issues in the Economic and Social Fields*; J. Martin Rochester's 1993 book, *Waiting for the Millennium*, and, most recently, Max Jakobson's *The United Nations in the 1990s: A Second Chance?*, the general tendency in recent years, especially at the level of international politics, has been to focus rather narrowly on administrative and financial reforms.[6] As these and other close observers of UN affairs have clearly pointed out, the administrative problems of the UN are severe and pervasive, and they significantly impact its activities. While not wishing to slight these reform efforts, current proposals do not seem to be based on a comprehensive, realistic, or holistic view of multilateral policymaking processes and structures. Without such a larger perspective, we should expect little in the way of meaningful reform.

Efforts to enhance coordination throughout the UN system need to be viewed from both a horizontal and a vertical perspective. Similar to domestic policymaking, multilateral policymaking entails the coordination of policy actions *horizontally* across the diverse domains, jurisdictions, and sectors encompassed by each of the autonomous institutions comprising the UN system. In the area of organizational reform, this involves creating ways to overcome the constraints on cooperation that arise because each individual agency has its own policy problems, parochial interests, and perceptions of global issues as well as its specific areas of expertise, capability, and experience. Among other things, these differences often lead to destructive rivalries over organizational turf.

At the same time, there is a need to facilitate greater cooperation *vertically* between the different levels of world society (a broad range of nonstate entities such as nongovernmental organizations, civic groups, and private businesses and institutions) from the micro-level of individuals seeking to satisfy needs and attain their goals through group or community action to the macro-level of interstate relations. The core problem for improving effectiveness vertically between the different levels of society entails integrating nongovernmental actors into the multilateral policymaking processes of intergovernmental organizations.

The principle of sovereignty is the most significant constraint currently hampering the integration of civic groups and other nongovernmental entities into the policymaking processes of multilateral institutions. While it is widely recognized that many, if not most, critical problems on the global agenda cannot be solved by states alone, the foundation of the UN system in the political and legal concept of state sovereignty dramatically limits the capacity of UN agencies to mount effective responses to those problems. The concept of sovereignty, as incorporated in Article 2(7) of the Charter, provides governments with the international legal right to restrict, manage, or otherwise control the involvement in multilateral policy processes of those elements of world society that fall within their political-legal jurisdictions. The exercise by states of their sovereign prerogatives continues to restrict the participation of the nongovernmental members of world society in multilateral policymaking processes, and it therefore hampers the search for equitable solutions to global problems.

Most importantly, the constraints placed by sovereign states on multilateral problem-solving cause particular difficulties in those areas encompassing some of the U.S. government's primary goals in the United Nations. Those issue-areas, which include spreading democracy, protecting fundamental human rights, promoting free markets, building sustainable development, furthering economic pluralism, curbing narco-trafficking, and assisting refugees, would all benefit from the greater integration of world society into intergovernmental policymaking processes.[7]

The challenges posed by the demands of multilateral policymaking for organizational coordination reflect the need to view the UN system as an interrelated though highly decentralized system-of-action, rather than as a unitary system that is managed from the center by the Secretary-General and the General Assembly. In reality, the UN system encompasses an exceedingly complex set of informal, legal, and institutional relationships among member states, intergovernmental bureaucracies, and a diverse array of other actors. Reform of the UN system needs to be based on an adequate understanding of how, when, and why these relationships take the form they do. Moreover, if the effectiveness of the UN system is to be improved, policy makers in Washington, D.C. and in other national capitals will need to manage their relations with UN agencies to reflect both the horizontal and vertical dimensions of multilateral policymaking.

UNDERSTANDING GLOBAL POLICY COORDINATION

The most important organizational problem hindering greater UN effectiveness is a lack of coordination or, perhaps more properly stated, the inability to foster an adequate level of cooperation among and between the specialized agencies and the numerous organs of the United Nations. Improved coordination would facilitate identifying gaps in programs, avoiding incompatible activities, eliminating unnecessary resource expenditures, and promoting more effective problem-solving by complementing or otherwise reinforcing the actions of widely differing institutions. But to accomplish these goals, coordination will have to be accepted as a multidimensional and multilevel process within the context of the more general processes of global policymaking.

It is helpful to understand the coordination of global policymaking in terms of at least four intersecting domains (as depicted in Figure 3.1): the inter-secretariat, intergovernmental institution, national government, and world society domains. The inter-secretariat realm encompasses the world of international administration and includes the numerous secretariats of the UN specialized agencies. Secretariats are the main organs charged with carrying out the day-to-day work of the

FIGURE 3.1
COOPERATIVE GLOBAL POLICY DOMAINS FOR COORDINATION

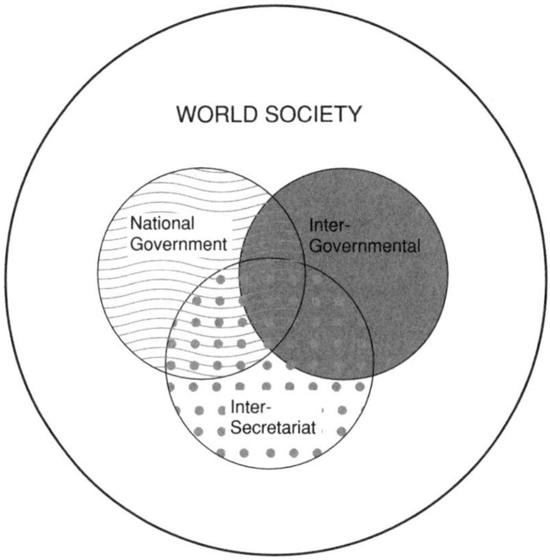

WORLD SOCIETY

National Government

Inter-Governmental

Inter-Secretariat

Source: Adapted from Mahdi Elmandjra, The United Nations: An Analysis (Hamden, Connecticut: Archon Books, 1973), p. 198.

organizations. The intergovernmental institution domain consists of the delegate bodies of multilateral organizations that are comprised of member states. In this realm are located both the primary governing bodies of the UN specialized agencies and the numerous sub-organs of those governing bodies. The primary governing bodies are responsible for approving, financing, and overseeing the work of the organization. The national government domain is the world of member states and incorporates governmental bureaucracies, legislative bodies, and the other units of national governments that may become engaged in either making or executing international policies and projects. Finally, world society envelops all of the preceding domains and encompasses the civic order within which all global policy processes occur. As discussed earlier, it is the civic domain of individuals and nonstate actors that together comprise world society.

Each of these domains and the respective points of intersection between them represent areas where cooperation is important for making and implementing multilateral policies. Interactions concerning almost any given issue may take place within each one or across all of these institutional settings simultaneously. Moreover, interactions taking place in any particular domain are likely to affect and to be affected by interactions taking place in one or more of the other domains. Accordingly, effective multilateral policy action, including the implementation of UN programs, usually requires complementary interactions across several of these domains.

Traditionally, the coordination of the UN system has been conceived of largely in terms of the *inter-secretariat domain*. The tendency of those seeking reform has been either to focus somewhat narrowly on programmatic and financial matters or, conversely, to deal at a relatively high level of abstraction. In the inter-secretariat domain, formal structures such as the Administrative Committee on Coordination (ACC) have been created over the years to facilitate interagency cooperation in formulating and implementing compatible or complementary decisions and programs. These permanent mechanisms have been subjected to periodic attempts to enhance their effectiveness, but nevertheless they have been rather unsuccessful at promoting and sustaining improved interagency cooperation.

The Charter assigns ECOSOC the role of coordinating the *intergovernmental domain* activities of the UN system in the economic and social fields. ECOSOC is authorized to fulfill its coordination function through consultations with the specialized agencies and subsequently through recommendations to the General Assembly and member states regarding the actions that might be taken to enhance the coherence of the system.

However, ECOSOC has never been endowed with the organizational capacity that would be required to effectively carry out that mandate.

The governing bodies that manage the diverse intergovernmental organizations comprising the UN system possess little real capacity to undertake systematic coordination beyond that provided by their respective secretariats. Within the central institutions of the UN system, however, a number of intergovernmental organs have been created to facilitate the coordination of UN activities in the economic and social fields.

Among the most important of these is the Committee for Program and Coordination (CPC), which works under the joint auspices of the General Assembly and ECOSOC. The CPC is supposed to help the General Assembly and ECOSOC avoid duplication and incompatible activities in the programs of UN bodies. Over the past several years, the CPC and the Administrative Committee on Coordination have begun holding joint meetings to overcome the administrative and political difficulties that inhibit system-wide coordination. In addition, the Advisory Committee on Administrative and Budgetary Questions (ACABQ) is supposed to facilitate greater efficiency and effectiveness by reviewing budgetary matters and the financial administration of the United Nations.

Another mechanism that has been used by both the General Assembly and ECOSOC to promote system-wide coordination in the intergovernmental domain has been the identification or the creation of lead agencies charged with facilitating and improving coordination in specific areas of UN work. The recently established Commission on Sustainable Development (CSD) is such a body, and its creation provides insight into the problems associated with this ad hoc approach to improving coordination within the UN system.

The CSD has been given the task of coordinating multilateral activities in the sustainable development area both inside the UN system and beyond the boundaries of that system. Exactly how the commission is to accomplish this mandate, however, was left rather ambiguous by the General Assembly. This ambiguity presents a problem because the UN Environment Program (UNEP), which was created in the early 1970s, has a similar mandate to serve as the UN institution overseeing system-wide "policy review and coordination" in the environment area, including development related issues. As a result, there are now two potentially conflicting "lead" UN agencies overseeing coordination in the environment field (the CSD and UNEP) and two agencies overseeing coordination of UN activities in the development field (the CSD and UNDP). In these two overlapping issue-areas, these institutions are now confronted with the tasks of deciphering their complex relationships with other UN institutions and designing complementary strategies to fulfill their respective mandates.

While there are small but important differences between the CSD and UNEP, as well as between their areas of work, sorting out which institution will coordinate what aspects of the environmental activities of the UN system will not be a simple process. In addition, there are likely to be significant problems in the process of deciding where the resources will come from to finance sustainable development activities, and so while the CSD has the potential to complement UNEP's activities, the two organizations may become rigorous competitors.

In some instances, the ad hoc approach may produce some degree of coordination, as evidenced by the practice of caucusing. Caucusing involves the formal and informal consultations among groups of governments, such as the Group of Seven, the Non-Aligned Movement, the Nordic Group, the Geneva Group, and other intergovernmental associations organized on the basis of geography, functional issue-areas, or shared interests. In addition, regional organizations such as the European Community or the Organization for African Unity provide forums for facilitating the intergovernmental coordination of UN activities. These associations transcend the boundaries of individual UN agencies and possess the potential for making important contributions in the realm of intergovernmental coordination. For example, the Geneva Group, which is the caucusing group of major financial contributors, has demonstrated a significant degree of success over the past decade in keeping the growth of agency budgets under control. Yet even in these bodies there remain major constraints on generating effective coordination, especially because the quality of member states' representation varies quite markedly across institutions and issue-areas.

Perhaps the single most important factor underlying the limitations of efforts to coordinate the program activities of UN institutions, however, lies outside the organizational boundaries of the UN system. The source of many organizational problems plaguing the UN system lies in the *domain of national governments,* and these problems can be traced to the failure of member states to effectively coordinate their own policies within the UN system. Foreign ministries, for instance, tend to focus on the traditional concerns of diplomacy and foreign policy, and therefore they generally do not possess the capacity to oversee and coordinate the program issues that dominate decisionmaking in the UN specialized agencies. Despite the cross-sectoral, multidisciplinary, and interdependent nature of contemporary global problems, member-state participation in the activities of international agencies still tends to be managed by individual ministries within national governments. Consequently, states do little in the way of coordinating their representation across the agencies of the UN system and, quite frequently, the national delegates to specific UN conferences or governing bodies are from particular government agencies and are unaware of the policy positions taken in other UN bodies by their counterparts from other government agencies. Unless states address the fundamental failures of their representation within multilateral institutions, efforts to reform the UN system—no matter how well designed—are not likely to generate more effective coordination at the international level.

The challenge of building effective coordination cannot be met without breaking through the constraints imposed by sovereignty on incorporating the *domain of world society* in global policymaking. Global policymaking processes that traditionally have included only intergovernmental organizations and national governments need to be expanded to encompass civic-based institutions. Finding ways to integrate the resources and expertise of civic groups into the policymaking processes of interstate relations presents a formidable challenge. Indeed, this represents one of the most perplexing problems now confronting UN bodies like the Commission on Sustainable Development. This is particularly true because the commission's ultimate success is widely recognized to be dependent on activating those people and institutions that lie beyond the scope of traditional interstate diplomacy.

The scope and complexity of UN coordination problems is brought more completely into perspective if we consider UN operations with respect to the domains illustrated in Figure 3.1. Traditional views of interagency coordination across the UN system, and the resulting proposals for reform, have focused largely on coordinating activities within narrow parts of the realm of multilateral policymaking. Such proposals have tended to concentrate on four areas:

♦   the inter-secretariat domain (administrative and financial reform)

♦   the intergovernmental domain (program and budget reform)

♦   the linkage between the inter-secretariat and intergovernmental domains (program, administrative, and budget reform)

♦   the junction between the inter-secretariat and national governmental domains (institutional reform at the field level)

Other areas such as world society have been ignored despite their importance for improving the long-term effectiveness of the UN system.

Most troublesome has been the lack of attention paid to the zone
where all of the policy domains converge (see Figure 3.1). This is the
area where the most complex, interdependent, and continuous linkages
exist, and it is here that system-wide coordination finds its greatest
long-term challenge. Effective coordination in this sphere will require an
approach that is compatible with the UN system's foundation in the
diplomatic and legal concept of state sovereignty. At the same time,
that approach will need to transcend the conventions of sovereignty by
bringing nongovernmental organizations, private business enterprises, civic groups, and other nonstate institutions into full working partnerships with international agencies and national bureaucracies.

Transcending the conventions of state sovereignty threatens the
sanctity of that cornerstone of the United Nations, which was articulated in Article 2(7) of the Charter. Yet, if we are to enhance the effectiveness of the United Nations, it will be necessary to overcome the
limitations imposed on the UN system by sovereignty. This represents
perhaps the greatest institutional challenge confronting the world organization as it moves into its second half century.

ENHANCING CAPACITY AND COOPERATION IN THE UN SYSTEM

A practical approach to reforming the United Nations that seeks to
improve system-wide coordination must transcend the limitations of
existing reform proposals, which tend to focus on either major structural
change or on minor administrative innovations. There are two reasons
for adopting such an approach: First, as Ronald Spiers argued in chapter two, major structural reform simply is not a political possibility in the
near-term. Second, and most importantly, micro-level reforms cannot by
themselves significantly improve the overall functioning of the UN system. Despite the horror stories about administrative practices and personnel problems in the United Nations, the most fundamental problems
constraining UN effectiveness are generally not found in the management of individual agencies.

One key to the successful reform of the UN specialized agencies
will be to select carefully a small number of objectives that are achievable and which, in turn, can serve as building blocks for further reform.
Pragmatism suggests that major structural reforms, no matter how necessary or desirable, are not likely in the current international political climate. This should not suggest that the community of states should not
discuss reforming the structures and procedures of ECOSOC, the

General Assembly, the Security Council, or particular specialized agencies. Debate is healthy and it can illuminate challenges and constraints and thus the potential for long-term change. However, at this point in time, the central institutions of the United Nations should not be the primary targets of serious reform efforts seeking to improve the operational effectiveness within the UN system.

There currently exists far too much ambiguity and discord about what member states collectively want and need from the UN system to achieve a consensus over major structural reforms that would be needed to improve the overall effectiveness of UN system bodies. Furthermore, existing proposals for centralizing the decisionmaking and the coordination of the specialized agencies within UN headquarters in New York are based more on wishful thinking than on a realistic appraisal of the structures and processes of the UN system. It is far from clear that greater centralization would be desirable even if it were achievable, which it certainly is not at this point.

In this context, a small number of important reform initiatives do appear to be *achievable* in the short-term, given adequate leadership and commitment. Most importantly, once achieved, these changes should help to facilitate additional reforms.

INTER-SECRETARIAT REFORM

In the inter-secretariat domain, reform discussions need to continue to focus on administration and finance, with the most immediate attention centered on easing the financial predicament confronting nearly every agency in the UN system. As argued by Ronald Spiers, this desperate financial situation originated largely from the failure of member states (and most notably the United States) to fulfill their legal obligations. The financial picture has been further complicated by rising peacekeeping costs and has taken on crisis proportions.

At the request of the Secretary-General, an Independent Advisory Group was created under the auspices of the Ford Foundation in 1992 to analyze and make recommendations about the financial situation of the United Nations. This group, headed by Paul Volcker and Shijuro Ogata (former senior central bank officials from the United States and Japan respectively), issued its report in early 1993.[8] While making a number of relatively minor recommendations related to procedures for the payment of assessed and voluntary contributions, increasing the UN's Working Capital Fund, and the peacekeeping budget, the group's mandate did not permit it to extend its review to cover the specialized agencies. The next step for those interested in improving the effectiveness of the UN system should be to bring the entire UN system more clearly into debates about the organization's financial crisis.

With respect to personnel policies, several reforms are of substantial importance. A merit-based personnel system is a prerequisite to effective action. Hiring and promotion should be based on a system of competitive examinations and performance evaluations respectively. Geographical balance is important in multilateral institutions, but it should guide recruitment practices rather than hiring decisions. The reform of personnel policies alone, however, will likely do little to solve the personnel problems of the UN system. Salaries throughout the UN system need to be made competitive with those in the international financial institutions and in national governmental service. Ronald Spiers thoroughly discusses these issues in his chapter.

Beyond the areas of finance and administration, three other short-term reforms should be pursued. First, the joint consultations of the ACC and CPC need to be formalized and expanded. In addition, the work of both of these committees needs to be linked through either joint or separate consultations with the ACABQ. In this way, the programmatic, administrative, and financial issues confronting the United Nations and the numerous specialized agencies can be brought into a more holistic UN system perspective.

Integrating the work of these committees should lay the foundations for a second short-term reform: the creation of a UN System Computer-based Information System (UNSCIS). Such an information sharing system would provide access to basic program and budget data, non-classified personnel information, data on field operations, and other information that is not easily accessible. The information system would be open to member states as well as agency secretariats and intergovernmental bodies. While deciding on an appropriate location for the information system will require careful consideration, it might be placed within the UN Statistical Division, under the direction of the Secretary-General as chair of the ACC, and/or within the United Nations University (UNU). A special ACC–CPC joint task force could be made responsible for overseeing the design and development of this UNSCIS by an independent commission or by contract to private institutions.

Third, as J. Martin Rochester argues in his recent study of UN reform,[9] the lead agency concept seems to be an appropriate model for coordinating operational activities in specific functional areas. In the past, lead agencies have been identified mainly on an ad hoc basis, with, for instance, UNDP tasked with coordinating UN technical assistance activities in the area of development, UNEP for the environment, UNDRO for disaster relief, and the Center for Human Rights in the field of human rights. This approach has worked with only partial success because these efforts lacked any system-wide coherence and few, if any, incentives for cooperation have been provided. An important task for joint ACC–CPC–ACABQ consultative efforts is to develop a more comprehensive system of designated lead agencies and to work to provide both the resources and the authority required for lead agencies to coordinate UN activities effectively. Also, these efforts should concentrate on identifying and putting in place a system of *incentives* for informal as well as formal inter-agency coordination. Centralized managerial coordination simply will not work in this highly decentralized system of autonomous organizations.

All of these inter-secretariat reforms will require leadership and vision from the member states and, especially, from the United States. These reforms also will require strong support from the intergovernmental bodies that must ultimately approve and fund them.

INTERGOVERNMENTAL REFORM

Recommendations for creating new intergovernmental bodies or for the major restructuring of existing institutions are not the most appropriate target for reform efforts at this time. Little would be accomplished by investing the tremendous resources and energy that would be required to reconfigure ECOSOC and/or the General Assembly, given the changing nature of the world political climate and the evolving and expanding definition of global peace and security. A few relatively small reforms, however, seem to be appropriate short-term targets for efforts to improve the coordination of the UN system. Each of these reforms must overcome significant constraints, and neither of them will be achieved easily.

First, as suggested by the UNA-USA panel in their report, *A Successor Vision*, a greater degree of rationality needs to be brought to the process of technical assistance project funding. This could be accomplished by merging the separate governing boards of the UNDP and other UN technical assistance funds into a single Technical Assistance Board.[10] In addition, this Board should establish a close working relationship with the international financial institutions with the goal of reducing needless duplication of programs across UN system agencies.

Second, the United States needs to use its position within both the Group of Seven industrialized countries and the Geneva Group of major UN financial contributors to achieve a consensus on reworking the UN scale of assessment. A maximum assessment on any single member state of fifteen percent (or less) of the overall regular budget of the

United Nations and the UN specialized agencies should be the U.S. target in these negotiations. This reform should be accompanied by a commitment by the United States to maintain the same level of overall UN system funding (assessed plus extra-budgetary contributions) as under the current formula. This would entail setting aside relatively larger amounts of funding for extra-budgetary purposes, which would give the United States increased flexibility and latitude to promote programs and projects that are deemed to be of greater importance.

Finally, referring back to the diagram in Figure 3.1, the key focus for short-term reform needs to be placed on capacity-building at the core of the policy process where all of the policy domains converge. The UN system of the twenty-first century needs to serve as a mechanism for synthesizing and integrating the diverse needs, interests, and capabilities of state, interstate, and nonstate actors alike. Working "partnerships" among these various elements of the global policy process need to be created and sustained.

In this regard, the newly created Commission on Sustainable Development (CSD) holds some promise as a model for such an integrating and synthesizing mechanism. While the commission is primarily an intergovernmental body, it is being challenged to find ways to integrate the contributions of hundreds of nongovernmental organizations into its work and consensus-building processes. While thus far falling quite short of what many might envision as an ideal "working partnership" model, the CSD experiment with expanding the IGO–NGO–private sector linkage is a step in the needed direction. Strong United States support of such civic-based involvement in the CSD would certainly be helpful in solidifying the partnership model in UN system activities in the face of strong opposition both within some elements of the international bureaucracy and from many member states.

These reforms, although minor compared to the much more ambitious proposals articulated by Maurice Bertrand,[11] the UNA-USA panel in the *Successor Vision* report, J. Martin Rochester, David Steele, and many others (including some of the authors in this volume), can be achieved only with concerted commitment, leadership, and vision. This brings us to a final prerequisite for building and maintaining effective multilateral action: commitment.

COMMITMENT: THE REFORM OF U.S. POLICYMAKING

The commitment to active and constructive engagement by member states in multilateral diplomacy is another key element for building effective multilateral policies in the UN context. While this is true in general, such a commitment from the UN's largest contributor and most influential member, the United States, is especially important. As the sole remaining military superpower and the member state making the largest contribution to the UN budget, the United States enjoys a rather unique status. It has held a position of leadership in the United Nations since the establishment of the world body, but for some time now the United States has been responsible for few major initiatives at the United Nations outside of the military realm and seems reluctant to assume a leadership role in pushing for a stronger and more effective United Nations. While the Clinton administration has demonstrated a willingness to use the United Nations to further U.S. interests, there is little evidence that the administration is ready to make a commitment to provide the leadership needed to build the consensus and organizational capacity required to make the UN system work effectively. (As Ronald Spiers argues, one important element of that commitment entails meeting the United States's financial and other legal obligations to the United Nations in a timely fashion. However, financial responsibility will not be enough by itself.)

For much too long, U.S. representation within the UN system has been oriented primarily toward damage limitation. As a result, ad hoc crisis management often tends to dominate U.S. policy within these organizations. Accordingly, a great deal of U.S. energy has been spent on intense efforts to fend off relatively innocuous and, in practical terms, insignificant actions by other states that U.S. officials view as contrary to American values. Consequently, the United States has often failed to exploit the existing opportunities to play a more positive and constructive role within the specialized agencies. This passive U.S. engagement in the specialized agencies also means that few major initiatives have been taken in recent years to enhance the interests of the United States in the social and economic work of the United Nations.

One of the greatest challenges for U.S. policymakers will be to treat multilateral diplomacy as a major instrument of U.S. foreign policy on a par with unilateral or bilateral action. While there are signs that the Clinton administration is moving in this direction, greater movement than that made to date will be required for the Clinton administration to achieve its most pressing foreign policy goals through the United Nations. In addition, the active engagement of the United States will need to be guided by a clear blueprint for policy action based on a sound understanding of the constraints on effective multilateral policymaking.

Effective leadership also will require the State Department, working in close association with other government agencies and nongovernmental organizations, to develop a consistent and comprehensive set of goals, objectives, and policies toward the UN system and its component institutions. Effective leadership also will require formulating and pursuing U.S. interests with an awareness of other member states's interests, goals, and policies. While these two requirements may appear rather modest, long experience with bureaucratic decisionmaking processes indicates that the coordination of policymaking is more complex than is often realized.

There is a need for a comprehensive and integrated set of U.S. policies for participation in the agencies that comprise the UN system. In particular, there is a need to develop a coherent policy for reestablishing U.S. membership in the UN Educational, Scientific, and Cultural Organization (UNESCO). When the United States withdrew from UNESCO in 1984, the organization suffered from very serious administrative, managerial, budgetary, and other problems. Over the past six years those problems have been greatly ameliorated, and as is openly acknowledged in the Bureau of International Organization Affairs of the State Department, UNESCO is today perhaps the best-managed agency in the UN system. The work of that agency is vitally important for dealing with many of the most important local, national, and international problems confronting the United States. UNESCO's mandate in the areas of science, education, culture, and communications encompasses four interrelated spheres of activity that are essential for confronting the most pressing challenges dominating the global agenda. UNESCO's work in these areas can contribute to promoting democracy, forging cooperative responses to environmental problems, battling pandemic diseases like AIDS, and fostering the universal application of individual human rights. A commitment to full reengagement in UNESCO will require formulating and pursuing U.S. interests in the context of what other member states want to accomplish in that organization. While this sounds simple, the past experience of the United States demonstrates that this process is extremely complex.

There is not only a need for a comprehensive set of strategies and policies for U.S. participation in the UN system, there is an additional need to build new structures and procedures for ensuring the effective integration of U.S. policies into the activities of the numerous UN agencies and facilitating the active participation of Americans in the work of those agencies. Previous U.S. policies toward the specialized agencies suggest that we need to distinguish clearly between official U.S. representation in UN agencies, on the one hand, and American participation (that is, the participation of U.S. citizens and civic-based institutions) in the ongoing activities of those agencies on the other hand.

Contrary to the antiquated image of international organizations as forums in which sovereign states interact in pursuit of defined interests and goals, the world of the UN specialized agencies in the 1990s is far more sophisticated and complex. The activities of UN agencies revolve primarily around the representation of member-government interests, yet those activities reach deep into societies in what has traditionally been termed the realm of domestic politics. American citizens as well as civic groups and institutions become active participants in solving the problems of the world principally through the activities of UN specialized agencies. There are many benefits to be gained from active engagement in UN agencies, and these result more from the participation of individuals and civic institutions than from official state representation. This distinction between official representation and civic-based participation is particularly important when it comes to designing the appropriate administrative and liaison mechanisms for the two functions.

While it is important for the United States to play an active role supporting efforts to reform the UN system of specialized agencies, a more immediate and important reform must take place in Washington. For many years there has been a major deficiency in U.S. representation at the UN specialized agencies. In theory, the State Department, operating through the Bureau of International Organization Affairs, is to provide central oversight of the program activities of all UN agencies. In practice, however, the State Department has failed for the most part to provide a strong oversight function. The officials of State's International Organization Bureau generally believe their main function is to monitor political, administrative, and budgetary issues involving multilateral organizations. This means that relatively little State Department attention is focused on the programs implemented by multilateral institutions, even though program activities constitute the principal work of those agencies.

The responsibility for program oversight traditionally has been dispersed across a wide range of federal agencies. However, the institutional structure of those federal agencies often inhibits their effective engagement with the programs of UN organizations. Some UN agencies like the World Health Organization have clearly defined and attentive domestic constituencies in the United States, both inside the U.S. government and within the broader public. The problem, however, is that the diverse individuals and government bodies that need to scrutinize UN agencies and programs are scattered throughout the federal bureaucracy. Moreover, many parts of that bureaucracy are only concerned with particular aspects of any specific program. Consequently, it has been hard for the U.S. government to effectively sustain its participation throughout the UN system.

A high priority for the Clinton administration should be to improve the coordination of the U.S. government's multilateral policy-making structures. The United States needs to coordinate more effectively its UN policy with the broader interests, programs, and goals of U.S. foreign policy. To be implemented effectively, UN policies must be directly linked with the other foreign policy management functions of the State Department as well as with the international and domestic concerns of other government agencies. In addition, U.S. policy toward the United Nations needs to be coordinated with the activities of U.S. embassies, AID missions, Information Service offices, and the other foreign offices of the U.S. government.

This is not to argue, however, that the UN policies of the United States should remain the exclusive preserve of the International Organization Bureau of the State Department. Experience indicates that relations between the United States and the UN specialized agencies must be given greater consideration by the State Department and the rest of the executive branch. In this regard, to deal with specific issues the State Department should, in cooperation with the National Security Council, designate lead agencies to be in charge of managing U.S. policies and the representation of the United States within individual UN agencies.

To oversee and manage U.S. representation within the UN system and to ensure that all the relevant federal agencies are involved in the policymaking process, interagency policy coordinating committees are needed. It is most important that each committee has a clearly established hierarchy of responsibility among the participating federal agencies. These interagency committees would serve a number of useful purposes, including:

+ providing a forum for keeping interested governmental agencies informed on a regular basis of general developments within specific UN agencies

+ serving as a vehicle for discussing specific program-oriented foreign policy initiatives

+ providing a sounding board for federal agencies to raise questions about UN programs that may require high-level intervention by the U.S. missions

+ serving as a mechanism for coordinating government-wide policies regarding the loan of U.S. personnel to UN agencies to deepen the involvement of the U.S. government in the work of UN agencies

◆ providing a device for ensuring a more adequate and balanced representation at delegate body sessions and, even more importantly, at the intergovernmental meetings of the various regions

◆ providing a means for coordinating the collection and reporting of statistical data for agencies' publications

◆ determining which UN organizations and positions should be staffed by U.S. candidates.

The structure and operation of these interagency committees will present complex questions. Since few federal agencies have an explicit mandate from the U.S. Congress to be involved in foreign affairs, the composition of each committee may require the approval of the National Security Council. In any event, an exceedingly diverse set of federal agencies will need to be included on each committee, and a lead agency or agencies will need to be identified for each multilateral organization or issue-area.

The State Department would remain responsible for the conduct of U.S. representation within the respective UN agencies, with the interagency committees providing assistance and recommendations on programmatic matters. A policy of establishing and pursuing well-targeted objectives would be a productive way to approach representation. In addition, the aspects of U.S. representation in the UN specialized agencies that involve program activities should also be developed in partnership with the relevant U.S. nongovernmental organizations. Given the preeminence of program activities in the work of these agencies, there is a need to institutionalize a close working relationship between government agencies and civic-based organizations.

In this regard, asserting an effective U.S. leadership role within the UN system and ensuring that Americans receive the many potential benefits of the UN specialized agencies will require a bold new initiative for managing American participation. Autonomous "national commissions," such as those called for in the UNESCO Constitution, may provide one way to build more effective structures for promoting American participation in those agencies. Moreover, in the UNESCO case, such a commission already has been authorized by a joint session of Congress. The commissions would be nongovernmental in nature and, while they would not be under direct government control, they would be administered through the State Department. Each national commission would be comprised of individuals representing selected elements of U.S. civil society that fall within the area of competence of a particular UN agency.

These national commissions could serve a number of important functions. They might serve in an advisory capacity to the U.S. delegations to the governing bodies and conferences of UN agencies, including conducting analyses of agency documents, proposals, and draft resolutions, and helping to plan long-term U.S. participation. The commissions also could become intermediaries between UN agencies and domestic constituencies in the United States. In addition, they could be responsible for preparing policy papers for meetings of the executive boards, delegate bodies, and conferences of the specialized agencies. They could solicit initiatives for new program activities, handle public relations, monitor agency recruitment activities, and identify and encourage qualified U.S. citizens to apply for positions within those UN bodies.

To implement these reforms of U.S. foreign policymaking procedures and processes a significant commitment to a multilateral approach to foreign policy will be required by the Clinton administration. These reforms are important and they should have the simultaneous effect of demonstrating to the world community that the United States is serious about its commitment to the UN system. They should help to reinvigorate the United States' leadership role in the United Nations. Also, these actions and the results flowing from them should encourage a greater commitment from other states, thus lessening the burdens on the United States of assuring the maintenance of global peace and security.

CONCLUSION

The efforts of the U.S. government to reform the UN system of specialized agencies and other institutions should begin in the United States. The member states of international intergovernmental organizations remain the most fundamental and important components of those institutions. A strong and effective system of UN specialized agencies will first require the strong and effective participation of major member states and the active participation of their civic-based organizations. Given the unique position of the United States as the largest and most influential member state in the system of UN organizations, many would argue that the United States has a singular capacity and responsibility to play a leadership role.

As Oran Young, a leading scholar of international relations, has argued, leadership has several dimensions—intellectual, entrepreneurial, and structural—each of which will need to be brought to bear in building the UN system's capacity for effective collective action.[12] Intellectual leadership—the power of ideas, values, and symbols—and entrepreneurial skill are crucial for consensus-building. Designing and constructing greater organizational capacity requires a special blend of vision, leadership, and the capacity to generate the needed resources.

This final element underscores the importance of the commitment dimension of U.S. leadership and it requires the demonstration of political will. Clearly, within the United States there is no inherent lack of vision, of entrepreneurial skill or of resources. The biggest uncertainties, however, are the political will and commitment of the United States to multilateralism and the United Nations. Indeed, demonstrating a serious commitment to seeking multilateral solutions to global problems represents one of the most fundamental challenges facing the Clinton administration in the area of U.S. policy toward the United Nations.

PART II

ISSUE-AREAS AND
POLICY RECOMMENDATIONS

≈**4**≈

THE MILITARY DIMENSIONS
OF COLLECTIVE SECURITY

BARRY M. BLECHMAN

*T*wice in this century, following the First and Second World Wars, the community of nations attempted to establish an institutional capability for controlling war and increasing international security. The effort failed each time, the victim of continuing conflicts among the great powers. With the end of the cold war, and with the paralysis imposed on the United Nations by the East-West conflict now a fading memory, a third opportunity is presented—perhaps a final chance for the international community to create a working system of collective security.

The countries of the world are turning increasingly to the United Nations to resolve both national and international conflicts. Since the November 1989 fall of the Berlin Wall—the symbolic end of the cold war—the United Nations has become involved militarily in twelve new conflict situations, increasing within four years the number of UN peacekeeping missions by two-thirds. During this period, the number of troops involved in UN peacekeeping missions rose even more rapidly, from 15,000 in 1989 to 78,000 in 1993.[1]

Yet, the depth of the international community's commitment to the UN collective security system is far from evident. Despite the greater potential freedom of action provided by the new international situation, it remains unclear whether the organization has the ability to cope effectively with the greater burdens now being placed upon it. While the member states of the United Nations have been willing to dump the problem of international conflict on the organization, they have not yet demonstrated a corresponding willingness to revitalize the military dimensions of the UN collective security system. The members of the United Nations have shown no great enthusiasm for sufficiently increasing the resources provided to the organization, so that it can deal with the greater demands being placed upon it, or for building the new institutions and procedures necessary to meet the new types of challenges that the organization now confronts. So far, world leaders have talked loudly and frequently about the need to improve the UN collective security system, but they have proven unwilling to invest the money, resources, and, most importantly, the political will that is required to bring about significant change.

Far-reaching reforms are necessary in the military dimensions of the UN collective security system. Unless those reforms are forthcoming in the near future, the international community will miss this third and final opportunity in the twentieth century to establish a working collective security system.

CHALLENGES FACING THE UN COLLECTIVE SECURITY SYSTEM

Many Americans believe that the United Nations already has been strengthened. The liberation of Kuwait is often cited as an example of the revitalized UN collective security system. The liberation of Kuwait was essentially a U.S. operation, however, and while carried out under the authority of the Security Council, Operation Desert Storm was undertaken without benefit of the mechanisms for enforcing collective security that are contained in the UN Charter. The United Nations again turned to the United States when its first humanitarian relief mission to Somalia failed in the fall of 1992. Yet again, the arrangement seemed to work for a while, at least in terms of the limited goals established for the U.S. intervention. But the United States cannot afford, and should not be expected, to serve as the world body's enforcer in every instance, as demonstrated most convincingly by the obvious reluctance of Presidents Bush and Clinton to involve the United States meaningfully in Bosnia.

In many recent instances where the UN Charter's mechanisms for enforcing collective security have proven inadequate, the United Nations has turned to the "peacekeeping" apparatus established during the cold war. Until recently, peacekeeping was seen as a relatively low-risk means of helping states that already had decided to make peace—

or at least to cease fighting—rather than as a way to impose a peace on recalcitrant parties. Historically, peacekeepers have simply implemented the mechanisms, such as demilitarized zones, that were intended to stabilize cease-fires and other negotiated solutions to conflict situations. When one of the parties to a conflict decided that it would no longer honor a cease-fire agreement, UN peacekeepers had little choice but to withdraw.

Not surprisingly, the procedures developed by the United Nations to implement these limited and relatively low-risk "peacekeeping" operations are proving far from adequate for the more ambitious "peacemaking" tasks now being thrust upon the organization. In addition to a sharp increase in the number of missions, the complexity of UN military operations has multiplied, and more to the point, the risks they pose to the soldiers and civilians involved have also grown immensely.

Despite these changes, the countries of the world continue to treat UN peacekeeping missions as if they remain the relatively simple and safe operations that characterized the cold war period. For example, the Secretariat's Office of the Military Advisor, which for years had a tiny staff of five, was expanded to thirty in 1993. Yet, the staff remains far smaller than the number of people required to plan and carry out the difficult peacekeeping assignments with which the United Nations is now charged. In addition, stocks of equipment for UN peacekeepers are virtually nonexistent, and troops are often inadequately equipped when deployed into dangerous situations. Finally, there is little specialized training for troops on UN peacekeeping duty, with only the Nordic states and a few other countries taking the need for such training seriously.

All but a handful of member states refuse to commit their armed forces for UN peacekeeping duty prior to the authorization of a specific mission by the Security Council. As a result, it continues to take months to create the forces required for each operation. For example, the third UN peacekeeping operation in Somalia (UNOSOM II) was first discussed in late 1992 and authorized by the Security Council in March 1993. The force was officially established in May 1993, but as of September, more than eight months after the force was first discussed, the full set of national contingents pledged to the force had still not arrived. The situation with respect to the Security Council's establishment of "safe havens" in Bosnia was even worse. In September 1993, more than one year since the proposal was first discussed and five months after the Security Council's affirmative decision, the troops needed to guard the safe havens had not even been identified. The consequences of such delays can be tragic, and these difficulties cast doubt on the whole concept of the United Nations as the guarantor of international security.

While the jury is still out, few observers would argue that the United Nations has had great success ensuring international security in the post-cold war period. To a degree, this negative perception may be the product of a single unresolved conflict: the civil war in Bosnia. Increasingly, however, the success of the United Nations in dealing with some conflict situations is offset by its failure elsewhere, or by the problematic long-term outcomes of the "successes" themselves. Thus, for example, the achievement of the United Nations in establishing a democratic government in Namibia has been shadowed by the organization's inability to deal effectively with the conflict in Angola. Even the expulsion of the Iraqi armed forces from Kuwait has been eclipsed by Iraq's continuing efforts to obstruct implementation of the cease-fire agreement, and by the continuing belligerency of Saddam Hussein's regime against the Kurds in northern Iraq and the Shiites in southern Iraq.

Of course, it is not the United Nations per se that is failing to contain conflict in the post-cold war period; rather, it is the community of states, the major powers, and, most particularly, the United States—as the world's leading military power—that have failed. The United Nations, after all, is not a supranational actor on the world stage; it is a multilateral organization with only the power and authority granted to it by its members. While the secretary-general can bring matters to the attention of the Security Council and appeal to the governments and peoples of the world, thereby bringing some moral force to bear, the organization has little real power and no military or other tangible resources of its own. As an effective force for maintaining global peace and security, the United Nations is utterly dependent on the resources and authority granted to it by its member states.

It is thus the leaders of the states that are members of the United Nations who are failing to grasp this third opportunity to build an effective international security system, and not the United Nations. Unless the United Nations is given the means that are necessary to carry out the difficult tasks now being assigned to it, the international community once again will fail to deal effectively with the problems of war and organized intrastate violence. Indeed, it can only be considered irresponsible for the world's leaders to give the United Nations the types of complex and dangerous tasks that are now routinely being assigned to it without also providing the organization with adequate resources.

The United Nations has not failed in all its recent attempts to resolve conflicts, and it should not be inferred from the discussion above that a total collapse of the UN collective security system is near. The United Nations has clearly succeeded in some cases, such as El Salvador and Namibia, and in other cases, such as Cambodia, the organization has made a significant contribution to peace even though the outcome remains uncertain. The dictates of national politics, moreover, will ensure that world leaders preserve at least a minimal role for the United Nations in maintaining international security. However, without significant changes in the way the United Nations is permitted to deal with the problems of building and maintaining international security, the four-year trend toward greater use of the organization's collective security apparatus will soon come to an end. Should this occur, the organization is likely to return to the indifference that characterized the military dimensions of collective security throughout the cold war. And once again, the international community will have failed to take advantage of an opportunity to create an effective system for protecting the security of all countries and for reducing organized violence within and between states.

Demonstrating the requisite will, as well as a moral and material commitment to the UN collective security system, is the greatest challenge that now confronts the United States and the other major powers. Meeting this challenge will require three types of reforms in the military dimensions of the UN collective security system: structural and political reforms, financial reforms, and reforms in the methods employed by the organization to prepare for, and to conduct, military operations.

Each of these categories of reform is discussed in the sections that follow, and in each section recommendations for overcoming the problems that face the UN collective security system are presented. The concluding section of the chapter addresses the U.S. policy toward the United Nations and the prospects that the Clinton administration can energize an effective effort to rebuild the international collective security system.

POLITICAL AND STRUCTURAL CONSTRAINTS

Most of the leaders of the international community appear to be ambivalent about the United Nations. On the one hand, they argue that the organization should become more effective in dealing with international security problems, thus relieving states of that task. On the other hand, to the degree that making the United Nations more effective requires yielding power to the organization, or providing substantial resources to it, the goal runs headlong into entrenched beliefs about national sovereignty and the independence of national governments.

Thus, the leaders of the major powers are reluctant to allow the emergence of an independent UN military capability, even if this would enable the organization to act more effectively in dealing with conflict situations.

The leaders of the less-powerful states are similarly reluctant to support UN intervention against tyrannical or even genocidal regimes in the fear that this would lead to a propensity for the United Nations to intervene in domestic affairs. Even small steps toward empowering the collective security system to act more effectively are resisted by many member states because they could establish a precedent that would further reduce national sovereignty and eventually lead to the creation of a truly supranational organization.

Nowhere is the ambivalence about the United Nations stronger than in the United States, where a traditional antipathy toward "entangling alliances" and a fierce sense of national independence both militate against any significant surrender of state prerogatives and power to international authority. Moreover, the disappointing record of the United Nations during the cold war places a special burden on efforts to muster support in the United States for giving more power to the organization. Finally, with the disintegration of the Soviet Union having made the United States the world's dominant military power, it takes a certain farsightedness to understand the benefits to U.S. national security of an effective UN collective security system.

The ambivalence of world leaders about giving the United Nations more power is the most fundamental constraint on the effectiveness of the international security system. Were threats to the security of states rare and isolated occurrences, and were the frequency of military conflicts as low as that which characterized earlier centuries, it might be possible to rely on a collective security system without permanent institutional mechanisms to make it work. In today's fractious world, however, where there are often dozens of conflicts going on at any given time and military action requires only hours or days to be successful, an ad hoc system cannot be effective. As members of the Security Council, now meeting virtually in continuous session, have come to realize, an effective international collective security system requires standing mechanisms with authority, resources, and established procedures for dealing promptly with conflicts as they occur.

A crucial consequence of this international ambivalence toward the United Nations is a lack of consensus concerning the types of situations in which it is legitimate for the organization to intervene. The two most important and long-standing parameters defining the limits on UN intervention have been pierced in recent years, but no new consensus has yet emerged concerning the boundaries that should take their place. As a result, great pressures are generated for the United Nations to intervene in virtually all conflicts, and the organization is being pushed into situations that it would be much wiser to avoid.

The first boundary that has been pierced involves the very nature of UN peacekeeping operations. As mentioned above, UN peacekeeping is no longer confined to cooperative situations in which previously warring parties have agreed to a peace; in recent years, UN peacekeepers have faced hostile adversaries in Bosnia, Cambodia, Croatia, and Somalia, to name just a few instances. Indeed, it is uncertain how much longer and to what degree the international community and, most importantly, the countries that provide the United Nations with military forces will be willing to place peacekeepers in harm's way. This blurring of the once-clear line between "peacekeeping" missions and "peace-enforcement" or "peacemaking" operations has significant implications for the kinds of structures and procedures that are required to strengthen the collective security apparatus of the United Nations.

The second boundary that has recently been pierced concerns the distinction between international and civil conflicts. In the 1990s, the United Nations has become involved in several conflicts where the disintegration of states has led to wars between religious and ethnic groups, or between new countries harboring old animosities. But the UN increasingly is also being asked to intervene in conflicts that are essentially domestic affairs. The UN attempt to oust the military government of Haiti is perhaps the clearest example of this change, but the peacekeeping operations in Cambodia, Mozambique, and Somalia also have far less to do with international than with civil conflict.

Defining the limits to be placed on the UN security role is a difficult challenge, but it is also an important step toward a more effective international collective security system. If the organization's role is defined too broadly, and in particular if there is too great a tendency for member states to request UN interventions in domestic conflicts, the organization may be doomed to failure. The international community is clearly not ready to invest supranational authority in the United Nations. Instances in which the United Nations is asked to intervene against established authority within a single country should clearly be limited to the few truly egregious cases that involve massive violations of human rights.

The anachronistic composition of the Security Council is a second political or structural constraint on the effectiveness of the UN collective security system. While the founders' wisdom in establishing a separate body to deal with security questions, and in assigning a special role within that body to the great powers, is even more evident in the 1990s than it was in the 1940s, it is also clear that the states having permanent membership on the Security Council no longer reflect the real distribution of power in the world. The organizational principle behind membership on the Security Council remains sound, but the implementation of that principle must be updated to bring the United Nations into the twenty-first century. Alternative proposals for reforming the Security Council are discussed by Ronald I. Spiers in chapter 2 of this volume.

A third political or structural constraint on the effectiveness of the UN security system stems from the management practices and organizational "culture" of the Secretariat and other UN agencies. Despite years of pressure, most observers agree that the United Nations continues to be poorly managed, preoccupied with appearance at the expense of accomplishment, and stultified by its own permanent bureaucracy.

There are, of course, thousands of UN employees who work hard, perform brilliantly, and conduct themselves with integrity and professionalism in service to the organization and to the world. Instances of UN employees' dedication far exceeding normal standards, to say nothing of tremendous personal courage on their part, have become commonplace in recent years as the organization struggles to maintain peace and provide for basic human needs in dozens of natural and man-made disasters.

Yet, anecdotes describing the inefficiency of the UN bureaucracy, complete with examples of "bureaucratese," unproductive "mind-sets," and waste on a huge scale, are legion. It is precisely because the United Nations was considered only a forum for propaganda and political conflict during the cold war that many of its agencies were permitted to develop these inefficient and wasteful procedures, and that some of its employees were able to conduct themselves in an unprofessional, and sometimes even corrupt, manner. Though no doubt a minority in the organization, some UN officials do view their appointments as sinecures, payoffs for political or personal connections. There are, moreover, among the employees of the United Nations, bureaucrats whose only interest lies in protecting turf and avoiding the turmoil of change, and outright incompetents who endlessly do more harm than good.

The management problems plaguing the UN bureaucracy constrain the organization in two ways. First, the UN's inefficiency hampers its ability to act decisively in situations where the organization receives a mandate to deal with a threat to world peace. Delays in the UN response to crises originate from many sources—most importantly, from constraints imposed on the organization by its members—but, to a degree, the frequent inability of the United Nations to act in a timely manner is a product of its internal organizational problems.

Second, and more importantly, the management problems of the United Nations cause many countries to be wary of investing greater authority and resources in the organization. Even when national governments are willing to make larger investments in the United Nations, the perception of the organization as being inefficient, wasteful, and sometimes corrupt makes it difficult to persuade legislatures to appropriate the necessary funds. This is a particular problem in democracies that must justify their UN contributions to domestic constituencies. In the United States, the problem has been endemic virtually since the founding of the organization, no matter who was in the White House and which party controlled the Congress. In 1992, for example, the Bush administration encountered a storm of protest when it sought to significantly increase the U.S. contribution for UN peacekeeping. It required some serious arm-twisting by Secretary of State James Baker before Congress approved the increase. The fate of a similar proposal by the Clinton administration in 1993 was unclear at the time this chapter was drafted, but it seemed virtually certain that not all the funds requested by the administration, reflecting the increased cost of UN peacekeeping, would be appropriated.

During the cold war, when the United Nations was not permitted to play a meaningful security role, the substitutions of debate for decision, appearance for action, and "studies" for operations were harmless traits of the UN "culture" that served various political purposes. The international environment has changed radically in the last few years, however, and if the third opportunity to build an effective international security system is going to be fulfilled, the UN "culture" will also have to change for the organization to become a more effective actor in world affairs.

FINANCIAL CONSTRAINTS

The amount of financial support available to the United Nations for peacekeeping and other military activities is much smaller than what is deemed necessary for most industrialized countries' national defense. As a result, UN peacekeepers routinely must get by on limited resources, carrying out their missions with far fewer troops than planners would have preferred, and often sending those forces into the field without the proper equipment, support, or specialized training. The United Nations is now being asked to carry out many more peacekeeping missions, and those missions are typically much more difficult than before, but the problems of financing those operations are only getting worse as member states balk at paying the higher costs generated by the new responsibilities they have placed on the world body.

The financial constraints on UN military activities go well beyond the amount of money available—or not available—to pay for peacekeeping operations. The financial procedures that the United Nations currently employs to raise the necessary monies and to reimburse the states contributing to peacekeeping operations evolved during the cold war period when UN peacekeeping was an ad hoc response to the few situations in which the organization could make a contribution to international peace. Now that UN peacekeepers are being deployed more frequently and are being given broader and more difficult roles, the procedures used to finance UN military operations are proving increasingly insufficient and are constraining the organization's ability to complete its new missions.

The vast majority of UN peacekeeping missions are budgeted and paid for individually. Every time the Security Council decides that the organization should undertake a new peacekeeping operation, the member states of the UN must first draw up and authorize the operation's budget. This is accomplished through a complicated and protracted procedure involving mission planners in the Secretariat, representatives of the permanent members of the Security Council (which must approve the mission's mandate), representatives of such other key states as the members of the General Assembly's Advisory Committee on Administrative and Budgetary Questions (which must approve the budget), and those countries directly affected by the operation. As a result, there are frequent delays in getting UN peacekeeping troops deployed, and the forces sent to deal with conflicts are typically much smaller than planners would have preferred.

The separate budgeting of each UN peacekeeping mission creates yet another problem. Because missions have been budgeted individually, there has been no general appropriation for peacekeeping, and funds have not been made available for the various support activities that are necessary for the success of any military operation, such as developing training standards, acquiring common equipment, and maintaining a command center and planning staff.

Finally, the individual budgeting of UN peacekeeping missions exacerbates the operational problems that the organization must confront. The operational constraints facing the UN collective security system are discussed in the next section of this chapter, but those types of problems are first and foremost the result of the organization's limited

financial resources. Enlightened decisions about the resources necessary for executing military operations effectively and professionally
will be made only when the financial requirements of UN military activities are considered in a comprehensive manner.

The special assessment scale that the United Nations uses to determine what each member state must pay for peacekeeping operations
constitutes another financial constraint on the collective security system. The permanent members of the Security Council pay about 22 percent more for the costs of peacekeeping operations than they would if
the regular UN assessment scale were used. Wealthier developing countries like Saudi Arabia and Brazil, on the other hand, pay about 80 percent less than they would under the regular assessment scale. The
poorest countries make an even smaller token payment for peacekeeping than they do for their regular dues, paying only one-thousandth of
1 percent (or one-tenth of their regular assessment rate) toward the UN
peacekeeping budget. Only the developed nations that are not permanent members of the Security Council pay for peacekeeping at the same
rate that they pay the regular expenses of the United Nations. As a
result, the permanent members pay a disproportionately large share of
the costs of UN peacekeeping operations, which weakens their support
for these missions and perpetuates the notion that peacekeeping is
exclusively an instrument of the great powers.

The higher peacekeeping assessment on the permanent members
of the Security Council causes particular resentment in the United
States, which in 1993 was assessed nearly one-third the cost of each UN
military operation. The special formula for peacekeeping assessments
was created in 1973 to finance the UN operations that helped to end
that year's Middle East War. The special assessment formula reflects
the then-contemporary sentiment that UN peacekeeping primarily
served the interests of the great powers and their regional allies.
Now that peacekeeping serves the interests of virtually all states—
particularly the smaller states that lack the means of protecting themselves individually—it seems clear that the special peacekeeping
formula should be abolished as part of any package of financial reforms.

The overall financial problems of the United Nations naturally
aggravate the problems associated with financing peacekeeping operations. If the secretary-general's Working Capital Fund had not already
been depleted, for example, resources could be made available from it
for special peacekeeper training courses, for acquiring stocks of equipment, or for finding ways to reduce delays in starting operations.

Some relief is in sight: Assuming new problems do not emerge,
the UN's financial problems will ease as the United States continues to

pay up its arrearage. Additional general financial reforms of the UN system, such as finding a solution to the problem of time lags between the start of the UN fiscal year and the dates when states actually provide their annual payments, would further ease the situation. Even so, UN military operations would be substantially strengthened by reforms targeted specifically at the methods used to finance peacekeeping.

The most far-reaching solution to the financial problems of the collective security system would be to incorporate all peacekeeping expenses into the regular UN budget, just as U.S. defense expenditures are part of the overall federal budget. Estimating the financial needs of peacekeeping activities, which are essentially contingency operations, is difficult but not impossible, as many kinds of organizations facing similar uncertainties can attest. In any event, any inaccurate estimates incorporated in a budget can be corrected. Surplus funds resulting from an unusually peaceful year could always be used for related activities (reprogrammed) or returned to members in the form of lower assessments in future years. And there is always the option of asking member states for supplemental appropriations for unforeseen contingencies—essentially the same procedure that is now used for all UN peacekeeping operations.

Integrating the costs of UN military operations into the organization's regular budget would have the advantage of making it clear that peacekeeping is an essential activity of the United Nations, rather than an ad hoc response to unusual circumstances. Such a change would greatly facilitate the establishment of a permanent and widely accepted international security system with some power, both symbolically and in terms of the decision procedures that member states would be forced to adopt. Most importantly, because the financing of each peacekeeping operation is an opportunity for criticism and posturing by national leaders and legislative bodies, the integration of UN military costs with the organization's regular budget would significantly reduce the problems that are currently encountered when financing for each individual mission must be requested from member states.

If the members of the United Nations are unwilling to make such a sweeping change in the method used to budget for peacekeeping, as now seems to be the case, they might instead consider a less ambitious but still useful set of recommendations proposed in early 1993 by an expert group convened by the Ford Foundation. Among other things, the Ford group called for the establishment of a larger revolving fund to give the secretary-general greater resources at the start of new peacekeeping missions, the provision of funds for training and other staff activities apart from the budgets for specific missions, and the creation of an integrated peacekeeping budget that, though still distinct from the regular UN budget, would at least avoid the need to finance each operation individually.[2]

A final reform that could ease the financial constraints on UN military operations would be to permit countries to pay some or all of their assessments for these activities in kind, by providing needed goods and services to the United Nations. Currently, member states are expected to pay their assessments in full, and then are reimbursed separately for the cost of any in-kind contributions that they have made to the operation. The developed countries, however, typically are not reimbursed for the entire cost of their contributions. For instance, UN reimbursement rates for troops participating in peacekeeping operations are far below the actual cost of the troops to many of the countries in Europe and North America that often provide them. Moreover, some services provided by developed nations, such as staff support, are often not reimbursed at all. If peacekeeping assessments could be reduced by the true cost of in-kind contributions, based on formulas worked out by the UN staff and member states, some countries might be provided with additional incentives to make military units and capabilities available for UN service.

Although problems with the methods used to finance UN military operations are not the most fundamental constraints on increasing the organization's contribution to international peace (that distinction being held by the political and structural constraints), finding solutions to those problems is a prerequisite for building a more effective international security system.

OPERATIONAL CONSTRAINTS

The United Nations has used several methods to secure the military forces that it needs to carry out both peacekeeping and peace-enforcement operations. For the largest and most difficult missions, the organization typically authorizes one member state either to carry out the operation, in effect serving as a kind of subcontractor to the United Nations, or to lead a coalition of members. Under such authorization, the United States organized and led the UN enforcement actions in Korea in 1950 and in Kuwait in 1990, as well as the second (December 1992) intervention in Somalia. In another example of this approach, the British Royal Navy was authorized to enforce the oil sanctions that the United Nations imposed on Rhodesia in 1966–79. In Bosnia, the United Nations again turned to this approach when it planned to use NATO forces to implement the aborted Vance–Owen peace agreement. In these cases, the lead military power operates under the general authority of the United Nations, and in official compliance with guidelines laid down by the Security Council. Nevertheless, the actual authority of the United Nations over tactical decisionmaking is minimal.

For most peacekeeping missions, however, the Secretariat historically has assembled an ad hoc collection of national military units and individual civilian specialists. Typically, several members contribute infantry battalions, others provide communications units and the necessary transportation, and additional members contribute the various types of civilian personnel (election monitors, police, etc.) that may be required. These assemblages of forces are usually put together quite hastily, and as a result, they leave a lot to be desired in terms of their ability to operate together. In most cases, few of the soldiers have received specialized training for peacekeeping operations or have had any experience in that kind of mission. The officers commanding the operation have typically not had previous opportunities to work together and, in addition, are frequently not familiar with standard UN procedures. Each unit usually brings its own equipment, moreover, impairing the ability of the national contingents to operate together effectively. With the demand for peacekeeping units rising quickly, these problems are being aggravated as the pool of trained and experienced national contingents is being diluted further by inexperienced units.

The command and control of UN peacekeeping operations represent a special problem, and not only because of incompatibilities in communications gear and other equipment from different nations. The national contingents assigned to a UN operation come under the command of a UN-appointed officer, but few countries are currently willing to yield real authority over their soldiers to the United Nations. This was demonstrated pointedly by the July 1993 dispute over tactics in Somalia between the UN mission commander and the commander of the Italian contingent; the disagreement eventually led to the withdrawal of the Italian forces from Mogadishu. Indeed, there are often better communication between national contingents and their home capitals than between the UN mission commander and his ostensibly subordinate units. The commanders of national units often consult with their national authorities before implementing any UN mission commander's orders that they find to be questionable or even just significant.

Faced with these types of problems, and in particular the difficulty of putting together an effective force on short notice, some observers have suggested that the United Nations should organize a quick-reaction military force. For example, in 1992 French President François Mitterrand proposed that the UN member states create a thousand-man standing force composed of national contingents that could be available within forty-eight hours of an alert. Secretary-General Boutros Boutros-Ghali seemed to support this proposal in his 1992 report on peacekeeping. And in 1993, Sir Brian Urquhart, the former UN under secretary-general for special political affairs, called for the creation of a standing UN military force composed of individual volunteers rather than national contingents.[3]

Recommendations like these make many governments uneasy. They fear that the creation of standing or ready capability would give too much power to either the secretary-general or the Security Council, or both, and lead to too great a propensity for the United Nations to intervene in conflicts. The firm rejection of these ideas and others like them by the United States suggests that a standing UN military force is unlikely to be created anytime soon. Yet, if the international community is not yet ready for standing UN military capabilities, how can it overcome the obvious deficiencies of the other two approaches that the United Nations has used to obtain troops for peacekeeping operations?

The approach of authorizing individual member states to undertake enforcement actions, as in the cases of Korea, Rhodesia, Kuwait, and Somalia, can work only under particular circumstances. Nor is this approach desirable if the goal is to improve the long-term effectiveness of the international security system. If the United Nations can be effective only when the United States or another great power is willing to back the organization with military forces, it suggests that the international community has neither the authority nor the legitimacy to guarantee world peace—that the United Nations can serve only as the instrument of the great military powers, and then only under special circumstances. Although this may in fact be the case at present, the goal should be to build a more truly international collective security system.

Similarly, the ad hoc approach utilized in the past to procure troops for most UN peacekeeping operations suffers from the problems described earlier that tend to beset any last-minute military coalition. When UN peacekeepers were rarely exposed to serious danger, these weaknesses may not have seemed terribly important, but now they are significant constraints on the effectiveness of UN forces, just as they are substantial constraints on the long-term effectiveness of the UN collective security system.

Fortunately, there is a solution to many of the problems associated with the ad hoc approach for securing peacekeeping forces that does not involve the creation of standing UN armies: Each member state could "earmark" forces that it would be willing to make available to the

United Nations for peacekeeping duty under the right circumstances. Each country would then provide those earmarked units with the special training and equipment necessary for them to operate in conjunction with the forces of other UN member states on peacekeeping missions. The earmarked forces need not be set aside solely for peacekeeping: Member states could also plan to use those forces for national military assignments. Earmarked forces would have to be assigned peacekeeping as a secondary mission, however, so that the special requirements of those UN operations could be incorporated into their training, equipment, and composition.

Earmarked forces would *not* serve at the beck and call of either the Security Council or the secretary-general. And creating such a force would *not* constitute a step toward an independent UN military capability. Earmarking units for *possible* service in peacekeeping would *not* mean that they were automatically committed to any specific peacekeeping operation. Member states would reserve the right to review each peacekeeping operation authorized by the Security Council and to decide whether or not to permit their own earmarked forces to participate in that particular mission. (The United States and the other permanent members of the Security Council would have the additional protection of being able to veto the initiation of any peacekeeping operation to begin with.)

With member states retaining complete control over their forces' participation in UN peacekeeping operations, the creation of earmarked forces probably would not help to ensure a more timely UN response to crises. Standing forces would be more efficient in that respect. But earmarked forces would be a major step toward a more effective peacekeeping capability for the United Nations. It would create a core force of national military contingents throughout the world that would be specially configured, trained, and equipped for UN peacekeeping duties. UN staff would work with national defense officials to ensure that a balanced mix of different types of forces were earmarked for possible UN duty. UN staff could also work with national military establishments to set training and equipment standards for earmarked forces, to organize staff exercises and planning sessions, and generally to encourage the professionalization and standardization of the inventory of forces from which peacekeepers would be drawn in the future.

For this "earmarked forces" approach to work, it would be necessary to create a far more serious military planning and command capability within the United Nations. This objective could be accomplished in part by breathing life into the Military Staff Committee (MSC), the organization established by the UN Charter to "advise and assist the Security Council on all questions relating to the Security Council's military requirements for the maintenance of international peace and security, the employment and command of forces placed at its disposal, the regulation of armaments, and possible disarmament." According to the charter, the MSC is to consist of "the Chiefs of Staff of the permanent members of the Security Council, or their representatives."[4]

In its role as professional military adviser to the Security Council, a functioning MSC could provide the expertise and influence required to ensure that the Security Council's decisions on peacekeeping operations were informed authoritatively as to the military requirements of the situation, and that member states fully understood the required size and cost of military forces, as well as the types of military activities and rules of engagement, that would be necessary to fulfill the mission's political objectives. Such prior clarification of the mandates for peacekeeping operations, including a tough-minded assessment of necessary rules of engagement, could help to avoid UN involvement in situations like Bosnia in 1992–93, when the world community was not prepared to carry out the military actions required to fulfill its ostensible political objectives, therefore dooming the UN mission to failure.

There is a need for greater realism and judiciousness in the Security Council's decisions regarding the authorization of UN peacekeeping missions. Professional military advice should help to ensure that the Security Council has a clear idea of the military requirements for prevailing in a particular conflict situation. Ideally, the Security Council would then authorize only those peacekeeping operations for which member states accepted the military requirements that were prerequisites for success. Such realism and judiciousness would become an important element in ensuring that an effective UN collective security system is created and sustained over the long term.

Transforming UN peacekeeping from an apparatus that is effective only in cooperative situations into the potent instrument of collective security that the international community now seems to want it to be, also requires greatly strengthening the military staff incorporated in the Secretariat. Virtually all military officers who have addressed this question believe that the MSC could not be an effective agency for the actual command of peacekeeping operations, as it would be a committee of five equals—the military chiefs of staff of the five permanent members of the Security Council. Unity of command is a primary principle of military organization. Thus, the strengthened collective security system should feature a rejuvenated MSC as an advisory body to the Security Council and to mission planners in the Secretariat. Once a mission is authorized, however, its organization and command would fall to a greatly strengthened military staff within the Secretariat.

The Secretariat's military staff would also carry out the various activities required in normal times to maintain forces around the world trained and equipped for peacekeeping operations. Among other tasks, the Secretariat's military staff might carry out the following:

◆ Negotiate agreements with member states to ensure that earmarked units represent a balanced inventory of military capabilities.

◆ Establish standardized requirements for the performance and composition of the national units earmarked for UN peacekeeping service.

◆ Establish reimbursement formulas for compensating states that participate in peacekeeping missions.

◆ Establish command-and-control facilities and procedures adequate to the task of carrying out contemporary military operations.

◆ Together with military officials of key contributing countries, develop doctrine covering the aspects of peacekeeping that differ from normal military activities, such as the relationships between peacekeepers and nongovernmental humanitarian assistance groups.

◆ Establish standardized courses, curricula, and educational aids for the training of earmarked units, and work with member states to ensure that the officers and enlisted personnel of those units are familiar with UN procedures and the special skills required for effective peacekeeping.

◆ Carry out command exercises to give the officers of earmarked units opportunities to work together and practice the types of procedures required by joint peacekeeping operations.

◆ Establish standards to ensure the interoperability of equipment, and work with member states to ensure that earmarked units are properly equipped.

◆ Stimulate the development of the specialized equipment that could aid UN forces in executing peacekeeping missions and, at the same time, could reduce the risks to the peacekeepers. (A variety of advanced military technologies could strengthen UN peacekeeping capabilities, from the enforcement of economic sanctions to the monitoring of arms embargoes and demilitarized zones.)

In the end, establishment of an effective international collective security system will depend on such a professionalization of the means available to the world organization to maintain international peace and security.

U.S. POLICY AND THE PROSPECTS FOR REFORM

The possibilities for strengthening the UN peacekeeping apparatus rest solely on the member states' willingness to provide the resources and to make the organizational and procedural changes that are necessary for effective action in this area. This is true because, as discussed above, the United Nations can only be as effective at reducing conflict as the international community will allow it to be. As is always the case with security matters, moreover, the desires of the permanent members of the Security Council will be decisive in determining the future of the UN collective security system.

The leadership of the United States is essential if the international community is going to create an effective UN collective security system. The United States cannot strengthen UN peacekeeping by itself, but neither will significant change take place without U.S. leadership. For most of the organization's history, the United States had remained relatively aloof from the operational aspects of UN peacekeeping. American officers have served as observers with UN peacekeeping missions, and the United States has provided airlift for many UN operations; the United States has also provided occasional staff support in New York. For the most part, however, U.S. presidents and other executive-branch officials have believed that there is little to be gained from American participation in UN peacekeeping operations, and they have operated on the belief that those missions should be viewed as independent of the great powers.

This view began to change in 1989 as the end of the cold war created new opportunities for the United Nations to contribute to international security. At the time, the Bush administration reviewed U.S. peacekeeping policy and concluded that a larger role for the United States was justified; accordingly, in September 1992 President Bush announced the new U.S. policy. Arguing that the importance of UN peacekeeping operations had increased, he directed the secretary of defense to establish a peacekeeping curriculum for U.S. military schools that would emphasize the training of combat, engineering, and logistic units for the full range of peacekeeping and humanitarian duties, including the participation of U.S. forces in multinational peacekeeping exercises. President Bush also called on all the members of the United Nations to join the United States in taking bold steps to advance the organization's ability to prevent, contain, and resolve conflicts across the globe.[5]

The Clinton administration has continued this rhetorical support for the strengthening of UN peacekeeping capabilities. Whether or not this rhetorical support can be translated into effective action remains to be seen. The new administration began its own review of U.S. peacekeeping policy soon after taking office in January 1993. While the review had not yet been released at the time this chapter was completed, according to press reports there had been spirited debate within the administration about how much to strengthen the peacekeeping capabilities of the world body. The debate seems to have been won by those who favor a modest approach. One official termed the new policy "evolutionary," rather than "revolutionary." Most importantly, the new Clinton policy is said to liberalize the criteria that govern when the United States potentially could become involved in UN peacekeeping operations, thereby broadening the range of situations in which U.S. military capabilities could be used in support of the United Nations. The new policy is also said to call for strengthening U.S. capabilities to support peacekeeping operations.

On the negative side, although the new policy is reported to state that U.S. forces could be assigned to UN commands led by foreign officers—legitimating and formalizing the precedent already set in Somalia—it also is said to list several conditions under which U.S. officers can disregard the orders of UN commanders. If true, such a statement of policy would establish a precedent and example that other nations could point to in justifying their own refusals to obey UN commanders, thus compounding the already difficult problem of command and control in peacekeeping operations, as previously discussed. The Clinton policy review apparently also managed to avoid most of the more fundamental problems discussed above that limit the UN's effectiveness in peacekeeping, choosing not to address the political, structural, and financial constraints on the organization's capacity to undertake military operations.[6]

The most controversial part of the Clinton policy review, and the issue that delayed its completion for months, was the question of placing

U.S. forces under the command of foreign officers. The controversy surrounding this issue reflects the deep ambivalence of the U.S. armed forces about multilateral operations in general, and UN peacekeeping in particular. Although the U.S. armed forces, and especially the army, have begun to take UN peacekeeping more seriously over the past few years, U.S. military leaders remain concerned that the needs of UN peacekeeping missions will divert limited U.S. resources from their more central missions. They also are fearful that strengthening the organization's military capabilities will eventually lead to situations in which foreign officials have the authority to place the lives of U.S. soldiers in jeopardy. While the leadership of the U.S. military understands why UN operations are favored by elected officials in the post-cold war international environment, their strong preference is for the United States to operate independently as much as possible.

The ambivalence of the U.S. military is a reflection of the even deeper ambivalence among the American people. While public-opinion polls continue to show substantial support for the United Nations, many U.S. citizens remain suspicious of the organization and skeptical of its potential. For example, the American people do not share the basic assumption of this chapter that a more capable collective security system would enhance U.S. security. Nor is it widely believed that the United States can help create a stronger collective security system without losing control over the UN decision to intervene in a conflict, or subsequent decisions concerning the participation of U.S. forces. The civilian opponents of a stronger UN security system are fearful, as are U.S. military leaders, that the United States will lose control of the decisions placing U.S. troops in jeopardy. Moreover, the citizens of the United States seem to find the rising costs of UN peacekeeping to be a burden, and they are growing resentful of the large portion of those costs that is shouldered by the United States.[7]

During the first year of its term, the Clinton administration has not been in a political position to push the more basic reforms required to fulfill the president's call for strengthening UN peacekeeping capabilities. The policy review just completed does not by any means provide the means necessary to strengthen the military dimension of collective security. Problems associated with the international collective security system will not go away with its release.

If nothing else, the rising costs of UN peacekeeping will compel the Clinton administration to seek larger appropriations to support the organization in future years. Any requests for additional UN funding are sure to stimulate further debate about how to improve the effectiveness of the international security system, and about the proper role of the

United Nations within that system. A bold initiative—one seeking not only greater resources but also the types of fundamental reforms that would enable the UN collective security system to function more effectively and would also make the system more acceptable to the American people—might be the only way to ensure that the U.S. Congress agrees to pay for additional UN peacekeeping activities.

President Clinton and other senior officials in the administration have stated clearly that they share this writer's belief that support for a stronger UN military capability is an important means of strengthening U.S. security. Time will tell whether the administration places a priority on this objective high enough to bring about significant change.

≈5≈

THE INTERNATIONAL ATOMIC ENERGY AGENCY: CAN IT EFFECTIVELY HALT THE PROLIFERATION OF NUCLEAR WEAPONS?

THOMAS W. GRAHAM

*T*he International Atomic Energy Agency (IAEA) is the key institution within the complex international regime devoted to the nonproliferation of nuclear weapons. Responsible for overseeing and implementing the 1968 Treaty on the Non-Proliferation of Nuclear Weapons (Non-Proliferation Treaty; NPT), the IAEA has in the past two years increased the effectiveness of safeguards for those countries that are parties to the treaty. The support of the United States for the continued strengthening of the IAEA by the community of states is essential, whether the goal of U.S. policy is to slow, manage, or counter proliferation.

The fundamental challenge that now confronts the IAEA is to maintain the positive evolution of its capabilities, procedures, and practices. Not only will this effort enhance the ability of the organization to halt the spread of nuclear weapons and technologies with respect to those states that are NPT parties, but more importantly, it should also improve the agency's ability to restrain proliferation in the half-dozen "problem countries" whose decisions to develop or to forgo nuclear weapons will determine the fate of the entire nonproliferation regime.

The principal constraints on improving the IAEA's ability to halt the spread of nuclear weapons are the organization's own culture and the insufficient levels of financial support and leadership provided by its most influential members, including the United States. Now that the spread of nuclear weapons has become the number one threat to U.S. security, the IAEA must increase its capacity to confront nuclear proliferation. For the organization to do so, however, its member states must seek to modify its institutional culture and provide the financial support and the leadership that are commensurate with the contemporary importance of its mission. The challenges facing the IAEA, their associated constraints, and a set of policy recommendations designed to overcome those constraints will be explored in this chapter.

The goal of strengthening the IAEA is complicated by the fact that within the United States, three different groups play important roles in the development and implementation of U.S. policy in the area of nuclear nonproliferation. These three groups are: experts on the IAEA, or those who work with and study the IAEA itself; nonproliferation specialists, or those policymakers and academic experts who focus on the broader issues of nuclear nonproliferation; and elites who follow U.S. foreign policy, including nonproliferation policy. Each of these groups has different perceptions of the IAEA's goals, its mission, and its effectiveness, and as a result, each group tends to recommend that different steps be taken to strengthen the agency. This chapter will also explore the impact of these three groups on the making of U.S. policy toward the IAEA.

CHALLENGES AND CONSTRAINTS FACING THE IAEA

The IAEA faces three distinct challenges. First, the IAEA must continue to uphold the safeguards which reduce the chances of proliferation in those states that are parties to the Non-Proliferation Treaty. Second, the IAEA must increase its involvement in and importance to international nonproliferation efforts directed against the problem countries. And third, the IAEA must establish itself as the centerpiece of the broader nonproliferation regime that is built around the NPT. Each of these challenges is accompanied by a diverse set of constraints that hamper the organization's ability to achieve its goals.

NON-PROLIFERATION TREATY SAFEGUARDS

The principal mission of the IAEA has been to verify that the nuclear materials and related equipment *reported to it* under the provisions of the Non-Proliferation Treaty are placed under safeguards and that those materials are not diverted to military purposes. Throughout its thirty-six-year history, the IAEA has been quite effective in verifying the compliance of the states that are parties to the NPT. More recently, however, the IAEA's mission has been expanded to include the search for *undeclared* nuclear materials at any location in the non-nuclear-weapons states that are parties to the NPT, a task which is much more difficult for the organization to accomplish.

Since its establishment in 1957, the IAEA has faced many constraints. The political rivalry of the cold war, the ambiguity resulting from the agency's mission both to promote nuclear energy and to safeguard nuclear weapons materials, and the diplomatic complexities inherent in the institutional structure of the IAEA as an autonomous UN agency run by an independent board of governors have added to the IAEA's difficulties. Furthermore, it has had to confront additional difficulties associated with applying safeguards to a growing amount of nuclear material with a budget that has seen little real growth in ten years.

Obstacles to the implementation of safeguards have been present since the beginning of the cold war. During the early years of the IAEA, the Soviet Union and India worked to inhibit the development of an effective safeguards system.[1] Although the Soviet Union began to change its attitude in 1962 and, shortly thereafter, cooperated with the drafting of the first safeguards regime in 1965 (INFCIRC 66), for many years the Soviets continued to obstruct IAEA efforts, such as the adoption of Western Europe's EURATOM system, to improve the effectiveness of its safeguards measures.[2]

In addition, the Soviet insistence on imposing IAEA safeguards on Germany and Japan, combined with the nonaligned countries' demands that safeguards be applied according to the principles of nondiscrimination, has produced a gross distortion in the allocation of IAEA resources.[3] As a result, 70 percent of the IAEA safeguards budget is expended on the monitoring of facilities in Western Europe, Canada, and Japan, all countries that present virtually no proliferation concern.[4] Unfortunately, this distortion in the use of the organization's resources persists to this day.

In addition to the constraints associated with the cold war, a few states have worked continuously to limit the effectiveness of IAEA safeguards. For example, throughout the 1970s, India effectively thwarted IAEA safeguards measures from prohibiting "peaceful" nuclear explosions (PNEs). Although the crude form of obstructionism previously employed by India has ceased, the representatives of both developed and developing countries continue to put their national interests above the interests of the international community. Within IAEA committees like the Standing Advisory Group on Safeguards, for instance, states seek to ensure that safeguards remain targeted at the lowest-common-denominator aspects of the proliferation problem.

Strengthening safeguards is further complicated by the manner in which the IAEA is managed. The agency's board has always contained states that were actively seeking to develop a nuclear weapons capability. This problem with the membership of the IAEA board has been compounded since 1973 when the number of seats was increased from twenty-five to thirty-five. For example, in 1974 following India's test explosion, the countries on the IAEA board that posed concerns about proliferation included Argentina, Brazil, India, Iran, Iraq, Pakistan, and South Africa. Similarly, in 1993 several countries with less than perfect non-proliferation records, including Algeria, China, India, Libya, Pakistan, and Syria, have had seats on the IAEA board. Those states seated on the IAEA board that were seeking to acquire nuclear weapons have typically sought to reduce the impact of safeguards on their activities, often joining forces with states having solid nonproliferation records in efforts to ensure that the IAEA maintains a "balance" between promoting nuclear technology and applying safeguards.[5]

Approximately one-third of the IAEA's regular budget, of which 25 percent is paid by the United States, is devoted to safeguards in any given year.[6] However, the precise share of total IAEA resources devoted to safeguards is rarely stated in clear language, in part because of disagreements among member states over whether the IAEA should use the majority of its resources for safeguards or for technical assistance. Even when the "off-the-books" expenditures donated by governments are included, there is no reason to believe that the IAEA spends more than 40 percent of its resources on safeguards. In fact, because technical assistance programs grew from $5.4 million in 1976 to $56 million in 1993,[7] a period when the safeguards budget has stayed relatively stable, the portion of total IAEA resources devoted to safeguards probably has remained closer to one-third.

The IAEA safeguards budget has seen no significant increase in real terms for the past ten years. The freeze in the real growth of the overall IAEA budget began in 1983, and it was maintained with respect to the safeguards budget until 1992, when the budget for the following year was increased by 4.6 percent. (The 1994 safeguards budget is scheduled to increase by 2.5 percent.) In the meantime, the demand for safeguards increased substantially over roughly the same period. When the NPT entered into force in 1970, the IAEA applied safeguards to approximately 90 facilities around the world. By 1978, the number of facilities under IAEA safeguards had reached 322, and a decade later, 920 facilities were under safeguards, representing a tenfold increase from 1970.

Although the growth in the number of facilities under safeguards leveled off in the 1990s (reflecting the fact that more nuclear reactors are now being decommissioned than are coming on-line), the amount of nuclear material to which safeguards are being applied has continued to increase. Defined in terms of the "significant quantities" (SQs)[8] necessary to produce a nuclear weapon, the amount of nuclear material under safeguards nearly doubled between 1985 and 1991, from 31,116 SQs to 61,463 SQs. As outlined in Table 5.1, by using another measure, the amount of separated plutonium under safeguards increased threefold from 1988 to 1991. During roughly the same period, however, only about twenty new inspectors were added to the safeguards staff of the IAEA.[9] Although safeguards costs are affected more by the number of facilities being safeguarded than by the amount of nuclear material under safeguards at each facility, the growth in the amount of separated plutonium also increases the difficulty of applying safeguards and thus drives up the costs for the IAEA.

The IAEA used to have an active research and development ("R & D") program devoted to developing improved safeguards measures. Due to budget pressures, however, virtually all safeguards R & D is now conducted and funded by the agency's member states. In addition, many safeguards training activities are now paid for by member states, and a trend is starting where some safeguards operations are being funded through voluntary contributions.

As IAEA budget pressures have increased, more and more safeguards expenses are being picked up by a small group of member states,

TABLE 5.1

APPROXIMATE QUANTITIES OF MATERIAL SUBJECT TO IAEA SAFEGUARDS
(IN SIGNIFICANT QUANTITIES)

	1988	1989	1990	1991
Plutonium in irradiated fuel	31,806	35,606	38,710	42,128
Separated plutonium	1,355	1,695	2,516	4,050
Recycled plutonium in fuel	65	136	220	362
Highly Enriched Uranium (20%+)	291	252	268	264
Low Enriched Uranium (<20%)	9,654	10,399	10,900	9,724
Source material	4,065	4,325	4,618	4,955
Total Significant Quantities	47,236	52,413	57,232	61,483
Non-Nuclear Material				
Heavy Water	73	73	89	72

Source: IAEA Annual Report, 1988–91.

including the United States and Japan. Each year, the IAEA establishes targets for voluntary contributions, which have not fallen under the zero-growth regular budget and which have usually been met. Although most of these voluntary contributions go into technical assistance, some are devoted to safeguards. In addition, several states provide the IAEA safeguards program with cost-free experts and devote national R & D resources to the development of safeguards technology for use by the agency. The United States, for example, spends about $7 million each year to strengthen IAEA safeguards through its Program on Technical Assistance (POTAS).

Several other developments have increased the burden on the IAEA safeguards budget. First, the agreement between Argentina and Brazil to apply comprehensive safeguards, which is administered by the IAEA, cost the agency $400,000 in 1991, $650,000 in 1992, and $1.2 million in 1993.[10] Second, although the direct costs of the nuclear inspections in Iraq are covered by the UN Special Commission, the IAEA has faced indirect expenses that are difficult to document and consequently not reimbursed. Third, the IAEA has conducted unique inspections in Romania, Iran, and North Korea using special procedures that have resulted in additional expenditures by the agency. Fourth, the IAEA will soon begin applying safeguards to the many nuclear facilities in the former Soviet republics.

Despite these constraints, in the past decade the IAEA has nevertheless improved its performance in the area of NPT safeguards measures. As a result, the number of cases in which the agency has fully attained its inspection goals has increased substantially, from 17 percent in 1978 to 53 percent in 1984, even with respect to its goals for plutonium and highly enriched uranium outside of reactor cores.[11] For these and other reasons, the IAEA's annual Safeguards Implementation Reports have noted steady progress, and the most recent NPT Review Conference passed resolutions that commended the IAEA for its work in assuring compliance with the NPT.[12]

IMPROVING STATE COMPLIANCE WITH THE NPT: EXPANDING IAEA SAFEGUARDS

The IAEA is now using an array of new inspection capabilities to force countries to either allow intrusive inspections or be branded a nuclear proliferator. As a result of these changes, the IAEA is now in a position to ensure that "timely warning" about a potential proliferation problem can be achieved for those countries that are parties to the Non-Proliferation Treaty. Although these new capabilities may not solve a particular proliferation problem, the IAEA secretariat now has a clear mandate to aggressively investigate emerging problems, report its findings to the board of governors, and, if necessary, communicate a finding of noncompliance to the UN Security Council, as outlined in the IAEA statute.

The most important new safeguards measure adopted by the IAEA has been an affirmation by the IAEA secretariat and board of governors that the agency has the right to conduct special inspections to detect undeclared material at any location in a state that is a party to the NPT.[13] Although the IAEA never pressed this interpretation of its statute and INFCIRC 153 before Iraq invaded Kuwait, this decision by the IAEA has fundamentally *transformed* the safeguards role of the organization.[14] As a result, countries such as North Korea, Iran, and Libya that may have joined the NPT thinking they could develop a separate nuclear weapons program and keep it secret from the IAEA face an entirely different situation.

The second important change involves a new reporting requirement that states inform the IAEA when they decide to construct or modify a nuclear facility, rather than the previous requirement that they wait 180 days before introducing nuclear material into a facility. This expanded reporting requirement allows the IAEA to verify that the information it receives from NPT states is accurate and that it can be updated throughout the construction of a particular facility. As a result, if the international community becomes concerned about a facility that could produce plutonium or highly enriched uranium in a state that is a party to the NPT, the IAEA now has a right to inspect the facility long before it becomes operational. When this capability is combined with extensive intelligence monitoring by major powers and with enhanced enforcement of export control regulations by suppliers, the entire NPT regime has greatly increased the chance that a facility oriented toward a covert nuclear weapons program will be discovered by the IAEA.[15]

The third change involves a radical shift in internal IAEA practice. Before the Iraqi invasion of Kuwait, the IAEA was reluctant to assemble all the information that existed *within* the agency and make it available to the safeguards division. Now, not only has the IAEA taken steps to pool its own information and reestablish the country desks that previously existed, but it has also requested intelligence information from member states and, moreover, has shown that it is willing to initiate extraordinary inspection procedures based on such information.[16]

In the past the IAEA received briefings from member states on the nuclear programs of suspect countries, but the reluctance of the IAEA to admit to this practice and to place special controls over this information made national intelligence services extremely reluctant to provide complete access to their intelligence information. This, in turn, made the IAEA much more reluctant to break from its past practice of applying safeguards on a nondiscriminatory basis. As a result of its activities in Iraq and North Korea, the IAEA has made great progress in breaking down this type of communication barrier.

The fourth change made by the IAEA in its safeguards program involves the more intensive use of environmental sampling techniques, as well as public acknowledgment that IAEA inspectors are using these techniques.[17] Since the IAEA is developing a working relationship with some member-state governments with respect to information sharing, for the first time potential proliferators are not in a position to know exactly how much the IAEA can determine through its environmental sampling techniques. Although it is too soon to know, the deterrent effect of this capability could greatly increase the effectiveness of the IAEA's safeguards measures.

Finally, the IAEA has adopted a voluntary system for reporting exports and imports of nuclear and selected nonnuclear materials and equipment. Although this particular change in the agency's safeguards measures is not as strong as that proposed by the IAEA secretariat, the new system will give the IAEA additional opportunities to receive early warning that a country is starting down the path to a military nuclear capability. While administratively separated from the agency's other safeguards activities, this voluntary system is being implemented by the IAEA at the same time that the Nuclear Suppliers Group has adopted a full range of safeguards requirements that are being applied to both completed nuclear facilities and to the materials and equipment included on its "trigger lists." Had these two systems been in place in the 1980s, Iraq would have had greater difficulty purchasing the array of nuclear materials and dual-use equipment that it acquired for its secret nuclear weapons program.

The IAEA has taken many steps over the past few years to strengthen its safeguards capabilities; however, the additional improvements necessary to make the agency effective in dealing with problem countries will be much more difficult to achieve.

DEALING WITH "PROBLEM COUNTRIES"

Countries that are parties to the Non-Proliferation Treaty have given the IAEA broad powers to inspect their nuclear programs. On the other hand, many of those countries that are considered "problems" with respect to building nuclear weapons, such as Israel, India, and Pakistan, are not parties to the NPT and therefore the IAEA has no jurisdiction to inspect their nuclear programs, nor does it have the right to "go anywhere and see anything." In addition, the IAEA has little direct leverage over those countries.

Since the success of the entire nonproliferation regime will be judged on the ability of the IAEA to make progress with respect to the most difficult "problem countries," the greatest future challenge for the IAEA will be to encourage greater cooperation from these problem states as it further improves the effectiveness of its safeguards system so that the agency can deal effectively with these situations.

In the past, the IAEA has been of marginal effectiveness in terms of dealing with these problem countries. Two principal factors reduce the IAEA's ability to deal effectively with problem countries: first, the incomplete membership of states in the Non-Proliferation Treaty and second, an IAEA culture that has resisted giving clear priority to the agency's nuclear safeguards activities.

These two factors have meant that the IAEA provides little assurance that the most difficult problem countries are not producing nuclear-weapons-grade material for clandestine military use. As a result, it has become apparent that the international safeguards system is extremely weak in cases where states that are not parties to the NPT seek to evade IAEA controls.

The incomplete membership of states in the NPT regime is a significant constraint on the IAEA's ability to deal with problem countries. The IAEA has no jurisdiction over the nuclear programs of non-NPT states, and thus the effectiveness of safeguards is of no relevance for controlling these countries' ability to produce nuclear weapons. Until only two years ago, in addition to India, Israel, and Pakistan, the list of problem countries would have included Argentina, Brazil, and South Africa. Thus, until recently, the top six problem countries were outside the full scope of the IAEA's safeguards mandate under the NPT.

The many gaps in safeguards coverage built into the standard IAEA safeguards documents (INFCIRC 66 and INFCIRC 153), and the limited effort made by the IAEA secretariat to change those constraints under the leadership of former Director-General Sigvard Eklund (1961–82), also reinforced the opinion of many nonproliferation experts that the IAEA is irrelevant when it comes to dealing with the "serious" proliferation issues presented by the problem countries.[18]

Until recently, even those states that are parties to the NPT could operate nuclear facilities under IAEA safeguards and still face no significant threat that their covert programs would be discovered as long as they did not mix their overt and covert programs together. The Iraqi case has clearly demonstrated the ability of an NPT state to build an

independent and unsafeguarded nuclear fuel cycle. The IAEA knew little about Iraq's covert program despite the fact that the existence of the
parallel Iraqi nuclear weapons program, though not its size, was known
to many officials in a number of governments long before the Gulf War.

The IAEA's difficulties in dealing with a few specific problem
countries served to reinforce the opinions of many policymakers, and
most especially nonproliferation specialists within the U.S. government,
that nation states rather than international organizations must deal with
the problem countries.

The first case that demonstrated the IAEA's inability to deal with
problem countries involved Taiwan. In the mid-1970s, there was concern that Taiwan was diverting irradiated fuel from a safeguarded reactor. This potential problem was handled through bilateral channels,[19]
rather than through the IAEA, because the United States felt that it was
not worth having the IAEA involved as the main actor and risking that
intelligence information would be leaked or that the job would be performed poorly.

Pakistan represents a second case: In the 1970s, there was reason to
believe that Pakistan might produce plutonium by diverting irradiated
fuel from its safeguarded KANUPP power reactor and use that material in its medium-size reprocessing plant at the New Laboratories. As
nonproliferation officials from several countries began to review the
adequacy of IAEA safeguards at the Canadian-built KANUPP reactor,
it became clear that several diversion paths existed and that the safeguards equipment at the facility—bundle counters, cameras, and seals—
was far from satisfactory.

Pakistan used every right that it had under the INFCIRC 66 safeguards agreement and the subsidiary arrangements that it had signed
with the IAEA to delay strengthening safeguards practices at the
KANUPP reactor. The IAEA secretariat worked diligently on the
Pakistan problem, finally reporting to the IAEA board that the agency
was no longer able to fully verify the provisions of the safeguards agreement. Nevertheless, national intelligence resources, rather than the IAEA,
were required to provide even a limited confidence that Pakistan had not
actually diverted fuel from the reactor to build nuclear weapons.[20]

Another aspect of the Pakistan case demonstrates the limited
capability of the IAEA when dealing with countries that are not parties
to the NPT or when supplier states do not provide the agency with
adequate information. Even though Pakistan had agreed to apply IAEA
safeguards to any reprocessing plant in the country which used solvent
extraction technology supplied from France, since neither Pakistan
nor France officially informed the IAEA of the existence of the New

Laboratories reprocessing facility, that particular plant was free to operate without safeguards. Thus, if Pakistan could divert fuel from its
KANUPP power reactor (which was designed to be refueled constantly), or from any other source, that country would have a very real
opportunity to produce plutonium for military purposes.

When we look into the causes of the Pakistan problem in greater
detail, it becomes apparent that the system of international safeguards
was extremely weak despite the best efforts of the IAEA. In spite of the
fact that heavy-water-moderated research reactors and small heavy-
water power reactors had been a primary proliferation concern for over
a decade, Canada had devoted inadequate financial and technical
resources to developing safeguards equipment for their medium-size
reactors like Pakistan's KANUPP. Instead, the Canadians gave priority
to developing safeguards equipment for their larger, export-oriented
600-megawatt reactors. U.S. safeguards officials were aware of this problem but did not want to push the issue and damage the close working
relationship they had developed with their Canadian colleagues. As a
result, the IAEA was unable to respond rapidly and effectively to the
Pakistan problem; moreover, the agency never considered conducting
a special inspection and it resented U.S. efforts to place Pakistan's reactor under a special status.[21]

The IAEA's record in dealing with problem countries led many
U.S. policymakers to believe that the agency could not stem the proliferation of nuclear weapons with respect to the most difficult problem
countries. In the past few years, however, the IAEA has improved its
ability to deal with some problem countries, such as Iraq and North
Korea, and it also has been more successful in less hostile situations
involving countries such as Argentina, Brazil, and South Africa. As a
result, the IAEA is becoming a more valuable player in dealing with
problem countries.

While some media reports have characterized the IAEA's inspection effort in Iraq as seriously deficient, the current view among U.S.
nonproliferation specialists is that after a slow start, the IAEA has
begun to get "serious."[22] The agency has made effective use of the intelligence information provided by its member states, it has brought
together highly qualified teams of inspectors on short notice, it has
conducted a large number of successful inspections, it has utilized
powerful environmental sampling technologies, and as a result it has
produced an extremely complete understanding of the Iraqi nuclear
weapons program.[23]

Most experts now believe that as a result of the safeguards program implemented by the IAEA and other organizations, Iraq's nuclear

weapons program has been effectively rolled back. Sensitive facilities and equipment have been destroyed, including dual-use equipment. These accomplishments have been achieved while maintaining a large degree of consensus among the membership of the IAEA. At the September 1991 IAEA General Conference, the resolution supporting the agency's efforts in Iraq was approved 71 to 1 (Iraq registering the only no vote), with only 7 abstentions (Algeria, Cuba, Jordan, Libya, Morocco, Namibia, and Sudan). In 1992, a similar resolution was approved 67 to 1 (Iraq again providing the no vote), with 9 abstentions (Algeria, Cuba, Kampuchea, Iran, Jordan, Libya, Sudan, Tunisia, and Zimbabwe).[24]

Much has been written contrasting the work of the IAEA and the work of UN Special Commission (UNSCOM) in Iraq.[25] Many observers have characterized the work of the IAEA in Iraq as ineffective and that of UNSCOM as effective, and some have even suggested that the IAEA should be transformed along the organizational lines of UNSCOM. I believe, however, that there is *less* to this story than one might think. The two organizations have different styles, strengths, and weaknesses, and they seem to be complementing each other in their work on the Iraqi problem. UNSCOM's single-focus mandate has allowed it to function without many of the institutional constraints faced by the IAEA.

The IAEA should not be reorganized so that it functions more like UNSCOM. There will always be limits to the ability of an international organization to function in a sensitive area like nuclear proliferation. Rather than attempt to recreate a "perfect" IAEA using the model of UNSCOM or the U.S. On-Site Inspection Agency, attention should be given to making sure that states supplement the IAEA safeguards efforts where appropriate in different regions around the world.

The IAEA has substantially improved its record over the past two years by working effectively to impose safeguards measures in countries other than Iraq. Although the IAEA's performance with respect to the Democratic People's Republic of Korea (DPRK) has not always been outstanding, recently it has been quite effective in its dealings with respect to that country.[26] The IAEA moved quickly in May 1992 to conduct the first of seven inspections after North Korea ratified its safeguards agreement with the agency and submitted lists of declared materials and facilities. The agency's environmental sampling helped to discover that the DPRK had reprocessed two batches of spent fuel to extract plutonium in 1990 and 1991.[27] During the sixth inspection, IAEA inspectors pressed their case and were not deterred from requesting invasive practices such as drilling into the basements of buildings to determine whether nuclear waste was being hidden from the agency.[28]

In the case of North Korea, for much of 1992 and 1993 the IAEA has performed as it should according to its statute. Once the agency obtained information that led it to believe that a safeguards violation had occurred, it requested additional information from North Korea. When the North Koreans refused to provide the additional information, the director-general found the DPRK in noncompliance and referred the matter to the IAEA board of governors and then on to the UN Security Council. While the IAEA's efforts may not solve the North Korean nuclear proliferation problem, the agency has provided the international community with timely warning, thus performing its function within the overall NPT regime.

The IAEA also has been effective in less hostile environments, conducting inspections in Argentina, Brazil, and South Africa. Those inspections have put the agency in a position to verify the *historic* transformations taking place in those countries as they move to abandon the construction of nuclear weapons or to implement safeguards on their nuclear weapons capabilities. The IAEA's successes in these three countries is the result of a decade-long effort to gain the confidence of those states and to demonstrate that applying safeguards will not hurt their nuclear programs but will provide the strongest assurance that each country is adhering to its agreement not to build nuclear weapons.[29]

After South Africa ratified the NPT and in 1991 provided the IAEA with a list of materials and installations to be safeguarded, the agency acted quickly to begin verifying whether the information that South Africa provided was complete. The agency conducted over eighty inspections and short-notice visits to South African nuclear and military facilities, reviewed fifteen years of detailed records relating to the production of enriched uranium, and conducted extensive environmental sampling.[30]

The IAEA inspectors and their support staff have worked hard to accurately understand the discrepancies between the amounts of feed material introduced into the enrichment facilities and the amount of weapons-grade nuclear material that the South Africans have reported producing. This effort has been aided by detailed statements made by the South African government concerning its past nuclear weapons program and by informal question-and-answer sessions held by South African government officials during nongovernmental conferences devoted to the subject of nonproliferation in Africa.[31]

The IAEA has been engaged in other activities that should give the international community increased, although still incomplete, confidence that states are not in a position to build nuclear weapons. In the case of Algeria, the IAEA has conducted several inspections since that country signed its safeguards agreement covering a small

15-megawatt research reactor.[32] Because these inspections were conducted before Algeria began operating nuclear facilities that have become the subject of some international concern, the agency should be able to develop a comprehensive baseline evaluation of Algeria's nuclear programs with which future developments may be compared. As a result, regular inspections should be sufficient to give Algeria's neighbors confidence that that country is not using its reactor to produce plutonium for nuclear weapons.

The activities of the IAEA with respect to Syria also demonstrate the agency's willingness to give nonproliferation concerns priority over its mandate to provide technical assistance when such action is warranted. The agency refused to provide Syria with the technical assistance requested by that country until it concluded a comprehensive safeguards agreement pursuant to its NPT obligations. However, once the agreement entered into force, the IAEA board of governors approved the transfer of a 30-kilowatt neutron source for use in research from China.[33]

The IAEA is also conducting ongoing visits to Iran to determine the validity of press reports that Iran is working to develop nuclear weapons.[34] While the agency has avoided calling these visits "special inspections," the actual inspection procedures have been unusual in that several sites have been visited that were not included on Iran's list of declared facilities.[35] In addition, the IAEA has visited Iran to add equipment and facilities to the list of facilities which had been declared as part of the country's peaceful nuclear program.

The IAEA's work in Iran has put the agency in a difficult position. Not only are the inspections technically challenging, but they are diplomatically sensitive as well. Given the fact that Iran's nuclear program has operated at a relatively low level until the past few years, even if reports of a covert nuclear arms program are true, the inspectors should not anticipate finding facilities and nuclear materials confirming a program at this stage. However, to maintain its credibility the IAEA must be seen as following up on credible leads even if a "smoking gun" is not discovered. Over the long term, the greatest test for the IAEA in this case will be to maintain good relations with Iran while proving to the Iranians that special steps must be taken for Iran to convince its neighbors that its nuclear intentions and capabilities are devoted exclusively to peaceful purposes.

A final development suggests that the IAEA has realized that ignoring unpleasant information undermines its credibility. In June 1974, after India detonated its "peaceful" nuclear explosion, the agency's board of governors debated the many serious issues which had been raised by this event. Nevertheless, during that year the agency's publication, the

IAEA Bulletin, made no explicit mention of India's nuclear explosion, and only included an oblique reference, not mentioning India by name, in a reprint of the director-general's November 1974 speech to the UN General Assembly.[36] Throughout 1974 and 1975 and well into 1976, the IAEA continued to publicize its efforts to promote "peaceful" nuclear explosions despite the fact that the world was quickly coming to acknowledge that a nuclear explosion by any name constituted a military capability.

In contrast, the IAEA has been extremely careful recently to publicly report safeguards violations, no matter how small they might be. In 1992, after the new government of Romania requested that the IAEA conduct a "special inspection," the agency reported to its board of governors and announced publicly that the previous Romanian government had violated safeguards by failing to report five grams of plutonium reprocessed from spent fuel.[37]

For all of the reasons discussed above, there is a renewed appreciation of the IAEA's ability to deal with problem countries, but, nevertheless, many experts and policymakers remain skeptical that any international organization can fulfill all the verification functions needed to keep nuclear weapons from spreading around the world.

THE BROADER PROBLEM OF NUCLEAR PROLIFERATION

Many components of the Non-Proliferation Treaty regime will have to come into play if the world is to achieve nonproliferation and move down the road to nuclear stability and the possible eventual elimination of nuclear weapons. In the past, senior officials at the IAEA have not seen their job as promoting nonproliferation; rather, they have seen their job as making sure that nonproliferation does not get in the way of promoting the diffusion of nuclear technology. Even if the diffusion of nuclear technology remains a principal mission of the IAEA, the agency must make nonproliferation its most important task if it is to revive international support for nuclear technology more generally.

The dominant institutional culture within the IAEA has been for several decades opposed to making nonproliferation the priority of the organization. In IAEA publications, for instance, the multimission role of the IAEA is emphasized, and the agency's role as the lead institution implementing nuclear proliferation safeguards is treated with as little emphasis as possible. Until recently, the IAEA treated nonproliferation initiatives as a threat to the successful diffusion of nuclear power technology. Through the 1970s, senior IAEA staff members openly criticized U.S.-led efforts to increase the effectiveness of the NPT regime, including strengthening export controls and deemphasizing the use of plutonium in the nuclear fuel cycle.[38]

By contrast, the nuclear power industry and many governments in Europe have encouraged the IAEA to become more active on nuclear safety issues, especially after the nuclear power accident at the Chernobyl plant in the Soviet Ukraine. This issue has received the highest level of attention from the agency's secretariat; as a result, special initiatives regarding nuclear safety issues are now swiftly funded, and the IAEA's public relations resources have been shifted to cover nuclear safety issues in much greater detail.

One important difference between the IAEA's ability to change in the fields of nuclear safety versus proliferation seems to be associated with the dominant ideology within the international nuclear power industry. Unlike the international chemical industry, which has taken an activist position to strengthen international controls against the development of chemical weapons (at some cost to itself), the nuclear power industry has remained trapped by its own inertia. As a result, the international nuclear power industry has not taken the lead in encouraging the IAEA to be aggressive with respect to nonproliferation; thus the industry and the agency have not been seen as contributing to the solution of the broader problem of nuclear proliferation.

Some of the antisafeguards attitudes within the IAEA have changed in the past few years. This certainly seems to be true of the agency's top leadership, and the organization seems to be slowly adapting to the technical and political realities of the 1990s. The slow rate of this change seems to be due to the culture of the institution—which in turn seems to be a product of the policy preferences of the international nuclear power industry—rather than to any inherent inability of the IAEA to change its attitudes on such issues.

U.S. POLICY AND THE FUTURE OF THE IAEA: THREE VIEWS

Three groups within the United States—experts on the IAEA itself, nonproliferation specialists, and the broader U.S. opinion elites who pay special attention to foreign policy—hold distinctly different views regarding the IAEA and its ability to halt the spread of nuclear weapons; consequently, each group tends to support different options for reforming the structure, operation, and practices of the agency.

Experts on the IAEA have historically concluded that the agency does a superior job in its principal task of accounting for nuclear material *placed under safeguards* in the 114 countries that are currently members of the Non-Proliferation Treaty. The IAEA experts believe that contemporary criticisms of the IAEA fail to take into account the constraints placed on the agency, and they feel that the agency is generally the most professional and the least politicized organization within the UN system.[39]

In contrast, nonproliferation specialists, most of whom work in the executive branch of the U.S. government, tend to evaluate the utility of various aspects of the nonproliferation regime in terms of whether each component slows, stops, or reverses nuclear weapons proliferation in the approximately one dozen "problem countries."[40] Until quite recently, the nonproliferation experts have publicly viewed the IAEA, like the NPT, as essential components of the international system for containing the problem of nuclear weapons proliferation, but privately they have seen the IAEA as marginal in terms of dealing with problem countries.

The nonproliferation specialists have traditionally believed that the IAEA is a credible organization in verifying that nuclear material is not diverted from low-risk nuclear power reactors in countries of relatively little proliferation concern. However, these experts believe that the IAEA has been safeguarding mostly irrelevant nuclear facilities, that the agency produces exaggerated projections of future growth in nuclear power generation, that the organization thereby indirectly justifies the dangerous processes of plutonium reprocessing and recycling, and that it wastes agency resources by maintaining an outdated ideology which believes that nuclear technology can provide substantial benefits to both the developed and the developing worlds. As a result, the nonproliferation experts traditionally have believed that the IAEA provides little assurance that the most difficult problem countries are not producing nuclear-weapons-grade material for clandestine military use.

Despite concerns that a country might want to develop atomic weapons with nuclear materials produced from their safeguarded civilian nuclear sectors, there have been very few cases where such a diversion has been suspected. One could argue that the lack of cases where civilian nuclear materials placed under NPT safeguards were diverted to weapons production demonstrates that IAEA safeguards are an effective deterrent, but nonproliferation officials with access to intelligence information are not reassured by the existence of the IAEA.

The traditional view of nonproliferation specialists has been that "serious" proliferation problems should be left to bilateral diplomacy, state-based intelligence resources, and military action. However, the nonproliferation experts have recently begun to revise their thinking about the utility of the IAEA, as safeguards inspections are beginning to have some effect on problem countries such as Argentina, Brazil, Iraq,

North Korea, and South Africa, and as the IAEA's record is beginning to show improvement in countries such as Algeria, Iran, and Syria. As a result, the nonproliferation experts now believe that the agency may be capable of making an important contribution to slowing or stopping proliferation in problem countries in the future.

Nevertheless, these observers still believe that substantial reforms of the IAEA's practices will be needed to transform the organization into a problem-solving agency with respect to safeguards. At the same time, one should be realistic concerning the maximum that can be accomplished by an international organization such as the IAEA. For a few de facto nuclear weapons states such as Israel, India, and Pakistan, and for a few potential proliferator states, the IAEA will not be the primary element of any nonproliferation "solution" in the near term.

The U.S. opinion elite, who pay special attention to foreign policy and which constitutes 5 to 10 percent of the population, has a view of the IAEA that is vastly different from the views held by the previous two groups.[41] The foreign policy opinion elite does not, for instance, distinguish between the IAEA and the nonproliferation regime as a whole, and therefore this large group judges the agency's effectiveness according to the degree to which it believes that nuclear weapons are spreading throughout the world. This group traditionally has been much more pessimistic concerning levels of nuclear proliferation than have either the IAEA experts or the nonproliferation specialists.

Most foreign policy opinion leaders do not follow either nonproliferation developments or the IAEA in any detail. To a large extent, they rely on the reporting of the international press. To help determine what type of information this important group may have concerning the IAEA, I reviewed the coverage of the IAEA by the major newspapers in the United States over the past several years.[42]

That review leads to the conclusion that the perception of the IAEA as an organization that is relatively ineffective at stemming the spread of nuclear weapons is understandable, even though such a view would be characterized as "uninformed" by IAEA experts. Given the influence of elite public opinion in post-cold war U.S. policymaking, the perceptions of this group as well as the media's influence on their views will be as important to the future vitality of the IAEA as the views of the IAEA experts or the nonproliferation specialists, who at most number only a few hundred people.

Several tentative findings are worth noting. First, before 1990, the International Atomic Energy Agency was not even listed in the standard reference book used by scholars to monitor the content of the print media in the United States, the *New York Times Index*. Although press stories mentioning the IAEA were published prior to 1990, they were relatively rare and were included in the larger category of arms control. For this reason, members of the foreign policy elite might be excused if they are not familiar with the constraints under which the IAEA has operated during its first thirty-five years.

Second, since 1990 the number of stories referring to the IAEA has increased substantially from approximately a dozen in that year to over a hundred in 1991, before declining slightly to about seventy in 1992. If press coverage of the IAEA continues in 1993 at the rate achieved during the first quarter of the year, over a hundred stories will focus on the IAEA. Thus, one should not be surprised if the U.S. foreign policy elite equates the IAEA with its current activities in applying safeguards to a handful of countries like Iraq, North Korea, and South Africa.

Third, during the recent period of relatively heavy press coverage of the IAEA, roughly 90 percent of the articles focused on safeguards activities. On the basis of this press coverage, members of the foreign policy elite would probably be surprised to find out that less than 40 percent of the agency's resources are spent on safeguards activities.

While a more detailed evaluation of U.S. press coverage of the IAEA is still needed, the contrast between the content of stories published by the IAEA in its own publications and the views presented to the public and the U.S. foreign policy elite by the national press is quite striking. The *IAEA Bulletin*, which is read primarily by specialists on the agency, is filled with articles based on an ideology first created in the 1950s when nuclear technology was seen as the most important technology of the future. In that publication, the multimission role of the IAEA is emphasized, while the role of the agency in providing nonproliferation safeguards under the NPT is treated with as little emphasis as possible.

Officials who are responsible for strengthening the IAEA should be greatly concerned about the radically different messages being sent to specialists and to leaders of U.S. foreign policy opinion. One way to help solve this problem would be to make the IAEA's own publications more forthright. To accomplish this goal, the IAEA leadership should bring knowledgeable critics of the agency into their network of advisers and not listen exclusively to the IAEA experts—who, though well intended, may have been too diplomatic in their effort to encourage the IAEA to change. The longtime friends of the IAEA may not be the most credible supporters if the agency is seeking to convince the broader U.S. foreign policy elite that the IAEA is actually changing and becoming more effective at stopping the spread of nuclear weapons.

IMPROVING THE ABILITY OF THE IAEA TO HALT
THE PROLIFERATION OF NUCLEAR WEAPONS

During the past two years, senior IAEA officials have been extremely successful in their efforts to make a series of changes that have greatly improved the efficacy of the agency's safeguards measures. These new measures have been particularly effective in the countries that are parties to the NPT. If the IAEA is going to further strengthen its safeguards efforts and thereby gain the enhanced political stature needed to achieve its broader mission of technical diffusion, the most important additional steps will require the active leadership of actors *outside* the IAEA.

The first most important additional step required for the IAEA to further expand its effectiveness is for the international nuclear industry to abandon its historical short-term worldview and begin to promote nonproliferation actively. This step would require the industry to admit that the future of nuclear power is primarily linked to a successful stemming of the proliferation of nuclear weapons.

While the nuclear industry has occasionally taken the lead in developing safeguards technology for specific facilities, on balance the industry has tried to avoid getting involved in the issue of nonproliferation. Only by demonstrating to the IAEA secretariat and the board of governors that it encourages an active effort in the nonproliferation area will the industry do its part to transform the institutional culture of the IAEA, which has resisted making safeguards the primary goal of the organization. The international nuclear power industry has been on the defensive for years as a result of India's 1974 nuclear explosion, as well as the major accidents at Three Mile Island and Chernobyl. Enlightened self-interest suggests that if the international nuclear power industry is seen as a leader in the field of nonproliferation, the industry will gain the renewed credibility that will enable it to play a more positive role.[43] By strengthening the safeguards role of the IAEA in the short term, industry will be building the renewed political support for nuclear power that it needs over the longer term, and thus it will be acting in its own self-interest.

The second most important change affecting safeguards is even more radical. Developing countries should initiate a comprehensive evaluation of the benefits and opportunity costs derived from the technical assistance provided by the IAEA. The majority of developing countries have typically viewed the IAEA much as they do any other UN agency: as a source of professional positions for their diplomats and as a source of international financial and technical assistance. The developing countries have resisted evaluating the relative costs and benefits of nuclear technology, in comparison with other advanced technologies now available in the 1990s, at least in part because such an examination might conclude that the technical-assistance mission of the agency is of little relevance for the current needs of the developing states.

For example, because of the small sizes of their electrical grids, their relatively low oil prices, their high capital costs, and the uncertainties over nuclear weapons proliferation, nuclear power will not be an option for most developing countries for several decades—if it ever is an option in the future.[44] With the long-term slowdown in the international nuclear power industry, there is little chance at this point that smaller nuclear reactors which would be much more appropriate for use in many developing countries will be designed and built.

Other examples involve the IAEA's technical-assistance programs. Approximately 20 percent of the organization's technical-assistance budget goes into agriculture. While the desire on the part of developing countries to use advanced technology to improve their agricultural development is understandable, those countries should be more realistic concerning which technologies can provide them with the highest payoff. Food irradiation, radioisotope production, and mutation breeding to improve plant genes may have been appealing in the 1950s, but in the 1990s, other approaches using chemistry and biotechnology may be more cost-effective and have a greater potential for technical spinoffs. The same can be said with respect to many other IAEA technical-assistance programs: How do developing countries believe they benefit from IAEA programs in nuclear fusion, spent-fuel storage, and reactor safety programs?

An independent cost-benefit analysis of IAEA technical-assistance programs by developing countries might conclude that the actual benefits are low but commensurate with the contributions they make to the IAEA budget. If this turns out to be the case, then an alternate diplomatic strategy should be used by developing countries to strengthen the IAEA's role in nonproliferation and, at the same time, to increase the benefits for developing countries in the context of sustainable development. The essence of such a strategy would be to create linkages across issue-areas within the UN specialized agencies. Developing countries could support strengthening safeguards regardless of the expense and its effect on the "balanced" IAEA program (which is paid by developed countries), in exchange for comparable increases in funding for sustainable development (perhaps given to other, more appropriate UN agencies).

For most of the developed countries that contribute to the IAEA budget, their contribution is part of national "international affairs" budgets that include other UN activities as well as foreign economic- and technical-assistance programs. The donor-country advocates of increasing the effectiveness of the IAEA's nonproliferation activities should ally themselves with those in developing countries who favor increasing foreign assistance budgets. By adopting such a linkage strategy, rather than demanding that the IAEA maintain a "balance" between technical assistance and safeguards, the discussion over technical assistance could move from a zero-sum game in the context of a relatively small IAEA budget to a positive-sum game with respect to development assistance more generally.

This initiative within the IAEA can come only from the developing countries. In the context of the Clinton administration, some senior U.S. foreign policy officials are sympathetic to development assistance needs of the underdeveloped states, but they are faced with severe budget constraints. However, they might argue that the developing countries' support for strengthening the safeguards function of the IAEA should be rewarded by increases in their development assistance. Such a quid pro quo could be justified with the argument that it would make a direct contribution to the national security of the United States. Thus, a new diplomatic strategy by developing countries within the IAEA could signal a "new realism" with respect to their participation in UN agencies and could contribute to a stronger United Nations, which is in everyone's interest.

The third most important change regarding safeguards involves the IAEA budget. During the Reagan administration, the United States advocated a zero-growth budget for all UN agencies. A decade later, this principle remains alive in the foreign ministries of countries such as Canada, Germany, and Japan that support nonproliferation but do not want to increase the IAEA safeguards budget because this would produce a commensurate increase in the safeguards "burden" placed on their large nuclear industries. While their logic is correct, their perspective is far too shortsighted.

The nuclear power industry will have a strong future only if the proliferation problem is solved. Countries such as Canada, Germany, and Japan must be willing to increase the resources they expend on nonproliferation because it is in their own self-interest. Although these additional amounts may be large in relation to past IAEA budgets, they are small in the context of current national defense budgets, and tiny in comparison with the amounts of money that will have to be spent on "counterproliferation" if the international nonproliferation regime fails.

For example, UNSCOM has required $25 million to remove slightly irradiated weapons-grade uranium from Iraq during the past year.

This expenditure constitutes approximately 40 percent of the annual IAEA safeguards budget. While this figure seems decidedly large within the context of the IAEA budget, it is rather small in terms of national security budgets.

Fourth, the United States must change its parochial view with respect to the IAEA budget. Not only has the United States been the moving force behind the zero-growth principle regarding the UN budget in the 1980s, but it has also failed to increase its support for the IAEA even as the agency has demonstrated its increased effectiveness in the area of nuclear nonproliferation. If nuclear proliferation is the number one national security threat facing the United States, as voiced by Les Aspin both before and after he became the Clinton administration's secretary of defense, why does the United States continue to fail to fund the IAEA accordingly?

The United States should increase its funding of the IAEA by an order of magnitude. One way to do this would be to move the IAEA account out of the international organization budget administered by the State Department and put it into the Defense Department budget.[45] An alternative strategy would be for leading private-sector organizations to establish a panel of international experts to review the IAEA budget and make recommendations for U.S. funding of the agency within the fundamentally new international environment in which the organization must now operate. Although the Ford Foundation recently conducted just such a review for the entire UN budget, the IAEA budget was not a specific focus of that study.[46]

PROSPECTS FOR REFORM

The world has changed so much during the past three years that predicting future reforms has become problematic in any area. If one were to base one's assessment on the logic of self-interest, one might predict that the developing countries, the international nuclear power industry, those developed countries with large nuclear power programs, and the United States could rethink their fundamental positions regarding the IAEA and reach a new consensus in favor of strengthening the agency. The amounts of additional financing that would be necessary are relatively small, and the level of attention that would have to be devoted to this issue by cabinet officials would be equally small. The expected benefits, however, could be quite significant.

The key question thus becomes, Can the professional policymakers who work on the IAEA and on nonproliferation modify their thinking about the agency and transmit innovative policy recommendations to senior U.S. decisionmakers, many of whom have a decidedly different and much more negative view of the IAEA?

While additional administrative changes should continue to take place within the IAEA to strengthen the agency's safeguards measures, none of these changes will increase the effectiveness of safeguards by an order of magnitude without strong support from important constituencies outside the agency. For this reason, the leadership of the IAEA would be wise to "think big." This will mean that people who are not experts on the IAEA or even experts on nonproliferation should be asked to review the standard operating procedures of the organization and recommend improvements that could make the IAEA the cornerstone in a realistic effort to win the battle against proliferation.

≈6≈

THE UNITED NATIONS, THE UNITED STATES, AND INTERNATIONAL HUMAN RIGHTS

MORRIS B. ABRAM*

*O*n October 19, 1976, I sent a memorandum to Jimmy Carter recommending that he distinguish himself from Gerald Ford by strengthening the U.S. commitment at the United Nations toward international human rights. I urged him to appear at the earliest possible date before the UN General Assembly to say the following words: "Henceforth, we shall call our shots in the vital area of human rights as we see them, exempting no one and inviting similar reactions to our own conduct." I now repeat my recommendation to President Bill Clinton because the message remains valid and, regrettably, largely unfulfilled.

This marks the thirtieth year of my association with the human rights structures of the United Nations. In 1963, when this association began, the organization was busy setting the standards for international human rights observance. The two covenants that construed and elaborated the 1948 Universal Declaration of Human Rights—the International Covenant on Civil and Political Rights and the International Covenant on Economic, Social and Cultural Rights—were drafted. Then, as the U.S. expert on the UN Subcommission on Prevention of Discrimination and Protection of Minorities, I

* I acknowledge the assistance provided by Dina R. Hellerstein, who was my special counselor during my tenure as U.S. permanent representative to the United Nations in Geneva.

participated in the drafting of the International Convention on the Elimination of All Forms of Racial Discrimination. By 1968, the end of my tenure as a leader of the U.S. delegation to four sessions of the Commission on Human Rights, the standard setting was largely complete. That year I attended the World Conference on Human Rights in Teheran. The Final Act declared that "much remains to be done in regard to the implementation of the rights and freedoms" of the international instruments. During my recent service from 1989 to 1993, I was a leader of U.S. delegations to another four sessions of the commission.

Now, as I step down from my four-year tenure as U.S. permanent representative to the United Nations in Geneva, I am motivated to review some of my ideas and philosophy toward human rights and the United Nations. There has been some advancement, much stagnation, and even a reversion of human rights practices during this time. The issues have become more sharply defined in the context of the recent dramatic changes in the world. Human rights, though now more prominent in U.S. foreign policy than when I wrote to Jimmy Carter, should receive increased attention from future U.S. administrations because those rights are the key to achieving and maintaining peace and stability.

The Charter of the United Nations of 1945 is a landmark, the first international treaty that affirms "faith in fundamental human rights, in the dignity and worth of the human person, in the equal rights of men and women and of nations large and small." It was neither a defense nor a trade alliance nor the usual international covenant, and it went far beyond the Covenant of the League of Nations and the post-World War I treaties that referred to minority rights or groups within newly created states. This novel undertaking by the United Nations was largely the product of effective lobbying by groups that were witnesses to the fascist era, groups that resolved that those atrocities would at least fuel a movement to make human rights a cornerstone of the new world edifice.

It is important to keep in mind that despite setbacks and failures, the United Nations has advanced the cause of human rights. There are those who will be dubious given the events in Bosnia in the summer of 1993, but the fact is that the United Nations has created a body of international law—including enforcement mechanisms—that, while far from perfect, provides a foundation upon which something enduring can be built.

The greatest impediment to improving the compliance of states with international human rights law, as was pointed out at the first World Conference on Human Rights at Teheran twenty-five years ago, involves implementation. In 1993, the United Nations held its second

World Conference on Human Rights in Vienna. The Vienna conference (June 14–25) highlighted by omission and by commission the present state of human rights as viewed in and from the United Nations.

The view of human rights presented at the Vienna conference remains strikingly similar to the view presented at Teheran a quarter century earlier. Although numerous states have ratified the many human rights conventions negotiated over the past thirty years, thus adding to the now substantial body of international human rights law, there have been major setbacks in human rights practice. During the twenty-five years since the Teheran conference, the world has endured the villainies of Pol Pot, Idi Amin, and Saddam Hussein, and now we are enduring "ethnic cleansing" in the former Yugoslavia. Those involved in the formation of the United Nations in 1945 believed they were setting up an organization to ensure that that kind of evil rule would never again happen. Unfortunately, over the past twenty-five years the implementation mechanisms erected by the United Nations have largely failed to improve state compliance with international human rights law.

As with the UN system as a whole, there remain enormous defects and inefficiencies in the human rights apparatus of the world body; these deficiencies are the result of political compromises, poor personnel practices, improper oversight, and the reluctance to restructure organs and procedures to meet conditions that have dramatically changed over the past half century. But while the UN human rights apparatus has many deficiencies, it is most important that states move to improve implementation—the enforcement of state compliance with existing human rights covenants.

What can be done? One primary goal should be to improve the effectiveness of the principal UN institution responsible for the enforcement of human rights, the Commission on Human Rights. The Security Council has been experimenting in the field of human rights, and further action should be explored. The dispatch of forces (under a Security Council mandate of Chapter VII of the UN Charter) to Somalia to restore peace so that food and medicine could be safely distributed would have been unthinkable only a few years ago. Another priority should be to strengthen the body of international human rights law, not through the negotiation of additional covenents, but by finding effective means to empower and enable the existing enforcement mechanisms. Finally, to address the fragmentation of nations and the upsurge in ethnic violence, the United Nations and all its member states should rededicate themselves to the protection of civil and political rights and, in particular, minority rights.

CHALLENGES FACING THE UN HUMAN RIGHTS SYSTEM

The fall of the Soviet communist empire raised hopes for world peace. Indeed, when communism began to fall in the late 1980s, the international human rights community had high hopes that with the end of the East–West conflict, which had brought the implementation of human rights to a standstill, there would be fewer obstacles to achieving universal observance of human rights. But those same events brought numerous regional, ethnic, and religious conflagrations within the communist states.

The UN human rights system currently faces several significant challenges that could determine the effectiveness and vitality of existing international human rights agreements and institutions. These challenges include the following: attempts to undermine the universality of basic human rights by making them mutable on the basis of cultural or traditional practices; efforts to put economic, social, and cultural rights, such as the right to economic development, on an equal footing with the long-established civil and political rights; the growing politicization of the Commission on Human Rights and other UN human rights bodies; and the need to help build and maintain democratic forms of governance around the world as the surest guarantee of human rights.

UNIVERSALITY OF HUMAN RIGHTS

Agreement on a definition of which rights are universal is one challenge that continues to face the United Nations. Despite the widening acceptance by states of the application of international human rights to their domestic practices, the Vienna conference was the stage for yet another round in the debate over what the content of those rights should be. Unfortunately, the negotiation and adoption of the 1948 Universal Declaration of Human Rights apparently did not settle the question of which human rights should be universal in character. As a result, many states continue their efforts to redefine the content of international human rights.

Some states claim that they should be held to different standards for the observance of particular human rights on the grounds of cultural differences between societies, which have come to be known in UN parlance as "particularities." Some representatives, for example, have argued that the international community should take account of traditions and customs when evaluating practices such as torture. Similar arguments have also been used to defend and thus maintain the lower status of women in some Islamic countries. In most cases, however, these same states have ratified international covenants that prohibit torture and discrimination on their territory.

The four preparatory meetings leading up to the Vienna conference sounded warnings that certain regimes were going to attack the greatest achievement of the UN human rights system: the universal acceptance of international human rights standards in the 1948 Universal Declaration of Human Rights. For some of the roughly 150 states attending the Vienna conference, this was the opportunity to dismantle the structure built around the cornerstone of the Universal Declaration. The attempts of these states to particularize human rights, or to make their application subject to cultural, historical, or traditional differences between societies, represent the post-cold war means employed by states to defend themselves against international scrutiny of their human rights records. This approach has increasingly replaced the sovereignty, or the "what-is-within-my-borders-does-not-concern-you," line of defense.

Despots will insist, as they tried (and failed) to do at Vienna, that human rights are not universal, but represent the use of "Western" norms to judge "non-Western" peoples. Since the notion that a law is meaningless if it is not applied equally to all is readily enough grasped, the citizens of functioning democracies, accustomed as they are to the principle of the single standard, ask why they should not feel the same way about human rights.

We should consider human rights to be universal. States from the Western democratic tradition find it easy to accept the rights contained in the Universal Declaration, which include the right to free expression, to free exercise of religion, to be free from arbitrary killing, and the right not to be tortured. These principles are consistent not only with the Western democratic tradition but with many religions, natural law, and the distinguishing qualities of all humanity. China, India, Chile, the Philippines, and Lebanon all were involved in the process of drafting the Universal Declaration. The rights therein were declared universal; they were, and remain, common to all peoples and states.

The "particularist" attack on the universality of human rights failed in Vienna because the West held firm. There is no way that practices such as female genital mutilation and the Islamic fatwa, or death sentence against the British author Salman Rushdie, can stand the scrutiny of international human rights standards. "Particularism," in short, represents not an argument for the respect of cultural differences, but rather the contempt of dictators for a single standard of justice. And when "politically correct" Western adepts of "Third Worldism" approve of phony particularisms like "African socialism" or "Islamic democracy," they are not showing respect for the peoples of the developing world or any other world. They are simply demonstrating their reluctance to confront authoritarian regimes.

There surely are traditions and religions that may conflict at times with universal human rights. Such "customs" might include "an eye for an eye," death by stoning, driving prohibitions for women, and lenient sentences for those who murder women. But by their adherence to the Universal Declaration, countries of all cultures and religions have accepted the equalization of rights in the name of civic peace and have agreed to work toward the elimination of practices, however sacred to tradition, that violate the Universal Declaration.

THE RIGHT TO ECONOMIC DEVELOPMENT

Another challenge to the UN human rights system is the specious argument that economic and social rights should have equal status with civil and political rights or that the latter cannot be claimed under conditions of economic deprivation. Unfortunately, the Vienna conference did not effectively turn back this particular diversionary tactic. When the framers of the UN Charter reaffirmed the importance of securing "fundamental human rights," they meant those civil and political rights contained in documents such as the U.S. Bill of Rights and the French Declaration of the Rights of Man. And what led the authors of the Universal Declaration of Human Rights to include splendid economic and social goals such as "rest and leisure" as basic human rights was more a matter of utopian fad and the great expectations generated by the end of the colonial era, rather than reason or logic. Too often despots use poverty as justification for an authoritarian form of government; this is self-serving and wrong. And it should be noted that there is not one state with long-enduring democratic traditions and institutions that is impoverished.

In the Declaration of Independence, in one of the best-known sentences in Western political rhetoric, Thomas Jefferson refers to the inalienable rights to life, liberty, and the pursuit of happiness. He meant that all persons have a right to seek their own happiness. This concept is radically different from the "inalienable right to development" now claimed by the developing world. The listing of rights in UN documents will not of itself achieve the aims implied by those rights. And there is a great downside to this practice, for when every social goal becomes a right, the claims of the fundamental human rights are debased.

At the Vienna conference, the claim of the developing countries to economic and social rights was emphatically endorsed—indeed, emphasis was placed on the "inalienable right to development." Thomas Jefferson would have choked had he known that his "inalienable rights" tag on civil and political liberties would be hijacked by the proponents of this new position.

The proponents of the right to development are unable to clarify whether that right is conferred by a state on its citizens or if it is a right possessed by the underdeveloped states themselves. If it is a right enjoyed by states, the question then becomes, On whom does the duty to fulfill this right rest? If the duty falls on the developed states, how is it quantified and proportionally assigned? These problems arise not only with the right to development but in the fleshing out of economic and social rights in general. For unlike civil and political rights, which require that governments *not* do ignoble deeds (such as censorship or denial of religious liberty), economic and social goals require that governments *do* noble acts.

The Final Document of the Vienna conference (which ran to some thirty pages) not only recognized the newly proclaimed "inalienable" status of the right to economic development, but also prescribed one way to achieve that right when it called on the international community to "alleviate the external debt burden of developing countries." Astonishingly, the United States went along with the other Western democracies in adopting a Final Document that calls for UN member states to alleviate international debt but nowhere unambiguously champions the freedoms of expression and religion.

Raising social and economic goals like development to the status of "rights"—to the level of legitimate claims on society—is detrimental both to the achievement of those goals and to the authority of established rights. When every goal becomes a right, then all rights are debased and subject to compromise. For when a goal becomes a right, when only the complete attainment of that now legitimate claim is acceptable, there cannot be any room for compromise.

Reasonable people may differ over a subject so eternal and fundamental to human societies as the causes of wealth and poverty. Respect for these differences requires that we find compromises in addressing the inequalities among nations, just as we have sought compromises between the rationality of the market and the claims of an ethic based on compassion. It is crucial, however, to understand that our ability to find broadly acceptable means for achieving economic and social goals— our ability to compromise—is jeopardized when we allow those goals to be raised to the level of the universal human rights.

Inevitably, the issue of the right to development becomes very murky, for the duty to individuals necessarily rests upon their own state. If it is a state claim, it amounts to a demand for the redistribution of wealth from the developed to the underdeveloped world. If one accepts that the economic progress of the underdeveloped world is a legitimate claim, there still remain the questions: How much redistribution? From whom? And, one might be permitted to ask, Does each underdeveloped state have to establish a reasonably stable and honest government to qualify?

There are multilateral institutions—such as the World Bank, the UN Development Program, and the International Monetary Fund—where the demand for development may be more properly deliberated and with perhaps more tangible results than at the Commission on Human Rights.

THE POLITICIZATION OF HUMAN RIGHTS

Another challenge for the UN human rights system is the need to become more objective in its treatment and condemnation of states for their human rights records. Since its inception, the human rights system of the United Nations has been abused by states seeking narrow political objectives. This practice must be curtailed because it undermines the legitimacy, universality, and effectiveness of the United Nations in the human rights field.

The annual agenda of the Commission on Human Rights comprises scores of items, many dated and of little or no consequence. Nevertheless, two perennial items on the agenda consume one-third of the commission's time: Israel and South Africa. Although some sessions concerning these two countries are adjourned for lack of speakers, they have retained their place on the commission's agenda. Yet, a 1993 attempt by the West to place the human rights tragedies in Bosnia ahead of Israel and South Africa on the commission's agenda was rebuffed.

Throughout its more than forty-year history, the commission has never taken action on the human rights violations of the five permanent members of the Security Council. Action was not taken against the United States when it practiced segregation by law, nor was there any response to the Soviet Union's operation of the Gulag camps (Stalin ruled during the first five years of the commission's existence), nor was action taken against China during the cultural revolution, nor against France during the colonial repression in Algeria. Finally, no action has been taken against the United Kingdom despite some Irish claims that the British occupy Irish territory.

A small group of states has received close attention and continuous condemnation from the Commission on Human Rights, including Chile, South Africa, and Israel. While no one should claim an exemption for any state from the scrutiny of the international community and the commission, an examination of the treatment of these three states is helpful in analyzing the objectivity of the UN human rights system.

The Chilean regime of the 1970s was indeed authoritarian, and it often deserved censure from the Commission on Human Rights. But in politics, as in almost all else, context is everything. During the 1970s, nearly every Latin American regime, and some of those in the immediate region, were equally authoritarian. South Africa was, until very recently, officially racist, and as such it was in contravention of the human rights principles of the United Nations. But the well-known and unspoken "secret" about Africa is that almost every regime that emerged from the colonial period has been plagued by tribal racism, and it is significant that the United Nations could not find even the rhetorical resources to say or do anything about this.

Chile has followed its Latin American neighbors in adopting a more democratic form of government. And South Africa may yet turn out to be the only major African country where multiparty and multiracial democracy takes hold, an outcome for which the United Nations may take some real credit. In view of these developments, world opinion has cooled off on these fronts, leaving Israel (a parliamentary democracy) as the one country to receive continuous condemnation from the "parliament of man."

In 1991, Israel was the object of no less than thirty-two accusatory resolutions in the United Nations. It is the object of a special section of the Secretariat and two special committees of the General Assembly: the Committee on the Occupied Territories, created in 1967 when Israel, having captured the West Bank of the Jordan while defending itself on three fronts, was weighing offers to return the territories to Jordanian control in return for peace; and the Committee on the Exercise of the Inalienable Rights of the Palestinian People, established in 1975 on the day the General Assembly passed the now infamous resolution equating Zionism with racism.

Although the "Zionism is racism" resolution was repealed in 1991, Jeane Kirkpatrick observed in 1992 that "on any given day a majority in the United Nations can be mobilized against Israel on any pretext." The Vienna conference highlighted the continuing unbalanced treatment of Israel. Even though there was agreement that no country-specific resolutions were to be adopted at the conference, on the final day of the meeting a cryptic but clear reference to Israel and its practices appeared in the Final Document. Pakistan, the Palestine Liberation Organization (PLO), and the United Kingdom inserted a reference to "occupied territory" that would lead one to believe the West Bank,

Gaza, and the Golan Heights are the only occupied territories of which the UN human rights system is aware. At the same time, while the Vienna conference roundly condemned racism, apartheid, xenophobia, and discrimination against women, children, the disabled, and migrant workers, it could not find the will to include anti-Semitism on its list of condemned practices. This was not surprising, because the conference also did not see fit to give the Dalai Lama a turn to speak, but the PLO's Yasser Arafat was again given a UN microphone to condemn Israel.

Indeed, millions of dollars are spent every year by the United Nations and its affiliated organizations on diplomatic and "educational" activities (some very slick propaganda) whose principal purpose is to isolate Israel from the world community. Apart from the waste of international funds involved, the continuing anti-Israel stance of the United Nations is having two pernicious effects. First, though not supported in the United States, these incessant attacks have created a climate of hate where it is now much easier to argue that Israel is different from other states and therefore deserving of special opprobrium. This is, in effect, a definition of anti-Semitism.

As it happens, of course, Israel is different from most of the countries that are members of the United Nations, and certainly from all of its Middle Eastern neighbors. Israel, unlike most of the member states of the United Nations, is a free society whose citizens and noncitizens are protected by the rule of law. Israel is different from most countries in the same way that the United States and Switzerland are different from a majority of the 184 countries that are members of the United Nations.

The second pernicious effect of the UN campaign against Israel is that that country has become the lightning rod of the antidemocratic camp in the international community. To the extent that the democracies do not defend one of their own when it is subjected to vicious and unfair attacks, the credibility of the United Nations as an institution for the advancement of a just international order becomes impaired. The effect of this campaign is that the United Nations is corrupted by its own weakness, in much the same way that a judge will eventually be corrupted if he permits corruption in his courtroom.

BUILDING DEMOCRACY

The last—and perhaps the most critical—challenge facing the UN human rights system is that of building democracy, because the creation of universally accepted and observed human rights standards depends primarily on the expansion of democratic forms of government. This belief is borne out by the fact that this turbulent century has never witnessed a single instance in which one true democracy has waged war against another democracy. This is the basis for the view of Natan Sharansky, the former Soviet political prisoner who is now an Israeli citizen, when he said, "I would rather live next to democracies that hate my country than next to dictatorships which love it."

The UN Charter does not require its members to have democratic forms of government for admission to the organization. It simply stipulates that members be "peace-loving" and that they "accept the obligations" contained in the UN Charter. The world body is primarily a collective security organization charged with building and protecting international peace and security, although new programs such as those providing advisory services and electoral assistance seek to strengthen democracy. Like the international community that it mirrors, the overwhelming majority of UN member states are not ruled by "democratic" forms of government.

However, the hope for human rights—and for a more peaceful world—depends on the development of a world in which more and more states are founded on the moral authority and consent of the governed. Edmund Burke, the eighteenth-century British statesman wrote that a tradition of moderation is a precondition of democratic government. If so, humankind may have a long wait before the UN Charter's goals are realized. Still, there is no other instrument, no other hope, in which to invest our energies than the United Nations system.

CONSTRAINTS ON THE UN HUMAN RIGHTS SYSTEM

Organizational and political realities exacerbate the difficult international challenges that today face the United Nations human rights system. The United Nations was constructed in 1945 to accommodate the 51 states that signed the UN Charter. With a present membership of 184 states, the United Nations has become both unwieldy and unmanageable. In the field of human rights, the world body is constrained by several factors: the structure and procedures of the Commission on Human Rights; a method for governing the UN human rights system that is based on appointing states to the commission by geographic rotation; the inadequate financing of the existing mechanisms for enforcing compliance with international human rights conventions; and constant battles over the boundaries of national sovereignty.

COMMISSION ON HUMAN RIGHTS

The Commission on Human Rights was once a major stumbling block to action by the UN human rights system, but it has become easier to respond to rights abuses through the commission now that the former Soviet republics and the East European states often vote with the Western democracies. A number of important changes have occurred within the commission. The once-tight alliances of the African and Latin American groups have been splintered as individual countries discover the political and economic benefits of democracy. At the same time, other alliances, such as the Asian and Islamic groups, have become more cohesive.

Regrettably, the work of the Commission on Human Rights seems destined to be overwhelmed by the bilateral political goals of some of its member states. Examples are numerous and include the Cyprus problem, in which Greece and Turkey support their respective ethnic populations, and the Arab-Israeli dispute, which often involves the manipulation of UN human rights institutions for distinctly political aims.

The membership of the Commission on Human Rights has grown from 21 states in 1965 to the current 53, a number larger than the original membership of the General Assembly. Much like the proportion in the General Assembly, 37 of the 53 are from among the nonaligned countries. The nonaligned countries can easily band together to defeat by majority vote those propositions they believe are against the interests of the developing world. Yet, when the recent proposal was put forth to add ten new members to the commission from among the nonaligned states, only the United States objected.

With regard to membership on the Commission on Human Rights, the regional groups recommend states to the Economic and Social Council, which then makes the final decisions regarding membership on the commission. There are no criteria used for the recommendation other than the principle of rotation—and that principle results in the anomaly of having members on the commission that have been condemned for massive human rights abuses by the very commission on which they sit. These human rights abusers often successfully campaign within their regional groups to gain a seat on the jury that will sit in judgment of their compliance with international human rights standards. This practice is defended by the spurious argument that representation on the commission allows these countries to defend themselves. Cuba and Iran, for example, while being investigated by the commission's special rapporteurs, still sit in judgment on other states. Moreover, at various other times during this decade, Iraq, Libya, Sudan, and Syria have been seated on the commission.

The United States was the first country to point out the aberration of seating human rights abusers on the commission; it may now be time for the United States to propose standards that would preclude human rights abusers from membership in the commission. The UN Charter contains standards for membership on the Security Council (even if they are not followed); Why not develop standards for the Commission on Human Rights? Just as the contribution of a member to the maintenance of international peace and security is a standard for membership on the Security Council, there should be a standard for membership on the Commission on Human Rights: the contribution of a member to the promotion of human rights. Both standards are stated purposes of the United Nations in Article 1 of the UN Charter and should be evaluated by the regional groups when members are nominated.

Alternatively, some simple measures could be taken to establish minimum standards for membership on the Commission on Human Rights. For example, any state that is under censure by the commission, or any state on which the Security Council has recently imposed Chapter VII sanctions, might be considered ineligible for membership. By either measure, some current members of the Commission, such as Cuba, Iran, and Libya, would be excluded from membership.

The subcommission of the Commission on Human Rights that exists today bears little resemblance to the institution that was established thirty years ago. At that time, it was intended that the subcommission be composed of experts independent of governments, and its members spent much of their time drafting treaties and studies. A 1963 study on the right to leave one's country, by the Philippine jurist Jose Ingles, eventually became the basis of treaties and accords by which the right to exit from the iron curtain countries was demanded and finally achieved. Now, some experts arrive fresh from service in their respective foreign ministries, with which they tend to remain affiliated even after they begin their service with the subcommission. For example, in August 1993 this body of "independent experts" had ten members who were either serving as ambassadors or held other posts within their governments. The subcommission currently works more like a minicommission that passes series of resolutions that duplicate the work of the commission. Unless the subcommission reforms its agenda and is reshaped into a body of experts who are independent of their governments, its ability to function as it should is questionable.

The subcommission's politicization was made clear at the August 1993 session when the Cuban representative moved to have the subcommission inquire into the violation by the United States of the human rights of some Christian ministers. The ministers had travelled to Laredo, Texas, with a school bus, food, and other items for shipment to Cuba; when the U.S. government prohibited the shipment of the bus without a license, the ministers chose to protest with a hunger strike. The U.S. expert on the commission attempted to amend the motion to include an inquiry into thirteen Cuban political prisoners named in a 1993 Amnesty International report. In the end, the subcomission voted down the U.S. amendment but passed the original Cuban motion.

The agenda of the Commission on Human Rights is another significant impediment to its effectiveness. The way in which issues are selected for consideration by the commission undermines its ability to deal with new problems. Certain of the commission's agenda items have remained unchanged for years and should be brought up-to-date. The world has changed dramatically; there is no reason for the commission to be addressing the same stale issues that it considered twenty-five and thirty years ago.

The expanded size of the Commission on Human Rights generates more speakers on each item, and the list of items grows as human rights are increasingly violated, particularly during ethnic and religious conflicts. It is therefore imperative that the commission's agenda be revamped. Otherwise, the commission will be out of step with the times and current events.

The Commission on Human Rights has also tended to focus on a small group of countries while ignoring the human rights problems of entire regions. Not until 1992 did the commission pass a public resolution on an African country other than South Africa: Equatorial Guinea. However, this practice may be changing with the passage in 1993 of resolutions regarding the human rights practices of Somalia, Sudan, Zaire.

A new mechanism available to the members of the Commission on Human Rights allows them to call special meetings when extraordinary circumstances arise between annual sessions. The United States successfully used this mechanism twice in 1992 to call a special session to consider the deteriorating human rights situation in the former Yugoslavia. The special session appointed a rapporteur to investigate the situation because of the allegations of concentration camps and mass graves. He has since reported to the commission, supplying valuable information, some of which will be used in eventual war crimes trials if they occur.

A revitalization of the agenda and a judicious use of the special-session mechanism would allow the Commission on Human Rights to fulfill its intended role as the body that spotlights and condemns contemporary human rights abuses throughout the world.

GEOGRAPHIC ROTATION

Another constraint is that the entire UN system overemphasizes geographic distribution, a practice that affects the quality of leadership in UN institutions. Instead of using competence as the standard for deciding which states and individuals will hold leadership positions, such assignments are made on the basis of geographic rotation. From the choice of secretary-general to the chairs of the regional groups, nearly every leadership position at the United Nations is rotated by region or country. If an African has held a certain position, for instance, it is accepted that an Asian should next hold that position.

The practice of geographic rotation has arisen independent of any requirement in the UN Charter and could be altered or even abolished. The only two references in the charter to geographic criteria make them secondary to other qualifications. For nonpermanent membership in the Security Council, "due regard [should be] specially paid, in the first instance to the contribution of Members of the United Nations to the maintenance of international peace and security and to the other purposes of the Organization, and also to equitable geographical distribution." With respect to the UN Secretariat, the charter states that "the paramount consideration in the employment of the staff . . . shall be the necessity of securing the highest standards of efficiency, competence, and integrity. Due regard shall be paid to the importance of recruiting the staff on as wide a geographical basis as possible."

The ability of the United States to play a strong leadership role within the United Nations has been hampered by the system of geographic rotation and the convention by which the permanent five members of the Security Council restrain themselves from seeking certain roles. As a result of this practice, the United States is hugely underrepresented in the UN Secretariat in terms of qualifications and expertise, rarely holds official roles or has its own experts appointed to commissions, and seldom leads the regional groups to which it belongs.

Furthermore, the international distribution of expertise is not necessarily reflected in the staffing of the United Nations because of the adherence to the principle of geographic distribution. Moreover, equal or proportional representation for all regions on the UN staff has often produced an extremely inefficient and ineffective bureaucracy. The principle of sovereign equality among all of the 184 member states of the United Nations creates further distortions in the staffing patterns of the Secretariat and in the appointment of experts servicing human rights organs, as well as the treaty and nontreaty bodies. It is also at variance with the importance and influence of those states that are major UN powers, in terms of the size of their populations, their contributions to the budget of the United Nations and its specialized agencies, and their political or moral authority.

The emphasis on representation by region prevents members who do not belong to any regional group from playing an effective role at the United Nations. Israel, for example, has been refused entry to the Asian group to which it belongs geographically. If it were accepted into that group, Israel would be one of the outstanding Asian democracies. (The Western European and Other group, though inclusive of non-European democracies such as the United States, Canada, and Australia, excludes the democratic state of Israel.) Since membership requires referral from a regional group, Israel is currently barred from holding a seat on the Commission on Human Rights. As a result, Israel is unable to respond effectively to attacks on its practices by countries that use their membership on the commission for purely political purposes. If the regional-groups system is to remain, it should not be permitted to selectively deny membership to some countries.

ENFORCEMENT MECHANISMS

The rapporteur and working group mechanisms employed by the Commission on Human Rights are another significant development. But even though their work can have a substantial impact on the implementation of international human rights agreements, they remain underfunded and understaffed, as do the other human rights operations in Geneva.

The rapporteur mechanism, which is now used rather extensively by the commission, has been a significant development for investigating and spotlighting international human rights violations. The rapporteurs can be country specific, such as the rapporteur on the former Yugoslavia and the rapporteur on Iraq, or they can be thematic, such as the rapporteur on torture. Their reports to the commission provide information culled from research and inquiries into the country or situation they are investigating. These reports, which are drafted by respected human rights experts appointed by the commission, not only provide information and assessments, but also draw attention to the topic or country under investigation.

The reports of the rapporteurs are often of great interest to the media, which can draw attention to human rights violations in forums other than the Commission on Human Rights. The media are capable of disseminating information about human rights violations to people around the world. Last year's devastating report on Iraq by the special rapporteur received substantial media attention, as has each report by the special rapporteur on the former Yugoslavia. The commission could use the media to publicize its other actions of condemnation, thus letting the world know which countries violate international human rights and, it is hoped, shaming those countries into compliance.

Strangely and happily, words can sometimes be used as a weapon. At the very least, even great powers seem to fear words that condemn their human rights practices. China went to extraordinary lengths to avoid condemnation and resolutions against its actions in Tiananmen Square, and continues its struggle to fend off the reproaches drawn up at the Commission on Human Rights. Some might question the idea that words are a real source of international power. But French, American, and Russian history furnishes abundant examples of the power of words: "Liberty, equality, and fraternity"; "No taxation without representation"; "Peace and bread." And, more recently, Did not the Ayatollah Khomeini bring down a monarchy with a tape recorder?

One method of investigation used by the commission, the "1503 mechanism," is secret. Under the 1503 mechanism, named for the Economic and Social Council (ECOSOC) resolution that created it, individuals or organizations may submit complaints about countries' human rights practices to the United Nation. The complaints are screened by a body of experts that determines whether there has been a pattern of gross violations of human rights in a given country. The government is then asked to respond to these allegations. Upon reference to the commission, the country can be condemned or an investigation ordered. The confidentiality phase ends at the stage at which the commission may recommend action in its annual report to ECOSOC. In turn, ECOSOC can accept the commission's recommendations, make its own proposals, or suggest resolutions to be adopted by the General Assembly.

The effect of the 1503 mechanism, the country rapporteurs, and other actions that the Commission on Human Rights can direct against a particular country lies with the dishonor experienced by a country identified as the subject of investigation. The strength of this effect has been proven many times through the efforts exerted by countries to avoid condemnation. Often, in the days leading up to country action by the commission, countries will release prisoners, they will make promises, or they will announce reform campaigns. While there can be no doubt that these efforts are not all taken in good faith, it is certain that some improvements result because of the fear and shame brought by inclusion in the commission's annual country actions.

The Commission on Human Rights has made greater use of the UN's advisory services in situations where human rights problems exist in a country but where assistance, not investigation or condemnation, is likely to be more productive. UN staff and outside experts can be made available to advise countries on how to rebuild national structures and democratic institutions or how to establish an impartial judiciary. Governments, including the United States government, should give full support to the work of the UN Center for Human Rights based in Geneva.

THE BARRIER OF SOVEREIGNTY

While the predominant international conflict of the past half century has subsided, regional conflicts have proliferated and now obstruct the potential movement toward wider observance of human rights. The cold war was a contest of nuclear armaments and security threats, whereas most contemporary conflicts around the globe are grounded in ethnic, religious, or nationalist rivalries. Within the UN system, security issues belong to the Security Council and the political organs of the world body, but conflicts that begin with ethnic and nationalist persecution or discrimination are violations of human rights and should therefore be initially addressed by the Commission on Human Rights. To deal with the growing number of essentially internal or civil wars, the United Nations has had to overcome the limits that were traditionally placed on its authority by the doctrine of sovereignty, which has undergone substantial evolution since the 1960s.

Writing about the Commission on Human Rights in a 1969 *Foreign Affairs* article, I observed, "Where issues involving human rights within national borders come up in the United Nations, few states hesitate to invoke Article II (7) of the Charter." That provision states, "Nothing contained in the present Charter shall authorize the United Nations to intervene in matters which are essentially within the domestic jurisdiction of any state."

Today, it is increasingly rare for states to argue that abuses alleged to occur within their borders are exclusively of domestic concern. (The Soviet Union gave up this practice in 1989.) With the barrier of sovereignty lowered, a closer examination of internal human rights practices is possible.

Those states that continue to rely on the doctrine of sovereignty to deflect international scrutiny of their internal human rights practices

are increasingly isolated. Saddam Hussein claimed that the United
Nations had no right to intervene in Iraq's domestic affairs when he
refused to comply with Security Council Resolution 688, which required
that Iraq provide international humanitarian organizations immediate
access to all parts of its territory. Cuba refuses on the same grounds to
allow entry to the commission's special rapporteur charged with examining human rights violations in Cuba.

Although a dwindling number of states continue to rely on the
doctrine of sovereignty to deflect international scrutiny of their human
rights practices, it can surely be argued that the United Nations has
helped establish what might be called "the right to learn the truth" in
defense of human rights.

Many states that have previously employed the sovereignty defense
would now welcome intervention to supply free food and medical care.
The declining boundaries of sovereignty have facilitated Security Council
action in the provision of humanitarian relief to desperate populations.
During my four-year tenure, the Security Council ordered, in the name of
international peace and security and without first requesting the consent
of governments, the delivery of humanitarian aid in Iraq, the former
Yugoslavia, and, most recently, Somalia. The claim of human rights on the
international conscience, coupled with the lowering of the sovereignty
barrier and the evident physical needs of many populations, has become
the basis for "the right to protect and meet the needs," which is rapidly
finding its place in international practice.

The High Commissioner for Human Rights

The Vienna conference on human rights reexamined and recommended to the General Assembly "as a matter of priority consideration" an idea that was first broached in the Commission on Human
Rights in the mid-1960s: the creation of a High Commissioner for
Human Rights. When that office was originally conceived by the United
States and urged by Costa Rica in the midst of the cold war, the Soviet
bloc instantly opposed it, surmising (correctly) that the first target of
the High Commissioner for Human Rights would be Soviet totalitari-
anism. After the collapse of the Soviet bloc, the United States revived the
idea because such an office could add visibility to the UN human rights
program and thus enhance its effectiveness.

In December 1993, after a thirty-year effort, the 48th General
Assembly established the post of High Commissioner for Human Rights
to have the principal responsibility for UN human rights activities. The
Secretary General has appointed José Ayala Lasso of Ecuador as the
first High Commissioner for Human Rights.

In chapter 10, Ambassador James Leonard expresses his hope that the High Commissioner for Human Rights can be insulated from the governmental pressures that have compromised the Commission on Human Rights. Fortunately, it appears that the first high commissioner is not personally tied to any contending and contentious theories of human rights or their exponents and, moreover, he does not share the views of the many authoritarian governments that tried to undermine the principle of universality at the 1993 World Conference on Human Rights. If he performs with independence and objectivity, he may become the eyes, ears, and conscience of humanity, deserving of the respect and attention of all.

The high commissioner will serve under the direction and authority of the secretary-general, and within the framework of the decisions and authority of the General Assembly, ECOSOC, and the Commission on Human Rights. The high commissioner's mandate is unclear as to whether he will guide these bodies or be their servant. The high commissioner will report annually and make recommendations to the Commission on Human Rights and, through ECOSOC, to the General Assembly. In particular, I hope he will encourage reform of the Commission on Human Rights' biased and outdated agenda and absence of criteria for membership.

The mandate of the high commissioner seeks to avoid duplication of the work of the Center for Human Rights—the high commissioner will supervise the Center for Human Rights and strengthen the provision of advisory services by the Center but have its own, independent staff. The commissioner's duty is to rationalize, adapt, strengthen, and streamline the existing UN human rights machinery to promote and protect all human rights and fundamental freedoms with a view to improving its efficiency and effectiveness. Most welcome is the directive that the high commissioner be guided by the principle that "it is the duty of States, regardless of their political, economic and cultural systems, to promote and protect all human rights and fundamental freedoms."

Because the mandate of the High Commissioner for Human Rights is general, the establishment of the position raises several questions. One must ask whether there are to be two centers of judgment and action—the commission and the commissioner—within the United Nations regarding human rights matters. Would the high commissioner's work advance, conflict with, or substitute for that of a special country or thematic rapporteur? These questions will be resolved favorably to the cause of human rights if the high commissioner carefully defines and exercises powers that are somewhat ambiguous.

The high commissioner's task will be fraught with tension, pulled in every direction, north and south, east and west. What he must not become is a mirror or endorser of the shifting majorities that character- ize the General Assembly or the Commission on Human Rights. Given the history of the politicization of the UN human rights organizations, one is entitled to ask whether a High Commissioner for Human Rights would follow the example of the Commission on Human Rights or set a new and objective course of equal treatment of "nations large and small." He will either be a leader firmly committed to the application of certain immutable truths to current circumstances or another tormented bureau- crat. As Mr. Lasso is the first High Commissioner for Human Rights, he will shape the office and the future of UN human rights promotion and protection. His crucial role in drafting the General Assembly resolution creating the position gives comfort to those who have yearned for a far more effective and less politicized UN human rights program

IMPROVING THE EFFECTIVENESS OF THE UN HUMAN RIGHTS SYSTEM:
THE ROLE OF THE UNITED STATES

In order to address the new threats to human rights that have arisen during the past five years, as well as those dangers that have persisted over the past thirty years, the international community need do little more than reassess and reform the institutions and frameworks that already exist. There is in place a body of international human rights law that could resolve many conflicts, including the continuing viola- tions of internationally recognized human rights standards perpetrated by marginal or fundamentalist groups and often sanctioned by gov- ernments. The problem is not with the law, but with its implementation by the international community and the UN human rights system.

Indeed, a series of international treaties protect civil, political, eco- nomic, social, and cultural rights, as well as prohibit racial, ethnic, and religious discrimination. There are conventions against torture and genocide, and there are also agreements that protect the rights of the vic- tims of armed conflict. These standards of conduct have been accepted by the vast majority of states that have, through their ratification of these agreements, pledged to grant rights, legislate and enforce laws, preserve and protect beliefs and traditions, and refrain from interfering with basic individual and group freedoms. Many of these treaties have associated assemblies of international legal experts that meet regularly to monitor the compliance of the states that are parties to the agree- ment. The work of these treaty organizations is important, although for the most part that work is relatively unknown and unappreciated.

The human rights elaborated in the numerous international treaties are held by individuals. Those rights must be implemented, however, by governments. If the existing international human rights treaties were truly observed by all states, there would be no ethnic or religious wars, no splintering of states by nationalist groups battling each other, and no questions involving the universality of human rights.

For those states signing international human rights agreements, national legislation should be in place that codifies the obligations that their governments have undertaken. Constitutions and laws are, however, just not enough. To merely acknowledge the existence and the evolution of international law by recording it in legislation does not represent a good-faith effort at observing those human rights. International human rights laws must be enforced if states are to meet their obligations.

If the international community can improve the effectiveness of the UN human rights system, there will certainly be more peace in the world. The fundamental connection between human rights and war was recognized by President John F. Kennedy when he asked, Is not peace, in the last analysis, basically a matter of human rights?

The United Nations must ensure that the universality of human rights is maintained. The universal acceptance of those rights in the 1948 Universal Declaration is the single greatest accomplishment of the UN human rights system. Those states that employ appeals to the "particularities" of their practices are simply attempting to validate their failure or lack of will in conforming to internationally accepted standards. If these efforts are tolerated by the international community, the Universal Declaration and the many human rights agreements built on that foundation over the ensuing years may unravel.

The United States and the other democracies were right to defend the principle of universality at the June 1993 Vienna conference on human rights, and it is imperative that this defense of universality continue within the Commission on Human Rights and the other organs of the UN human rights system. It is just as important, moreover, that the High Commissioner for Human Rights be a staunch supporter of the principle of universality, and indeed the high commissioner's mandate so directs him.

The members of the United Nations should seek to ensure that civil and political rights—the basic freedoms (such as speech, assembly, and religion) on which democracy is founded—retain their primacy over economic, social, and cultural rights (such as education, health care, and a minimum wage). The importance of this point should not be obscured by our desire—indeed our obligation—to help the less fortunate countries of the world improve their standards of living. The United States should continue to assist the developing states through bilateral and multilateral programs, but the creation of democratic institutions and governments is the surest path to development.

As long as the economic rights are claimed by citizens against their governments and not against the international community, they are consistent with U.S. values. It is only when "economic rights" are used by states as an excuse for the denial of civil and political rights, or as an argument for a redistribution of wealth from the richer countries to the poorer, that the term "rights" becomes objectionable. This is particularly true if those claiming a right to development use the human rights organs of the United Nations for this effort.

Reforming the Commission on Human Rights should remain a priority of the United States and the other members of the United Nations. As the principal international body charged with overseeing the UN human rights system, the commission is the key to the effectiveness of that system. A number of specific reforms would improve the structure and operations of the commission. The High Commissioner for Human Rights will have a role and unique opportunity to influence commission reform.

The Commission on Human Rights needs to become a more objective body. It should be the institution within the UN human rights system that does not replicate the diplomatic quarrels of international politics. Over the years, the commission has been subverted by individual countries, including the United States, seeking to further their national interests. As a result, the commission is accountable to governments and is neither independent nor objective. The member states of the United Nations should therefore work to curtail the politicization of the commission and its use by states as a tool of diplomacy.

Several specific measures may help to reduce the politicization of the Commission on Human Rights. First, the commission's agenda must be reformed. Persistent political issues—such as Israel's occupation of the West Bank, Gaza, and the Golan, or South Africa's racist policies—must not be allowed to dominate the agenda of the commission. The issues placed on the commission's agenda must reflect the full range of human rights issues that concern the international community at any given time, and the agenda must deal with abuses of human rights in proportion to the threat they pose to justice and human dignity.

A second reform that would improve the effectiveness of the Commission on Human Rights involves its membership. The system of designating membership by geographic rotation, which has resulted in abuses of the right to sit on the commission, should be abandoned; it frequently leads to states that abuse human rights being seated on the commission and serves to undermine the legitimacy and effectiveness of the UN human rights system.

The United Nations should establish minimum standards for membership on the Commission on Human Rights. Such standards could include the stipulation that any state under censure by the commission, or any state on which the Security Council has recently imposed Chapter VII sanctions, be ineligible to hold a seat. Standards such as these would ensure that states permitting the abuse of human rights will not have an opportunity to sit on the commission.

Another measure that would improve the effectiveness of the Commission on Human Rights is the reorganization of the subcommission to allow it to play its intended role in support of the commission. As noted previously, the subcommission was designed as an independent body of experts who conduct research and draft treaties for the commission. The subcommission should return to this role, ending the current duplication of activities entrusted to the commission.

The establishment of a High Commissioner for Human Rights may prove to be a step in the wrong direction. The member states must be careful to specify the high commissioner's role within the UN human rights system, as well as that official's relationship to the other institutions within that system. It is particularly important that a new and duplicative layer of bureaucracy not be added to the already cumbersome structure of the human rights system. These risks can be avoided only if the first High Commissioner for Human Rights uses his powers independently, objectively, and creatively.

The UN Center for Human Rights based in Geneva can and should play a greater role within the UN human rights system. To do this, however, will require both additional funding and an improvement in the quality of its personnel. The Center for Human Rights could justify these changes if it expanded its role within the UN human rights system. The existing program of advisory services—a UN program of limited technical assistance in the field of human rights, currently managed by the assistant secretary-general for human rights and provided with a limited budget—should be better financed and expanded. The expanded program should focus on the training of law-enforcement, judicial, and prosecutorial personnel, who are needed for countries that are willing to observe human rights standards but lack the means to do so.

While the United States is viewed as a military superpower, it is also thought by many to be a moral superpower. States around the world have modeled their constitutions and laws on those of the United States, and the United States is expected to speak out against injustice everywhere. If the United States is to fulfill its expected role as a leader of international moral conscience—and it should—it will have to act forcefully on issues of international human rights.

The United States should not be ashamed of either the military or the moral power it wields. The international community relies on the United States to lead, and even when the United States is not using its power, other states often assume that it is acting behind the scenes. By actually leading, the United States merely lives up to its reputation. Senator Daniel Patrick Moynihan, a former U.S. ambassador to the United Nations, wrote in 1981: "The United States helped found the United Nations, mostly wrote the Charter, has largely paid for the place. United States representatives have an obligation to insist that there are standards written into that Charter." We should not be ashamed when we recommend the standards that shaped our own democracy.

The UN human rights instruments are a web of law that links states all over the globe and binds them to uniform standards of observance. Therefore, to prove the seriousness of the U.S. commitment to international human rights at the United Nations, the United States should consider ratifying additional UN human rights instruments. Last year's ratification by the United States of the International Covenant on Civil and Political Rights was an important first step. However, it should not have taken so long to ratify a treaty that the United States helped to draft and that contains basic U.S. principles.

Ratification has both symbolic and substantive implications. Through its ratification of a treaty, the United States agrees to observe international human rights law on a par with the scores of other states that have so bound themselves. U.S. adherence to international standards in practice does not obviate the need to ratify the relevant agreements. Would we take all other states upon their word? That some parties ignore their treaty obligations does not minimize the significance of the treaty. Those errant states can be called upon to explain why they have neglected their international legal obligations. As a party to the treaty breached, the United States could more credibly join in criticism of the errant governments. With ratification, the United States could nominate its nationals as experts to the treaty bodies. American international lawyers would thus be better able to contribute their expertise to the international law that is created by the treaty bodies interpreting the human rights instruments.

The United States, as a leader in international human rights practice, should join and contribute to this expanding body of international human rights law despite the differences in philosophy that still exist between the United States and other countries when it comes to international human rights. These differences impede universal application of that law—and they fuel debate in the Commission on Human Rights. The United States should never compromise its principles merely for the sake of consensus, but in the interest of furthering universal observance in accord with America's democratic tradition, there are ways the United States can reconcile its differences with other states.

The United States is in a position to forge some common ground in other areas of controversy within the international human rights community. In response to arguments that cultural "particularities" must be accounted for in the implementation of universal human rights, the United States should point to its experiences with cultural differences. In response to the rise of ethnic nationalism, the United States should present its successful multiethnic society. The United States honors the varied backgrounds of its citizens and encourages them to preserve their differences while contributing to the indivisible democracy that is the American nation. Indeed, the United States was founded on the principle that security increases with greater diversity. James Madison, in The Federalist Papers, No. 51, wrote in 1788:

> In the federal republic of the United States . . . the society itself will be broken into so many parts, interests and classes of citizens, that the rights of individuals or of the minority, will be in little danger from interested combinations of the majority. . . . The degree of security . . . will depend on the number of interests and sects.

In pointing to U.S. experience as a method of conciliating controversies, we should acknowledge our domestic problems. Take, for instance, the riots in Los Angeles in 1992. One might view that situation as an example of U.S. inability to mediate between the different elements of society. The government's response was not to segregate these groups and discourage their interaction, but to conciliate between them and to encourage unity through nonviolent means of expression. This example demonstrates, I believe, that even America's problems can be proffered to the international community as strengths.

The United States has much to contribute to international human rights at the United Nations through its experience, human expertise, and moral conscience. If the United Nations is to serve the United States into the twenty-first century in human rights as well as in security matters, it is imperative that the United States—to paraphrase the words of Senator Daniel Patrick Moynihan—proudly and unabashedly impart its standards to the human rights structures of the United Nations.

≈7≈

THE UNITED NATIONS, THE UN HIGH COMMISSIONER FOR REFUGEES, AND THE GLOBAL REFUGEE PROBLEM

GIL LOESCHER

*I*n recent years, the international community has been confronted with one refugee emergency following another in rapid, and sometimes overlapping, succession. Refugee crises in Africa, Asia, the Middle East, the Balkans, and the former Soviet republics have strained the capacities of the United Nations almost to the breaking point. In particular, the Office of the UN High Commissioner for Refugees (UNHCR), the international community's principal institution for protecting and assisting refugees, has been stretched to the limit of its capacities.

Refugees have become a persistent feature of the international environment, and never before in the history of the United Nations has the demand on the organization to protect and assist refugees been as high as it is today. Nor has there ever been a greater readiness to blame the United Nations when humanitarian problems go unresolved. As the United Nations becomes increasingly involved in brutal civil wars such as those in Bosnia, Croatia, Angola, Somalia, Sudan, and Mozambique, there is a growing perception that the organization cannot meet the greater responsibilities placed on it by the international community in the post-cold war era.

A solution to the global refugee problem will require the sustained attention and financial support of the entire community of states. While the plight of refugees has an understandable claim on the conscience of the world, it is less often appreciated that refugee flows have become more than an episodic problem requiring solely humanitarian solutions. The members of the United Nations must begin to perceive the global refugee crisis as an essentially political problem, and not as a problem of international charity. Refugee flows are in fact intensely political, and the causes and consequences of refugee movements are linked intimately to political issues.[1] One of the principal lessons of the Bosnian conflict is that the humanitarian mandate of the UN High Commissioner for Refugees cannot be viewed as a satisfactory substitute for wider-ranging political solutions.

This chapter examines the unique features of contemporary refugee movements, it explores the international political environment within which UNHCR must work, and it considers the challenges that these two sets of factors pose for the UN system and, in particular, the High Commissioner for Refugees. It then describes how UNHCR, as the institution leading the UN response to these new challenges, must overcome a number of organizational and other constraints that hinder the capacity of the international community to act quickly and effectively. Finally, the chapter proposes an agenda for action on the part of the UN system that will require a more comprehensive and preventive strategy for dealing with the global refugee problem.

Multilateral cooperation to solve the growing refugee problem ultimately will depend upon the commitment and political leadership of the United States and the community of nations. Recent events demonstrate that dealing effectively with the refugee problem requires not only building a stronger humanitarian regime but also creating a working international security system that can help prevent refugee disasters from occurring in the first place. The global refugee problem cannot be dealt with enduringly without multilateral efforts, and the United Nations is most effective when it has the clear support of the United States and other major countries. Thus, by responding more actively to the global refugee problem, the United States not only could alleviate substantial human suffering, it also could contribute to greater stability and security in the future.

REFUGEE MOVEMENTS AND THE POST-COLD WAR WORLD

Fundamental political and economic upheavals in the international system over the past decade have produced unprecedented mass movements of refugees. These migrations have, in turn, affected political, economic, and strategic developments worldwide. For instance, the global refugee problem has forced the international community to rethink the entire notion of state sovereignty, the founding principle of the Westphalian state system.[2] The best example of this was the plight of Iraq's Kurdish population, which precipitated a precedent-setting UN intervention in the internal affairs of that country.

In the Middle East, the Horn of Africa, the Balkans, and elsewhere, the mistreatment of minorities, the forced displacement of peoples, environmental damage caused by refugee flows, and war-induced famines have demonstrated the truly international nature of civil conflicts, and most importantly, they have demonstrated that the traditional notion of state sovereignty may actually impede effective international action.

One of the most significant developments in recent years has been the growing number of refugees and internally displaced peoples caused by civil wars or internal conflicts. The end of the cold war has increased the violence and intensity of internal conflicts around the world. In the 1990s, internal conflicts have become the most common form of warfare as local tensions in the developing world and in the states of the former Soviet empire are fueled by the availability of modern weapons, sharp socioeconomic inequalities, and abuses of human rights.

Most contemporary refugee movements are the result of traditional differences such as the ethnic, communal, or religious antagonisms between Armenians and Azeris, Somalis and Amharas, Tamils and Sinhalese, Serbs and Croats and Muslims, or Palestinians and Israelis that have resulted in increasing levels of civil conflict and greater numbers of internally displaced persons. Most importantly, the substantial increase in the number of refugees and peoples displaced by internal conflicts has had a particularly severe impact on UN refugee assistance and protection programs.

One major problem is that the United Nations simply was not designed to deal with internal conflicts.[3] While the organization has had some important successes in El Salvador, Namibia, and Nicaragua, where it helped to end protracted internal conflicts by disarming the opposing forces and monitoring elections, the United Nations will find it difficult to resolve all civil wars. In countries like the former Yugoslavia, Somalia, or Angola, the United Nations is dealing with bitter internal strife brought about by age-old communal, ethnic, and religious tensions. The political will that is required for UN intervention to succeed in these situations is often absent because there is a limited international consensus on issues of self-determination, state succession, and humanitarian intervention. In addition, success is made all the more difficult because UN member states remain reluctant to commit their soldiers to missions that are of little direct relevance for their own national security interests.

A second problem is that the Office of the UN High Commissioner for Refugees was designed to work primarily with refugees who have fled their home countries. Formally established in 1950 at the height of the cold war, UNHCR was initially charged with protecting and assisting people displaced by the Second World War and communist persecution in Europe. Since the 1960s, the focus of UNHCR activities has shifted away from Europe to the Third World, where many refugees are the victims of local rivalries. Until recently, however, the emphasis of UNHCR remained primarily on working with those refugees crossing state borders.[4]

Internal conflicts exacerbate the types of problems faced by UNHCR and the international community in providing assistance and protection to refugees. In many internal wars, the opposing forces prevent international aid from reaching people living in areas of conflict, and UNHCR staff have experienced serious difficulties in gaining access to refugees and displaced peoples. In addition, the international community frequently is unable to intervene to provide assistance, and the influence of international organizations over the behavior of the warring factions in internal conflicts is often quite limited. Finally, in situations of internal conflict, UNHCR is called upon to do much more than simply provide relief assistance. For example, in the former Yugoslavia UNHCR not only distributes relief supplies, it must also try to restrain the opposing forces and protect human rights. However, faced by the cynical manipulation of all the parties to the conflict, UNHCR's humanitarian efforts are, at best, nothing more than stopgap measures.

Although contemporary refugee flows are usually the result of internal conflicts—of persecution by brutal regimes or the indiscriminate violence that accompanies the collapse of civil authority—external powers can influence some of the forces that generate these flows. Outside powers have exacerbated local conflicts, prolonged regional instability, increased internal repression, and diverted scarce resources away from economic development to military activities by arming violent dictators like Saddam Hussein of Iraq, Slobodan Milosevic of Serbia, Pol Pot of Cambodia, Mohammed Siad Barre of Somalia, and Mengistu Haile Mariam of Ethiopia. The arming of militaristic regimes like these has been a major source of increased refugee flows. Moreover, this illustrates how the global refugee problem will not be given sufficient priority and resources until governments and international institutions address the issue in its international political context.

Notwithstanding the problems discussed above, there is a growing appreciation among UN member states of the difficulties UNHCR faces when addressing the problems of refugees, internally displaced peoples, and other victims of conflict. However, there is a continuing need for more constructive analyses of the possible solutions to those difficulties and of the capacities that the UN system requires to more effectively address the global refugee problem.[5]

CHALLENGES FACING THE UNITED NATIONS AND UNHCR

The rapidly changing international environment and the highly political character of refugee problems will determine both the humanitarian challenges of the 1990s and the limitations under which the UN High Commissioner for Refugees will be forced to operate. While outbursts of political persecution and ethnic violence have produced large-scale movements of refugees throughout history, there are many new and unique features to the contemporary refugee crisis. Each of these features provides novel challenges for UNHCR in its efforts to aid refugees and internally displaced peoples.

First, refugee emergencies—characterized by massive, sudden movements of people in extremely difficult and desperate conditions—have become a hallmark of the post-cold war period. In recent years, refugee emergencies in many countries have vastly increased the numbers of people dependent on UNHCR assistance. These crises include the former Yugoslavia, where the number of people receiving assistance from the organization rose from half a million to more than four million; Somalia, where hundreds of thousands of people became refugees in neighboring Kenya and Yemen as a result of vicious inter-clan conflict; Armenia and Azerbaijan, where more than a million people have been displaced by the conflict over Nagorno-Karabakh; Tajikistan, where sixty thousand people fled across borders and half a million have been displaced by civil war between clans; Burma, where a quarter of a million Muslim refugees fled to poverty-stricken Bangladesh; and Bhutan, where nearly a hundred thousand have fled ethnic strife. As a result of these emergencies, the capacity of UNHCR to mount an adequate response to new refugee movements has been stretched to the limit.

Second, contemporary refugee crises tend to be complex emergencies that combine political instability, ethnic tensions, armed conflict, economic collapse, and the disintegration of civil society. In addition, refugee movements frequently aggravate existing social, political, and environmental problems, such as environmental degradation, resource depletion, and food shortages. And refugee emergencies often affect entire regions, as has been the case in the Horn of Africa, southern Africa, Central America, and the Balkans. Moreover, in recent years, few refugee crises have been fully resolved, meaning that the resources devoted to one crisis are often not available for use in the next crisis.

Third, by the most conservative estimates there are currently about 25 million people displaced within their own countries (see Table 7.1). In contrast, there are just over 18 million refugees worldwide. Although there is a clear international mandate and specific institutions—most prominently, UNHCR—to assist and protect refugees, no institution has been given the responsibility for addressing the needs of the internally displaced. This is a critical weakness of the international humanitarian system. In addition, the body of international law governing the treatment of internally displaced persons is entirely inadequate. The community of states has yet to fully appreciate the international

TABLE 7.1
SELECTED LIST OF SIGNIFICANT POPULATIONS OF INTERNALLY DISPLACED
(AS OF DECEMBER 31, 1992)

Sudan	5,000,000	Rwanda	350,000
South Africa	4,100,000	Croatia	340,000
Mozambique	3,500,000	Colombia	300,000
Somalia	2,000,000	India	280,000
Philippines	1,000,000	Cyprus	265,000
Angola	900,000	Azerbaijan	216,000
Burma	750,000*	Sierra Leone	200,000
Bosnia-Herzegovina	740,000	Cambodia	199,000
Ethiopia/Eritrea	600,000	El Salvador	154,000
Liberia	600,000	Guatemala	150,000
Afghanistan	530,000	Zaire	100,000
Sri Lanka	530,000	Kenya	45,000
Peru	500,000	Turkey	30,000
Iraq	400,000	Moldova	20,000
Lebanon	400,000	Georgia	15,000
Tajikistan	400,000		

Note: This table identifies selected countries in which substantial numbers of people have been displaced within their homelands as a result of human conflict or forced relocations. Although they share many characteristics with refugees who cross international borders, they are generally not eligible for international assistance. Because information on internal displacement is fragmentary, this table presents only reported estimates, and no total is provided. It is important to note that even this selected list includes nearly twenty-five million people, and that the total number of internally displaced civilians is undoubtedly much higher.

*This figure may be off by as many as a quarter of a million because of extreme restrictions preventing international access.

Source: World Refugee Survey, 1993 (Washington, D.C.: U.S. Committee for Refugees, 1993).

consequences of internal displacement, and as a result, these people are not protected by the international system precisely because they do not become refugees but remain within the boundaries of their own countries.

Despite the absence of an adequate response to the plight of internally displaced people, in an increasing number of civil conflicts the high commissioner is assuming new roles while taking on a de facto expanded mandate. In the former Yugoslavia, for example, UNHCR is the lead UN agency providing humanitarian assistance to both displaced people and populations under siege, and it operates in partnership with UN peacekeeping troops. In northern Kenya and Tajikistan, moreover, UNHCR has launched cross-border operations with the intention of stabilizing populations at home so that refugee flight is unnecessary. In these cases, and in many others around the world, the responses demanded of UNHCR extend far beyond the organization's traditional legal and humanitarian role of working only with people who have already crossed international borders.

Fourth, in addition to protecting and providing assistance to the internally displaced, more immediate short-term issues include dealing with the consequences of refugee movements and determining when and how repatriation and reintegration are most appropriate. Even as new refugee crises emerge, there remain numerous long-term refugee populations in the Third World—with some dating back ten, twenty, or more years. Unlike earlier forced migrations, which were ultimately resolved by the repatriation or the overseas resettlement of refugee populations, over the past decade Third World refugees have found only temporary asylum in neighboring states. During most of the 1980s, the majority of refugees languished in camps or survived illegally without any hope of a permanent place of settlement or eventual return home.

This situation may be changing, however, as the international community has begun to give much greater attention to repatriation and even to returning refugees to countries which continue to experience widespread conflict. As a result, some 2.4 million refugees returned home in 1992 (see Table 7.2). If large numbers of refugees continue to be repatriated in the coming years, the focus of concern must inevitably shift from repatriation to more long-term considerations involving reintegration and economic development. It is increasingly evident that in countries like Cambodia, Afghanistan, Mozambique, and Ethiopia, one of the preconditions for successful return is development aid and reintegration assistance aimed at alleviating poverty in countries of origin. Without careful reintegration and reconciliation, returning refugees will compete for scarce developmental resources, which in turn may well result in fierce political and economic competition with local populations.

Table 7.2
Significant Voluntary Repatriation in 1992

To	From	Number
Afghanistan	Pakistan	1,500,000
Afghanistan	Iran	300,000
Angola	Zaire and Zambia	45,000
Burma	Bangladesh	900
Burundi	Zaire and others	38,000
Cambodia	Thailand	249,000
Chad	Sudan, Cameroon, and Central African Republic	4,400
Croatia	Slovenia and Italy	22,700
El Salvador	Honduras and others	3,130
Ethiopia	Sudan and Djibouti	23,000
Guatemala	Mexico	1,700
Haiti	Cuba and others	3,750
Iraq	Syria and Saudi Arabia	1,300
Laos	Thailand and China	4,700
Liberia	Côte d'Ivoire and Guinea	50,000
Mauritania	Senegal	5,000
Mozambique	Malawi	40,000
Nicaragua	Costa Rica	1,850
Sierra Leone	Guinea	1,600
Somalia	Ethiopia/Eritrea	100,000
South Africa	Tanzania and others	7,750
Sri Lanka	India	5,850
Suriname	French Guiana	4,470
Uganda	Sudan	2,700
Vietnam	Hong Kong	12,570
Vietnam	Thailand and others	5,200

Note: These numbers reflect estimates of refugees who participated in formal repatriation programs administered by UNHCR as well as those who spontaneously returned to their homelands.

Source: World Refugee Survey, 1993 (Washington, D.C.: U.S. Committee for Refugees, 1993).

Repatriation and reconstruction raise new and exceedingly difficult challenges for UNHCR.[6] These challenges involve important considerations such as how long the organization should provide protection to returning refugees, and particularly in situations of continuing conflict. Should UNHCR have the capacity to engage in human rights monitoring in countries of origin? How much and what kinds of assistance are required for returnees to reestablish themselves successfully? Should international economic development agencies, such as the UN Development

Program, provide development assistance targeted specifically at refugees in the early stages of a repatriation? Should development assistance be extended not only to returning refugees but also to needy local populations? While there are as yet no answers to these questions, they are of critical importance if UNHCR is to respond effectively in the future.

Moving beyond traditional refugee assistance to focus on reintegrating returnees into the social and economic fabric of their home countries will involve additional challenges. The United Nations and the community of states will be forced to rethink the respective roles and mandates of both multilateral institutions and nongovernmental organizations (NGOs). These changes will require that the agencies charged with assisting refugees shift their operational priorities from the receiving countries to the countries of return, and that there be closer cooperation among development, human rights, and refugee organizations.

Fifth, the Western industrialized states are increasingly reluctant to let refugees enter their countries to apply for asylum. The attitudes of Western receiving countries toward refugees have become increasingly xenophobic and racist as the number of people seeking asylum in the West has risen from 90,000 in 1983 to about 825,000 in 1992. In all, some 3.7 million asylum applications were made during 1983–92 (see Table 7.3). To date, the political debate in the industrialized world concerning migrants and asylum seekers has largely been informed by government concerns with border controls rather than by human rights concerns. In Central and Eastern Europe, the collapse of communism has greatly increased the numbers of asylum seekers and migrants and has opened up the possibility of mass migration from the eastern part of the continent into the industrial states of Western Europe (see Table 7.4). As a result, the movement of refugees and economic migrants has become an extremely contentious issue in post-cold war Europe.

The refugee problem has reached such a critical point in some Western countries that the very institution of asylum is being threatened. Confusions abound, both at the institutional level and within the general public, regarding definitions, standards of treatment for nonnationals, and methods for the management of their movement, reception, resettlement, and return. In addition, in shaping policy responses to the asylum crisis, many Western leaders have been influenced by extremists who seek to exploit anti-immigrant feelings and tensions. What is required is for UNHCR and political leaders to articulate clear policies that will help guide public opinion through the complexities of the refugee problem, as well as the short- and long-range measures that will address the problem. This will require both intelligence and political courage.

TABLE 7.3

ASYLUM APPLICATIONS IN WESTERN EUROPE, NORTH AMERICA, AND AUSTRALIA, 1983–92

	1983	1984	1985	1986	1987	1988	1989	1990	1991	1992	Cumulative 1983–92
Australia	—	—	—	—	—	—	500	3,600	16,000	4,100	24,200
Austria	5,900	7,200	6,700	8,700	11,400	15,800	21,900	22,800	27,300	16,200	143,900
Belgium	2,900	3,700	5,300	7,700	6,000	5,100	8,100	13,000	15,200	17,800	84,800
Canada	5,000	7,100	8,400	23,000	35,000	45,000	22,000	36,000	30,500	37,700	249,700
Denmark	800	4,300	8,700	9,300	2,800	4,700	4,600	5,300	4,600	13,900	59,000
Finland	—	—	—	—	50	50	200	2,500	2,100	3,600	8,500
France	14,300	15,900	25,800	23,400	24,800	31,600	60,000	56,000	46,500	27,500	325,800
Germany	19,700	35,300	73,900	99,700	57,400	103,100	121,000	193,000	256,100	438,200	1,397,400
Italy	3,000	4,500	5,400	6,500	11,000	1,300	2,200	4,700	31,700	2,500	72,800
Netherlands	2,000	2,600	5,700	5,900	13,500	7,500	14,000	21,200	21,600	17,500	111,500
Norway	200	300	900	2,700	8,600	6,600	4,400	4,000	4,600	5,200	37,500
Spain	1,400	1,100	2,300	2,300	2,500	3,300	4,000	8,600	8,100	11,700	45,300
Sweden	3,000	12,000	14,500	14,600	18,100	19,600	32,000	29,000	27,300	83,200	253,300
Switzerland	7,900	7,500	9,700	8,600	10,900	16,700	24,500	36,000	41,600	18,100	181,500
United Kingdom	4,300	3,900	5,500	4,800	5,200	5,100	10,000	30,000	57,700	24,600*	151,100
United States	20,000	24,300	20,000	18,900	26,100	57,000	100,000	73,600	70,000	103,400	513,300
Total	90,400	129,700	192,800	236,100	233,350	322,450	429,400	539,300	660,900	825,200	3,659,600

*Excluding dependents.

Source: UNHCR.

TABLE 7.4

EMIGRATION FROM CENTRAL AND EASTERN EUROPE AND THE FORMER USSR, 1984–92

	1984	1985	1986	1987	1988	1989	1990	1991
Asylum seekers	25,000	30,000	41,000	48,000	91,000	127,000	156,000	245,000
Jews from USSR	1,000	1,000	4,000	6,000	30,000	71,000	220,000	173,000
German settlers	77,000	64,000	69,000	98,000	240,000	720,000	397,000	222,000
Others (estimate)	6,000	6,000	10,000	25,000	50,000	300,000	150,000	160,000
Total	109,000	101,000	124,000	177,000	411,000	1,218,000	923,000	800,000

1992

Asylum seekers	170,600
Jews from former USSR	115,000
German settlers	230,500
Ex-Yugoslav asylum seekers	250,000
Ex-Yugoslavs temporarily protected	350,000
Others* (estimate)	700,000
Total	1,816,100

* Albanians, Baltics, Bulgarians, Pontian Greeks, Romanians, Russians, and some other groups.

Source: Secretariat for Intergovernmental Consultations, Vienna.

Finally, it is important to recognize that the nature of migratory movements is changing worldwide. The refugee problem is part of an emerging global crisis of mass migration generated by deep structural economic, political, and social changes throughout the world, but particularly in the developing world and in Eastern Europe and the former Soviet republics. The growing interdependence of national economies, the transnational impacts of the global communications, information, and transportation systems, and the expanding gap between poor and rich countries have led millions of people from the developing countries to seek jobs and security in the wealthier countries of the world.

In another new development, widespread poverty in the developing world is leading increasing numbers of people to seek entry not only to the industrialized states of North America and Western Europe, but also to the newly industrialized states of Asia and the oil-producing states of the Middle East. Poverty and underdevelopment also exacerbate the political and social instability that generates refugees, and thus serve to further globalize the refugee problem.

As the numbers of all kinds of migrants increase throughout the world, it is becoming difficult to clearly distinguish between refugees, other forced migrants, and economic migrants. The motives of the individuals involved are seldom purely political or economic, and the factors generating migration often grow out of similar political and economic forces. However, as domestic reactions against migrant flows produce more restrictions around the world, the distinction between political and economic refugees has become increasingly important, affecting access to political asylum, relief aid, and the protection of international institutions and laws.

CONSTRAINTS FACING THE UNITED NATIONS AND THE UNHCR

The UN High Commissioner for Refugees faces substantial constraints on its ability to coordinate and manage the international response to major refugee emergencies. Until recently, the Office of the High Commissioner was not adequately equipped either to coordinate major logistic operations or to assume an effective role in overseeing relief operations because of significant deficiencies in the areas of funding, personnel, supplies, logistics, management, and accountability. Consequently, in several recent emergency situations UNHCR has been unable to meet the basic needs of refugee populations, resulting in unacceptably high levels of malnutrition and mortality, as well as public criticism of the organization's performance.

In the past, UNHCR has been criticized frequently for its slow response to the larger and more rapidly evolving refugee emergencies. It also has been disparaged for its inability to coordinate its activities with other international relief agencies and NGOs. These types of deficiencies were clearly displayed, for example, by the initial UNHCR response to the Kurdish exodus following the Gulf War, as well as by its response to refugee problems in the Horn of Africa (Somalia, Sudan, Ethiopia, and Kenya).

Funding is the greatest constraint on the effectiveness of the High Commissioner for Refugees. The most significant weakness of UNHCR is its dependence on *voluntary* contributions to carry out its expanded responsibilities. Apart from a modest annual contribution from the UN regular budget toward administrative expenses, all of UNHCR's funding depends on voluntary contributions. This has reduced the flexibility of UNHCR and therefore its ability to respond quickly and effectively to new refugee emergencies.

UNCHR's refugee activities are divided into general and special programs. The UNHCR Executive Committee approves each year's general program budget, which comprises annual program activities as well as those financed through the emergency fund. After approving the general program budget, UNHCR appeals to all UN member states to provide the resources needed to cover the annual programs. These resources are allocated primarily to the traditional areas of UNHCR competence: emergency relief, voluntary repatriation, integration into host societies, and resettlement.

In addition to activities financed through the general program budget, at the request of the secretary-general or the General Assembly, UNHCR undertakes special programs like unforeseen emergency operations (such as those in Bosnia or Kenya) or transportation and rehabilitation assistance to refugees and displaced people who have been repatriated (such as in Mozambique). The special programs are financed through fund-raising appeals to interested governments, and each program receives financing from a trust fund established for it. As a result, UNHCR must raise funds separately for each new refugee problem, typically through special pledging conferences that take time to organize and may not secure all the necessary funds.

In the 1990s, UNHCR has been faced with several new refugee emergencies that have caused its overall expenditures to increase significantly. In 1991, as a result of emergency relief operations in northern Iraq and the Horn of Africa, total voluntary fund expenditures (including both general and special programs) by the office were $862.5 million, an increase of almost 60 percent over 1990.[7] In 1992, new refugee and

humanitarian crises in the former Yugoslavia, Bangladesh, the Horn of
Africa, and southern Africa, in addition to ongoing responsibilities in
northern Iraq and new repatriation programs in Cambodia, Ethiopia,
and Mozambique, pushed UNHCR expenditures to just over $1 bil-
lion.[8] The total funding required for UNHCR's 1993 operations is estimated to be in the range of $1.5 billion.

While the funds available for UNHCR special programs have
increased substantially, donor-country contributions to the general program budget have not kept pace with increasing financial requirements
over recent years. In fact, despite the growing numbers of refugees, the
level of financial support for UNHCR general programs has remained
almost unchanged during the past decade (see Figure 7.1). The lack of
support for UNHCR general program activities threatens to reduce or
postpone repatriation programs, cancel needed improvements in
refugee facilities, and force the organization to make cuts in nutrition
and education programs.

Figure 7.1
UNHCR Expenditures 1984–93
(Voluntary Funds in Millions of US$)

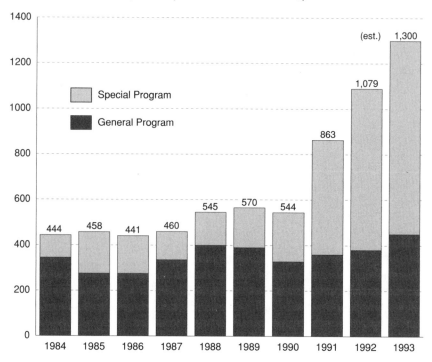

Source: UNHCR.

Several specific problems constrain the flow of assistance from donor countries. The voluntary funding provided by governments is often earmarked for particular uses, and this does not allow for sufficient operational flexibility. And, frequently, voluntary funding is not provided in a timely fashion, which exacerbates the office's difficulties in providing adequate funding to field operations. In addition, the funding of humanitarian activities often has a substantial political element. During the cold war, for example, the United States and other Western donors funded refugee assistance programs to express their condemnation of communist repression, which was forcing many people to flee those countries.

Many contemporary refugee movements, however, are seen as local or regional problems that present few foreign policy or security concerns for the major donor governments. Without compelling strategic or ideological incentives, there is an increasing danger that the industrialized donor states will reduce their funding for refugee programs in favor of more pressing domestic priorities.

The effectiveness of UNHCR is also constrained by a lack of trained personnel. The organization has always found it extremely difficult to undertake long-range planning, policy analysis, and multisector programming because the personnel assigned to these tasks must constantly be redeployed from their normal functions to emergency operations in countries such as the former Yugoslavia, Iraq, Somalia, and Bangladesh. This has changed somewhat, however, as positions of preparedness and response officers have been created to lead five newly established regional emergency response teams. In addition, a roster has been compiled of standby technical experts and relief workers for deployment in emergency situations. At the same time, UNHCR Emergency Management Training Programs (carried out since 1985) recently introduced an emergency response component.

The Office of the High Commissioner has had a very limited capacity to procure, store, transport, and distribute large quantities of relief assistance within a short time period. Recently, however, UNHCR sought to rationalize international humanitarian relief operations by improving its emergency relief preparedness and response mechanisms and bolstering its capacity to provide emergency staffing, relief supplies, needs assessment, and emergency program implementation. In addition, the high commissioner has signed an agreement with the World Food Program to clarify and simplify the coordination of all food relief. Finally, stockpiles of relief supplies have been amassed for use in new emergencies.

Another major constraint on the Office of the High Commissioner, one that plagues the entire UN system, is the lack of accountability for the performance of program activities. For one, UNHCR does not place a high-enough priority on ensuring that policy planning systematically takes into account the lessons of past operations. Furthermore, UNHCR does not routinely subject its programs and policies to independent assessment and evaluation to ensure that mistakes are not repeated in future operations. Although some UNHCR operations are now scrutinized by a small central evaluation unit, the experience gained in past operations continues to be inadequately exploited for the lessons that can be used to improve the agency's future performance. Even if mistakes are uncovered, there is no effective system of control and accountability. Like most UN agencies, many UNHCR officials are protected by their home governments who protest vehemently when their nationals are disciplined or sacked.

While UNHCR and other humanitarian organizations have made a promising start in strengthening their ability to respond quickly to future mass movements of refugees, it is too early to gauge the effectiveness of the new measures. Moreover, the scope and scale of post-cold war refugee and internal displacement emergencies suggest the urgent need for fundamental changes in the international system for humanitarian relief. In the future, it will be necessary to develop new strategies for dealing with refugee problems and for strengthening the capacity of operational agencies to accomplish their new tasks.

In the 1990s, the international community must place a greater emphasis on addressing the underlying causes of refugee problems in countries of origin through a preventive policy which includes early warning, preventive diplomacy, and the protection of human rights. The high commissioner recently adopted a comprehensive strategy designed both to address the root causes of refugee flows, with the aim of preventing the underlying conditions that force people to flee, and to contain those refugee movements already under way by providing immediate protection and assistance to lessen the need for further displacement.[9]

Yet another constraint will make it difficult for UNHCR to shift to a preventive strategy. The Office of the High Commissioner is simply not well suited to working in internal conflicts. Consequently, a preventive strategy for dealing with refugee problems will not be put in place easily or quickly, because the involvement of multilateral institutions in internal conflicts requires skills and competencies which many UNHCR staff do not possess. In conflicts such as those in Bosnia or Tajikistan, UNHCR has been forced to rely on procedures and techniques similar to those used by the International Committee of the Red

Cross (ICRC), but UNHCR staff have neither the special training and skills, nor the experience of the ICRC in dealing with internal conflicts.

In countries of asylum, UNHCR has a well-established history of providing protection and assistance to refugees on the basis of its own mandate as well as those contained in international agreements. In contrast, in countries enduring civil war, the Office of the High Commissioner must work not only with recognized governments but also with opposition groups and guerrilla forces. Rebel leaders frequently are fighting for their political and physical survival, and control over civilian populations is a principal objective of many internal conflicts. In regions where ethnic conflicts are raging, and especially in Bosnia, the Caucasus, and central Asia, there is little knowledge of or concern for the international humanitarian laws governing warfare.[10] In many civil conflicts, for instance, hostage taking and the murder of prisoners of war is routine.

In internal conflicts—which often are characterized by the breakdown of civil authority, the absence of viable government institutions, and chronic political instability—UNHCR and UN peacekeeping forces must protect civilians against reprisals and forced displacement, evacuate people from conflict areas, and provide relief to besieged populations such as those in Sarajevo. However, there is no formal authority for the organization to undertake these types of activities under either its own constitution or under current international law.

Internal conflicts require UNHCR personnel to direct entirely new types of activities, and most of UNHCR's employees are neither recruited nor trained to work in the cross fire of civil conflict. In such conflicts, internally displaced people are often treated as the enemy and UN assistance as biased in support of one side to the disadvantage of the other side. UNHCR personnel who lack the training and independence to work in internal conflicts not only face great physical danger, they also are vulnerable to manipulation by warring parties who view humanitarian assistance as a weapon. If UNHCR is to respond effectively to these new internal-conflict situations, there is an urgent need both to reorganize the staffing, training, and operations of the office to reflect its new roles, and to give it the necessary resources, tools, and mandate to properly do the job.

While it is increasingly clear that action to deal with refugee problems must extend into political, diplomatic, and economic realms if it is to be successful, it is equally important that humanitarian action on behalf of refugees not be held hostage to politics. With some internal conflicts, particularly those where UN troops cannot effectively defend civilian populations or protect humanitarian workers, it may be necessary for

UNHCR to acknowledge its limitations and be willing to withdraw or scale down its operations. In situations where hostilities continue unabated, humanitarian assistance may become an excuse for the international community to not deal with the underlying causes of the conflict.

The High Commissioner for Refugees should also be cautious about agreeing to sustain forcibly displaced populations within "safe areas" where refugees are entirely dependent on international aid and subject to attack. The problems with this policy are obvious. When the acquisition of territory by force and "ethnic cleansing" are central aims of a conflict, safe areas inadvertently help to realize these goals. Moreover, as a method for protecting civilian populations, safe areas require enormous resources to police and maintain them. Safe areas also prevent persecuted or threatened peoples from fleeing their homes to seek protection in other countries.

A final constraint that will make it difficult for UNHCR to take preventive action in countries of origin is the organization's inability to intervene against governments that abuse human rights *before* people are forced to become refugees. As presently structured, the High Commissioner for Refugees lacks any capacity to take action against governments that violate international human rights standards. The international refugee system of which UNHCR is a part was designed to focus strictly on the provision of humanitarian assistance and to avoid politicization. This is extremely important for relief organizations to gain permission to work in host countries and to secure funding from donor governments. The High Commissioner for Refugees must therefore avoid raising political issues like human rights abuses for fear of overstepping its mandate and damaging sensitive relations with governments, many of whom consider such intervention an interference in their internal affairs.

A Framework for Action

For most of the past forty years, the UN High Commissioner for Refugees primarily served people who fled across international borders to neighboring countries where they required relief assistance. UNHCR's staff has thus focused its activities on assisting refugees in camps, negotiating with host governments regarding protection and assistance, and seeking "durable" solutions to refugee problems. Traditionally, the search for durable solutions has included repatriation, local integration, and resettlement in third countries.[11]

In contrast, UNHCR is now committed primarily to meeting the immediate needs of refugees and internally displaced people living under conditions of ongoing communal conflict. This change in the focus of UNHCR activities has severely strained the organization's capabilities. In the former Yugoslavia, for example, UNHCR has dedicated approximately one-quarter of its staff and one-third of its resources to providing assistance and protection to nearly four million people. A real danger exists that UNHCR will be swamped by its involvement in internal conflicts, that the interest of donor governments in funding these protracted operations will wane—even in high-profile situations like the Bosnian war—and the organization will be left with insufficient resources to provide assistance to dependent and vulnerable civilian populations for indefinite or prolonged periods.

Achieving a durable solution to refugee problems is increasingly difficult because of the priority given to providing extended emergency relief in prolonged refugee situations in the Balkans, the Middle East, Africa, and parts of Asia. These prolonged situations now absorb the vast majority of UNHCR resources, and they present enormous challenges to the organization in planning, managing, and funding its worldwide network of protection and relief programs.

The end of the cold war gives the United States and the international community a unique opportunity to lay the foundations of an action program that includes the following elements.

IMPROVED FLOW OF FUNDING

As a first step toward improving the effectiveness of the High Commissioner for Refugees, the organization must be given a resource base that will permit greater autonomy and flexibility. The United States and other donor governments must resist the temptation to promote their own political priorities by earmarking funds for specific programs and activities. The global refugee problem, as a persistent feature of international affairs, will require the continuous financial support of the entire international community. To meet this challenge, serious consideration should be given to funding UNHCR programs through assessed rather than voluntary contributions, thereby acknowledging the permanent character of the refugee problem and the need to deal with it systematically.

A more comprehensive and effective UN response to humanitarian emergencies will require that adequate resources be available at short notice. Only one-quarter of the $4 billion requested by the Secretariat's Department of Humanitarian Affairs (DHA) in 1992–93 has been made available to fund humanitarian operations worldwide. Lack of donor support raises serious concerns about the effectiveness and credibility of

UN humanitarian relief programs. The Department of Humanitarian Affairs, the High Commissioner for Refugees, and other UN agencies cannot accomplish their missions unless the United States and other major donor states are prepared to bear a greater financial burden, albeit one that is hardly substantial when compared to the money spent on defense during the cold war.

A MULTIDIMENSIONAL RESPONSE

Hindered by its dependence on voluntary contributions and the need to obtain the acquiescence of host governments before intervening, UNHCR cannot resolve the global refugee problem by itself. Not only is there a need to acknowledge and deal with the political issues raised by refugee movements, but more attention needs to be focused on the range of actors—in addition to the traditional relief organizations—which must become involved in finding solutions to the global refugee problem. These organizations include development agencies, human rights networks, and peacekeeping and conflict resolution institutions—all of which must become involved in finding solutions to conflicts and the population displacements that they produce.

The refugee emergencies of the post-cold war era have highlighted the fact that combating the causes of forced migration cannot proceed solely within the mandate of international humanitarian organizations. A multidimensional response to refugee crises must involve the entire UN system, as well as regional organizations and nongovernmental organizations. In addition, it will require enhancing these organizations' capacities to defuse, deter, and mediate incipient crises before they require more serious and costly intervention. The United Nations must be able to respond more quickly and effectively in order to address humanitarian needs in a growing number of emergency situations.

The effectiveness of repatriation and reconstruction programs, which are discussed below, will require close cooperation between nongovernmental and intergovernmental organizations. This is especially true because U.S. NGOs are the principal providers of official U.S. assistance to refugees. The presence of NGOs also constitutes a form of protection for returning refugees, by serving as a deterrent to human rights abuses and as a source of early warning for the international system about emerging crises. Enhancing the capacities of NGOs will be crucial and will likely determine the ability of UNHCR to carry out the massive repatriation programs it is likely to confront in the future.

AN EFFECTIVE EARLY WARNING SYSTEM

Early information regarding impending refugee crises is critical not only for preventive action, but also for initiating effective and timely humanitarian responses to complex ethnic and communal conflicts. An effective central monitoring body should be established within the Secretariat to provide an early warning mechanism to alert the secretary-general, the Security Council, the Department of Humanitarian Affairs, and the High Commissioner for Refugees about potential conflicts and humanitarian emergencies.[12]

The Secretariat also should establish a small corps of permanent staff to serve as monitors in tense situations, to help deter situations from leading to displacement, and to act as an essential element of an early warning system. These UN emergency teams would be particularly useful in circumstances where response capacities are not already in place (such as in Georgia or Tajikistan) or where the capacities of UN agencies are limited (such as in Angola and, until recently, Somalia). Members of the monitoring body should include UN officials, NGO representatives, and the representatives of governments.[13]

To augment this central UN early warning mechanism, the early warning capabilities of UNHCR should be bolstered, and full support should be extended to initiatives to share the information obtained at the interagency level. Some steps have already been taken in this direction. For example, at the interagency level, the UN Department of Humanitarian Affairs, acting on an October 1992 decision of the Administrative Committee on Coordination, has begun to develop a system for advance warning of new flows of refugees and displaced persons.[14] Moreover, the Office of the High Commissioner for Refugees is in the process of institutionalizing a Refugee Emergency Alert System designed to provide the office with early warning of the likely scope, nature, and needs of refugee emergencies. These mechanisms need to be more fully developed and given sufficient resources.

In addition, the capabilities of other UN agencies to provide early warning of humanitarian and refugee emergencies should be bolstered. For instance, the UN Center for Human Rights needs to be strengthened to enable it to monitor and collect accurate and timely information on human rights abuses, to identify situations that have the potential to produce mass refugee flows, and to bring these to the attention of the international community.[15] In addition, the special representative of the secretary-general on internally displaced persons should be responsible for detecting early signs of displacement, submitting reports to the

Commission on Human Rights and, through the secretary-general, to the Security Council.[16]

The United Nations now has the ability to send fact-finding missions to defuse disputes and prevent major crises from expanding; this is among the most important instruments that can add to the organization's capacities.[17] Fact-finding missions will play an important role in the early stages of conflict development. They may prevent the misunderstandings that result in more rigid positions, and they can deter those considering actions that cause forcible displacement. Nongovernmental organizations, such as Amnesty International or the Helsinki Watch groups, may be more effective than UN monitors in collecting information and bringing human rights abuses to the attention of the international community. The United States and other countries should therefore systematically share information with the United Nations and nongovernmental organizations about potential forced migrations.

It is not enough to send monitors or for information to be widely available about potential refugee movements: Early warning programs must be connected to decisionmaking and response mechanisms within governments as well as within relief, development, and human rights organizations. In many recent refugee crises, though information concerning the impending conflicts and mass migrations was available in advance, there was little willingness or ability to act on this information. In Yugoslavia and Somalia, for example, international agencies anticipated these disasters before they unfolded, but there were no mechanisms for averting these tragedies by dealing with them while they were manageable.

Unless mechanisms are established for triggering prompt action regarding potential refugee problems, and the existing tools of diplomacy, human rights protection, and conflict resolution are reinforced, any measures that could be taken to prepare for future refugee flows will be of limited value.

REINFORCEMENT OF EXISTING UN MECHANISMS

The United States and other countries have repeatedly called on the United Nations to deal more actively with the consequences of conflict, including refugee movements. Recent events in the former Yugoslavia make it increasingly obvious that the international community also must address the causes of displacement before people are forced to flee. In addition, the increase in internal wars has highlighted the problems of coordinating effective humanitarian operations, especially in the opening days of an emergency.[18] Until recently, these problems were exacerbated by the lack of a focal point for humanitarian affairs within the UN Secretariat and of effective structures for consultation and action by UN agencies on the global refugee problem.[19]

In December 1991, the UN General Assembly created the Office of the Disaster Relief Coordinator, giving it the function of providing a central focal point for governments, intergovernmental bodies, and nongovernmental organizations concerning UN emergency relief operations. In early 1992, the disaster relief coordinator, Jan Eliasson, was given the status of under secretary-general in the newly formed UN Department of Humanitarian Affairs. This new UN bureaucracy is an important step toward coordinating the responsibilities of UN agencies in complex emergency situations, toward prompt UN decisionmaking on coordination mechanisms at the field level, and in negotiating access for UN agencies without waiting for a formal government request.[20]

Unfortunately, the DHA has been called on to coordinate the humanitarian response to crises at a time when the mechanisms for interagency coordination are still being established and remain largely untested. In addition, a lack of adequate field staff and the rapid succession of humanitarian crises in the post-cold war period have caught DHA unprepared, making it impossible for the department to fulfill its planned lead role in recent emergencies.

The legitimacy of humanitarian intervention has been growing within the United Nations over the past few years. The UN resolution establishing the Office of the Disaster Relief Coordinator allows humanitarian assistance to be provided with "the consent of the affected country,"[21] rather than at its request, as was previously the case. Thus, while governments have not fully endorsed humanitarian intervention, the resolution supports intervention strategies that are part of an emerging humanitarian diplomacy. "Corridors of tranquility," through which relief convoys are allowed to pass without interference, and "humanitarian cease-fires" and "zones of peace," which allow assistance to be provided in conflict zones, are pragmatic mechanisms that have been used extensively in recent years by the United Nations and NGOs.

The United States and other governments should encourage the Department of Humanitarian Affairs and other UN institutions to expand their capabilities and build on the precedents mentioned above to deal with the global refugee problem. In particular, the United Nations must seek to create modalities for protecting and assisting vulnerable populations and to devise further mechanisms to ensure freer humanitarian access.

Repatriation and Reconstruction

New emphasis needs to be put on improving conditions in countries of origin so that refugees can either remain secure at home or be repatriated in safety. Repatriation is not a realistic solution until economic and political circumstances are improved in countries of origin. Local integration is almost impossible in situations of mass refugee influxes where land and other resources are scarce or where ethnic and religious tensions exist. Resettlement in third countries, moreover, is a solution for only a small percentage of the world's refugees. (Less than 1 percent of the refugees were resettled during 1992.) Finally, faced with domestic economic difficulties and growing xenophobia, Western countries are becoming very reluctant to admit large numbers of people who are not easily assimilable.

The tasks of returning people safely to their home countries and reconstructing war-torn regions is beyond the mandate and resources of UNHCR. For instance, the cost of administering the UN peace plan in Cambodia—a country of eight million people—is estimated at well over $2 billion. The financial requirements of reconstruction in Afghanistan, Central America, the Horn of Africa, southern Africa, Liberia, and Western Sahara will be immense. As a result, one of the most meaningful short-term actions the United States could take to alleviate the global refugee problem is to increase its development assistance to those countries experiencing large-scale repatriations.

The focus of refugee-related development activities should be to create the proper conditions for return. Policy analysts have already called for the establishment of an international fund for reconstruction that would channel funds to war-torn areas through existing multilateral mechanisms such as the G–24, the World Bank, or the UN Development Program.[22] This new funding mechanism would support regional initiatives, such as the International Conference for Central American Refugees (CIREFCA) or the international fund for reconstruction in Cambodia, that are now financed by separate trust funds. Development funding should concentrate on rural reconstruction, training and education, and infrastructure such as roads and transportation. In addition, some analysts have argued that national and international agencies should submit "refugee impact" statements, similar to existing environmental ones, on major new initiatives in trade, aid, and arms sales when potential refugee problems exist.[23] To increase its effectiveness, refugee-related development funding could be tied to local compliance with cease-fires and peace accords, as well as to the observance of human rights standards.[24]

A failure on the part of the United States and other donor states to adequately fund repatriation and reconstruction programs will probably lead to increased local conflict and a worsening of the global refugee problem.

ASYLUM

The most fundamental principle of refugee protection—the right of refugees to flee their countries to seek asylum and not to be returned into the hands of their persecutors—must be preserved.

The commitment of the United States and other states to the protection of human rights should be judged by their willingness to provide asylum to the victims of conflict and persecution. The growing reluctance of many states to open their borders to people forcibly driven from their homes or subject to murder, physical abuse, and starvation illustrates the vital importance of maintaining the principle of asylum. The most important lesson that the international community can learn from its previous efforts to deal with the global refugee problem is that building walls will not deter people who are compelled to flee their homes.

The refugee problem cannot be managed through the tightening of border controls and asylum procedures. This problem instead requires unprecedented cooperation between countries of asylum and countries of origin. There is now a more active insistence by the international community that sovereignty also carries certain responsibilities of states toward their citizens. As a consequence, there is less willingness within the international community to tolerate flagrant abuses of power and widespread persecution by violent and lawless governments. The human rights mechanisms of the United Nations should now be used more effectively to persuade states either to fulfill their responsibilities to their own citizens or, if necessary, to accept help to carry out those responsibilities.

The countries of the world, and especially the United States, have a responsibility to offer refuge to those persecuted and threatened individuals and groups who flee their countries to seek asylum. The United States must be prepared to accept a greater share of the world's refugees, especially those with the most acute needs. Moreover, if the United States and the countries of Western Europe pursue a policy of restricting the entry of asylum seekers, Western leaders will not be able to encourage other states to protect and assist refugees when they stream across their borders. The United States and other industrialized democracies cannot, on the one hand, insist that Third World and East

European states provide refuge to victims of conflict and persecution, and on the other, claim that they themselves do not have the means to provide asylum.

In addition, a generous commitment to asylum is not simply a matter of charity or burden-sharing; it is also a way of regularizing and stabilizing large numbers of people whose irregular situation creates interstate tensions and regional instability. Unduly restrictionist U.S. and Western policies lead to greater isolation and deprivation in those countries forced to play host to rejected refugees and migrants. An angry, excluded world outside the West will inevitably give rise to conditions where extremist or aggressive groups and governments can pose new political and security threats.

THE IMPORTANCE OF U.S. LEADERSHIP

Never before has it been so appropriate to launch bold initiatives to deal with national and international policies and practices toward the global refugee problem. Although the leadership of the UN High Commissioner for Refugees is crucial, it is not enough. The president of the United States and other political leaders also must be involved in any effort to strengthen the UN humanitarian and refugee systems, and the secretary-general must be prepared to proceed with imagination and political courage to invigorate these multilateral mechanisms.

The several strategies discussed above would draw attention to the serious deterioration that has occurred in some states with respect to the treatment of citizens and refugees. The preventive approach suggested would attempt to deal comprehensively with the causes of refugee flows, rather than with their consequences. To win international support for a more comprehensive approach to the global refugee problem, the U.S. president and other leaders must be candid about the consequences for the international community of either ignoring this growing problem or relegating it to the traditional humanitarian and relief organizations. Dealing effectively with refugee movements is in the interest of the United States and other nations and coincides with their search for long-term global stability.

The United Nations is still the only organization capable of managing the complex global problems of the post-cold war era. The international community needs to take advantage of both the structural and technical reforms that have occurred within the UN system and the higher expectations for the United Nations that now exist. But events in Iraq, the former Yugoslavia, and Somalia have demonstrated that the United Nations is incapable of imposing order by itself, nor is it capable of achieving success in every endeavor.

The United Nations cannot resolve global problems when the United States and other countries lack the political will to act. The United Nations is only the sum of its member states, and the leadership of the United States and other Western countries will be a key factor if the organization is to achieve significant results. Despite the considerable concern among the developing countries about the uneven distribution of world power and the increasing activism of the United States and the other Western powers in UN humanitarian and peacekeeping initiatives, the United States remains the only country whose leadership many other states are willing to follow. It is also the country most capable of initiating international efforts toward such a major collective goal. Without active U.S. involvement, the international community will be limited to reactive damage-control responses to humanitarian crises.

The political stakes involved in creating an effective UN capability to respond to humanitarian emergencies and their accompanying refugee problems are high. A failure by the United States and the international community to increase the capacities of the United Nations, and in particular the Office of the High Commissioner for Refugees, will inevitably lead to a reduction in international security, to costly military interventions, and to further needless drains on aid programs to deal with refugee movements. Not since the end of the Second World War has the international community been presented with a better opportunity to make substantial progress toward resolving humanitarian problems. That opportunity should now be seized.

≈8≈

THE WORLD HEALTH ORGANIZATION:
SECTORAL LEADER OR OCCASIONAL BENEFACTOR?

LEON GORDENKER

*J*udged solely by its name, the World Health Organization (WHO) might seem the least controversial of the international institutions established immediately after the Second World War. Yet from its earliest days, the organization has from time to time generated disputes around its international programs. Internal battles have spilled out into the public realm and have served to spotlight important issues concerning international health programs and U.S. policy toward the organization. The debates over WHO programs often revolve around complex social-policy questions that require member governments to make difficult decisions. Nevertheless, these vigorous debates should be seen as evidence of an institution actively striving to fulfill its mandate.

From its beginning, the United States has been a principal participant and supporter of the World Health Organization, despite some disagreements over specific WHO programs. Its advanced biomedical establishment and public health structures have usually offered the United States easy access to the levers of leadership within the organization. Today, after years of growth in the organization's membership and in the scope of its activities, U.S. policymakers face an increasing number of choices that will either augment the U.S. contribution to WHO or instead lead to a more passive U.S. role within the organization.

The chapter opens with a brief review of the motivations behind the creation of the World Health Organization as well as its structure and programs. It then examines WHO's "organizational ideology," or the set of assumptions, beliefs, and routines which provide the institution with its own particular style. It is this ideology, more than anything else, that compels WHO to confront the constraints placed on it by some member states and the international system. The chapter takes up the challenges and the constraints that the organization must now confront, with a special focus on several recent issues that were particularly controversial. Finally, it considers U.S. policy toward WHO and international health issues.

The process of establishing the World Health Organization began in the earliest days of the United Nations at the 1945 San Francisco conference. Following three years of negotiation, the WHO Constitution[1] entered into force with its ratification by the United States in 1948. The constitution, which is legally binding on the members of the organization, sets out an extraordinarily broad program for international cooperation in the field of human health. At the most general level, WHO's mandate reflects that breadth in its call for the organization to foster "the attainment by all peoples of the highest possible level of health."

The impulse behind the creation of WHO came from public health officials and biomedical specialists. Prior to the Second World War, these groups, which traditionally have had access to each other's work through professional journals and societies and through existing institutions, such as the Pan American Sanitary Organization and the League of Nations, had become accustomed to international cooperation in the fields of epidemiology and disease control. Following the war, the movement to create new multilateral institutions supported the desires of medical professionals for a new global organization to expand cooperation in the field of human health. The strong support of the international public health and biomedical communities for multilateral cooperation continues to set the tone for the way WHO approaches its mandate.

Medical professionals hardly gave the same emphasis as conventional foreign affairs specialists to the jealous protection of national institutions from outside influence. Rather, they took it for granted that international cooperation to promote better health care would benefit all the countries of the world.[2]

Most generally, the World Health Organization has served as the instrument of governments for finding cooperative international solutions to public health problems. A considerable part of its role has been informational, such as providing global access to health statistics and scientific publications and providing opportunities for health professionals to share experiences through its meetings. WHO has worked to set international health standards through the establishment of both international laws and, more commonly, recommendations for national government responses to public health issues. In this way, WHO has extended the previously existing international controls on communicable diseases and has kept governments informed about how they should construct their communicable-disease programs based on new research and relevant experience. The organization also has advised governments extensively on the creation and organization of national health services, and it has provided substantial direct assistance to states and other international organizations during health emergencies. On occasion, WHO has tried to regulate the international commerce in medical and pharmaceutical products. It has sponsored and supervised research of interest to public health organizations. Finally, WHO has worked with the other agencies of the UN system to foster economic development and to cope with such medical and social issues as drug abuse.

The World Health Organization in many ways remains the institution that it was when it was founded in 1948. In particular, it must continue to deal with long-standing structural and programmatic issues. The organization's constitutionally mandated structure is highly decentralized. Six regional suborganizations generally undertake important administrative responsibilities, share in drafting the overall WHO budget, and, to varying degrees, assist in formulating policies and proposals. Each regional affiliate has its own director, secretariat, and regional assembly of member-state representatives. The relative capacities of the regional organizations are somewhat uneven, with insiders pointing to the Americas Regional Organization (which also carries the title of Pan American Health Organization) and the European Regional Organization as especially competent, the Western Pacific Regional Organization as satisfactory, and the large African Regional Organization as the least reliable.

This organizational structure obviously involves much complexity in the making of international health policy, as well as in the application, supervision, and accountability of those policies. For example, a strong relationship ties the Pan American Health Organization (PAHO) to the United States, which contributes directly to its budget. This special relationship has frequently placed WHO and PAHO in competition for the scarce financial resources provided by Washington.

The organizational structure of international health programs is further complicated by the fact that almost every WHO activity is filtered through 184 national public health systems to the people who are the ultimate consumers of health services. These national systems vary enormously from the quite primitive to the highly sophisticated. In addition, parts of the WHO program inevitably overlap with the wider development programs mounted by other multilateral agencies and bilateral donors in developing countries. This overlap impels efforts to coordinate, and thus adds another level of complexity.

ORGANIZATIONAL IDEOLOGY

Any organization develops a set of institutional beliefs which guide the work of its personnel and which can be described as an organizational ideology. This ideology provides a conceptual foundation for the organization's activities and tends to remain relatively constant over long periods of time. As a result, it is possible to identify the organizational ideology by examining the statements of senior officials and the nature of specific programs and activities. Alterations in underlying organizational assumptions can also be identified.

The greater part of the World Health Organization's ideology echoes the social goals of official public health services in the Western countries (especially the United States) because of the organization's descent from the international public health community, its continuous association with that community, and the medical community's ongoing contributions to WHO activities.[3] The directors-general of the organization have without exception been medical doctors, as have the majority of the organization's leading officials. National representatives in the World Health Assembly and the Executive Board, which together oversee WHO programs and activities, also are recruited from the same medical ranks. This common medical orientation is strongly echoed in WHO's primary objective, the highest possible level of health for all people.

The preamble of the WHO Constitution, however, includes principles that only rarely enter the conventional medical school curriculum. For instance, it defines health not as the absence of disease but as "a state of complete physical, mental, and social well-being." The enjoyment of health, the constitution asserts, is "one of the fundamental rights of every human being," which suggests a link between WHO and the broader efforts of the United Nations to protect social and economic human rights. Until recently, attributing legitimacy to social and economic rights was resisted by the U.S. government, which suggests a point of friction between the United States and the fundamental goals of WHO. The constitution asserts, moreover, that enjoyment of health by all peoples is essential for the attainment of peace and security.

How seriously the rhetoric contained in the WHO Constitution is taken by government decisionmakers as a guide to policymaking remains undetermined but not entirely untested. One commentator has noted, for example, that little has been done to develop international law to foster a right to health and to expand the participation of WHO in lawmaking.[4] If the development of international laws placing obligations on governments in the area of health were the sole test of the success of WHO's organizational ideology, then WHO would have to be judged as relatively unsuccessful.

The first three WHO directors-general made a point of elaborating aspects of the basic ideological elements that accompanied the formation of the organization. They were generally applauded for their efforts, which may be taken as evidence that the organization is in need of both leadership and the continuing attention to its ideology. In recent years, that ideology has fit well with the emphasis of the UN system on economic and social development, which began with the expansion of developing-country membership in all global intergovernmental organizations.

In 1977 the World Health Assembly defined the broad goal of the organization as "health for all by the year 2000." This definition represented an abrupt redirection of the WHO ideology toward a broad focus on health care and its role in development and away from a technical approach to improving human health.[5] Director-General Halvdan Mahler unceasingly sought to develop specific programmatic paths to this goal. During his fifteen-year tenure, the introductions to Mahler's biennial reports[6] adopted a theoretical approach to the organization's programmatic efforts and contained a forthright elaboration of WHO's organizational ideology. Mahler's biennial reports and other pronouncements were never rejected or severely criticized by WHO deliberative organs and they therefore contain the best expression of WHO's organizational ideology. By comparison, the reports of the current director-general, Hiroshi Nakajima, have much less ideological and programmatic content, instead striking a more managerial tone.[7] This may be evidence of another change in the organization's ideology, or it may indicate a lack of interest or of ability in formulating broad policy goals.

Mahler understood WHO's task to be that of providing practical guidance to governments in achieving the goal of "health for all by the year 2000." The central mechanism for achieving this goal was the development of primary health care, which was elaborated in a series of WHO strategic recommendations to governments. In addition, the organization directly assisted governments in developing their own primary health programs and in monitoring the results of those programs.

One consequence of the "health for all" program was that the WHO guidelines became a springboard for broader and more general development efforts. Within the UN system, in particular, human development took on greater importance than mere economic growth, even if some important member governments declined to endorse that focus. In addition, WHO began cooperating more extensively with other development agencies, but nevertheless it remained the primary source of the health policies and principles urged on its members.

Though Mahler's reports clearly enunciate the "health for all" slogan of the World Health Organization, the specification of that goal did not necessarily induce the undiluted support of the international public health community or of national policymakers. In fact, Mahler himself noted that there was some resistance in the WHO secretariat to the altered ideology.[8] A number of governments, including the United States, explicitly opposed parts of the "health for all" program. Mahler was thus forced to walk a fine line between assembling the voluntary cooperation of governments and more interventionary policies that relied on WHO leadership and assistance. This distinction reflects a tension that runs through all WHO programs, involving the extent to which the WHO secretariat should serve as an independent actor in forging world health policy.

In 1991, Nakajima informed the WHO Executive Board that the organization had yet to find a "realistic health-for-all paradigm."[9] After some criticism by members of the WHO board and following a wide-ranging discussion, the board asked the director-general to "flesh out" the prevailing model.[10] To this date, however, the existing "health for all" paradigm that is the cornerstone of the WHO ideology remains rather ambiguous. This ambiguity has dampened the organization's sense of mission and thus also its effectiveness.

CHALLENGES AND CONSTRAINTS FACING THE WORLD HEALTH ORGANIZATION

In the early 1970s, Harold K. Jacobson, one of the most practiced observers of international organizations, described the World Health Organization as a "strong, stable system."[11] Jacobson attributed the agency's stability to several factors: the positive, though financially limiting, attitudes of the United States, the Soviet Union, the United Kingdom, and France; the effective leadership of the agency's directors-general; the participation of the international biomedical community in the organization's programs; and the services provided by WHO to its poorer member states. Within the context of the UN system, WHO remains a relatively strong and viable agency. Yet potentially destabilizing cracks can be found in the organization's foundation.

Its multiple constituencies pull the agency in many conflicting directions, and the political climate within WHO is now unusually fluid. The developing countries, which make up the great majority of WHO members, expect and receive health services from the organization. China has become a more active, though still not a significant, presence within WHO. The once substantial role of the Soviet Union has been replaced by the weak role now played by Russia. The international biomedical and public health communities continue to participate extensively in WHO programs. Nevertheless, the priorities of the biomedical and public health professions are not necessarily in accord with the "health for all" goals that take the agency into nontechnical areas such as human rights and economic or social development.

Three larger challenges or problems confront the World Health Organization. First, the most important member state of the organization, the United States, has from the outset been ambivalent about the depth of its participation in WHO, as well as its leadership role within the international medical community. Although the United States has historically been a supporter of international health programs, the U.S. medical community and U.S. policymakers have frequently been reluctant to take on a strong leadership role within WHO. This ambivalence has had a severe impact on the organization.

Second, like all UN organizations, the World Health Organization is hampered by a lack of adequate funding. WHO relies on assessments on its member states, their voluntary contributions, and some additional support from the private sector to finance its broad range of research and program activities. In recent years, moreover, costly new health problems such as the global AIDS epidemic have increased the burdens on the organization's limited resources. In addition, with medical procedures and technologies advancing ever more rapidly, the organization faces the significant challenge of simply keeping up with changes in the health care field, while at the same time it seeks to broaden the focus of its activities well beyond earlier conceptions of public health. As a result, the demands on the agency have increased beyond the current limits of its budget and staff, and this is of concern to U.S. policymakers.

Finally, the history of the World Health Organization contains a series of major controversies over its mandate, programs, and leadership that have affected its ability to achieve its primary goals. While international cooperation of any kind involves smoothing out friction, some issues in WHO's history have produced especially wide concern in Washington, frequently generating publicity that has gone beyond the inner circle of medical professionals. Among the most problematic issues in this regard have been the regulation of the quality of drugs in international commerce, the sale of infant formula in developing countries, the abusive sale of pharmaceuticals in the Third World, the role of WHO in the UN system's increasing emphasis on development programs, the organization's programs to control disease, the development of a response to the AIDS pandemic, the reelection of Director-General Hiroshi Nakajima to lead WHO in 1993, and the participation of Israel and the Palestine Liberation Organization in WHO activities.

In each of these cases, policy issues that can be defined as extraneous to public health practices became salient. Such issues obviously constrain the organization from freely applying the standards consistent with the thinking of its professional biomedical elite, even if the eventual outcome of such political strife may not differ substantially from the policies that were initially proposed.

AMBIVALENCE OF THE UNITED STATES

The United States played a leading role in the construction of the World Health Organization, though it was hardly the only government responsible for the organization's establishment. Nevertheless, the participation of the U.S. government in the management and work of WHO has reflected a certain ambivalence toward the organization. There are several reasons for this ambivalence. Within the United States, the American Medical Association (AMA) has always been against any U.S. affiliation with "socialized medicine," which the AMA views as a true evil and which it has suspected WHO of promoting at times. In addition, when WHO was founded, the United States and the Pan-American Sanitary Organization had a long and successful relationship; as a result, the United States discouraged interference in the latter institution's work. And finally, the U.S. Senate objected to portions of the WHO draft constitution, in particular the provisions regarding withdrawal from the organization and the size of the U.S. financial contribution.[12]

The misgivings of the United States concerning the World Health Organization have had a serious impact on the organization because the United States has always been both the principal source of medical leadership in the world and the largest contributor to the WHO budget.

The views of such an important member state cannot be simply brushed aside. The United States is represented at every level of WHO management supervision and professional consultation. Leading WHO officials are often drawn from the United States and usually have experience and close contacts with the biomedical establishment there. The U.S. government thus has a high level of access to WHO when it wants to send a message to the organization. The large financial contribution of the United States to the WHO budget tends to make it a leader on budgetary issues, whether or not its representatives seek that role. The U.S. diplomatic mission to the UN office in Geneva has a brief to monitor WHO activities, and as a result, U.S. officials remain in close contact with WHO personnel and other leading state delegations. Moreover, the United States is a principal member of the Geneva Group, the informal consultative body whose deliberations deeply influence the decisions of the important financial donors concerning their contributions to the budgets of the UN specialized agencies.

FINANCING

The World Health Organization's goal of achieving the highest possible standard of health could consume almost unlimited resources. Moreover, the WHO Constitution specifically lists no fewer than twenty-two organizational functions, some of which are as broad as assisting governments to strengthen health services, promoting and conducting research on human health, furnishing the necessary aid to governments during emergencies, and the most general, taking all necessary actions to achieve these goals. Of course, WHO must design the specific programs to limit and make the work of the organization efficient.

In the 1994–95 biennial program budget, the agency's activities were grouped into ten specific subprogram areas within three main program areas.[13] Those subheadings are: health system development; the organization of health systems based on primary health care; the development of human resources for health; public information and education; the promotion and development of research; the protection and promotion of general health; the protection and promotion of mental health; the promotion of environmental health; the development of diagnostic, therapeutic, and rehabilitative technologies; and the prevention and control of disease. All but the last two of these are predominately developmental in nature.

For the entire range of WHO programs in 1994 and 1995, the director-general proposes to spend roughly $1.84 billion. Of this total, $872 million will come from the assessed contributions of member states. The United States pays 25 percent of the assessed contributions, or about $219 million. Aside from assessments on member states, the remainder of the organization's expenditures come from voluntary contributions and payments by other UN organizations.[14] Thus, over half of the proposed WHO expenditures for 1994 and 1995 are covered by "extrabudgetary" contributions.[15]

The reluctance of WHO member states to provide increased funding places real constraints on the organization's ability to fund its broad agenda of health activities. Not all of the programs are equal in size and scope: for example, the trust fund for the Global Program on AIDS, at $178 million, dwarfs the resources provided for maternal and child health, the control of river blindness, or emergency assistance. And while WHO promotes medical research, it does not operate its own laboratories but contracts out for limited services. Like every other member of the UN system of institutions, the World Health Organization must continually seek to fill its mandate with insufficient resources.

CONTROVERSIAL PROGRAMS AND PRACTICES

The prosaic titles of WHO budget documents have hidden the existence of severe controversies over the contents of several of its programs, including the degree to which the organization may specify the content of AIDS educational programs, or the extent of the controls that it may recommend and supervise on the international commerce in prescription drugs. Even the hypothetical possibility of providing medicines to poor countries caused an intense controversy and elicited a U.S. effort to limit this type of activity.

The United States has not been alone in blocking the development of specific WHO programs. The governments of some Roman Catholic member states, for instance, were able until 1966 to keep WHO from accepting family planning as part of the global health program. Nevertheless, more recently the Bush administration demanded assurances from WHO that no part of the organization's work on human reproduction went to support research on RU-486, a French commercial drug that induces early abortion.[16]

REGULATION OF COMMERCE

Three of the controversies mentioned earlier involve the regulation of international commerce: regulating the quality of drugs in international trade; the sale of infant formula to developing countries; and the sale of pharmaceutical products in the Third World. The regulatory issues dealt with by WHO have typically been politically sensitive matters for the U.S. government. As a result of positions taken by the medical profession and the pharmaceutical industry, the United States has ceaselessly opposed regulatory action by the World Health Organization. In a sense, this stand contradicts the principle of the highest standard of health for all, because it leaves the promotion of efficient health practices to the market and offers no assistance to weaker or poorer member governments in dealing with undesirable commercial practices. It is the governments of those developing countries that now strongly back standard-setting action by the organization. In addition, the efforts of member governments to create a standard-setting role for the organization are increasingly being supported by nongovernmental organizations (NGOs), some of which have a transnational reach.

Currently, WHO does have limited responsibilities to develop binding regulations for controlling epidemic disease and for setting standards for food safety. Nevertheless, what WHO can in fact do to regulate commerce is limited by the willingness of governments to control industries within their jurisdictions and to follow WHO guidelines. If the organization recommends binding international commitments to member governments to regulate commerce, they would still have the right to refuse to accede. Generally, however, the United States has been able to soften proposals for standard setting, but not to avoid them altogether.[17]

Concern with the quality of drugs in international trade has been on the WHO agenda continuously since the early 1960s. The United States has blocked proposals to establish independent international monitoring mechanisms by successfully advocating alternatives such as the provision of training and advisory services to member governments. In 1970, the United States did acquiesce in the adoption of international guidelines on manufacturing, labeling, quality control, and reports of adverse reactions. However, these guidelines were far weaker and vaguer than those originally proposed by advocates of strong international regulation.

The infant formula (mother's-milk substitute) issue had a far more emotional, controversial, and public character. In this controversy, the developed-country producers of infant formula were accused of deliberately promoting the sale of their products in poor countries, where they were likely to be misused and produce severe infant health problems. Many developing states and medical experts argued that the result of increased infant formula sales would be surges in malnourished and dead children in poor countries, as well as high profits for the producers. After extensive consultations with drug companies, governments, and advocacy groups, the World Health Assembly in 1981 recommended a marketing code for infant formula. The United States alone voted against the new code.

The U.S. position clearly reflected both the continuing nervous-ness of the U.S. government about international regulation and the ide-ological position of the Reagan administration. Since then, the issue has declined somewhat in salience and it now attracts little attention, but it remains on the WHO agenda.

Like the infant formula issue, questions involving the marketing of pharmaceuticals in the Third World generated a great deal of contro-versy in the late 1970s and early 1980s. This particular issue also reflect-ed the growing concerns about these practices on the part of the organization's membership as well as on the part of advocacy groups in the developed countries, including the United States. The underly-ing complaint against the methods used to market pharmaceuticals was neatly put by Director-General Halvdan Mahler, who charged that the drug companies of the developed world promoted "drug imperi-alism." The drug companies located in the developed states use their dominant positions vis-à-vis the developing countries, Mahler alleged, to engage in shoddy practices—from the dumping of outdated or obso-lete products and the withholding of low-cost generic products to out-right bribery.

As with the infant formula controversy, the United States strenu-ously opposed WHO attempts to regulate the international trade in pharmaceuticals. The United States responded by encouraging drug companies to regulate their own industry. In addition, the U.S. gov-ernment had its representatives to WHO use tactics that sought to weak-en the proposed regulations and codes, sought agreements between the drug companies and individual Third World governments, and more generally tried to reduce the WHO role in this area. The United States, however, was unable to block the 1978 adoption by the World Health Assembly of an action program intended to strengthen international regulation of drug companies and setting standards for their products.

DEVELOPMENT SERVICES

That WHO would be engaged in the direct furnishing of services to governments was obvious from the adoption of its constitution.[18] The character and extent of its engagement, however, emanate principally from the tumultuous expansion of development activities in the UN system that accompanied the growth of the world organization's mem-bership beginning in the 1960s.[19] This eventually led to the creation of the UN Development Program (UNDP) and the growth of the devel-opment lending programs of the World Bank. Both of those institutions increasingly encouraged WHO involvement in the public health aspects of their development projects.

The World Bank estimates[20] that $4.8 billion in development aid went to the health sector in 1990. Of this, only $800 million came from nongovernmental sources, and therefore the remainder was contributed by governments, much of it through WHO, the World Bank, and other multilateral institutions. The World Bank plans to disburse as much as $1 billion in health projects by 1995, but at this time its health lending program totals only $350 million. Although an increasing share of health aid is being distributed through multilateral channels, it has comprised a declining share of development assistance since 1980.

The United States has been a trendsetter with respect to development assistance financing. It began to restrain further expansion of its contributions to multilateral development programs as early as the mid-1960s. At the same time, its far larger bilateral programs came under increasing restraints due to political criticism and financial stringency in the United States. These more restrictive policies have affected the multilateral agencies, including WHO. During the last decade, U.S. policymakers have pushed the no-real-growth principle for UN and other international organization budgets and a limitation on U.S. contributions to a level of 25 percent of the total budget for most multilateral agencies.

It is in this context that the WHO program of "health for all by the year 2000" has led to controversy. That program has implied the creation and financing of development programs of a size that the U.S. government and other major donor states are not willing to support. The emphasis on development also presents the broader issue of coordination between WHO and the rest of the UN system. As discussed by Roger Coate in chapter 3 of this book, coordination issues never have been adequately resolved by the UN system of institutions.[21] Senior WHO officials are known to have taken the position that their organization ought to have special dispensation to execute public health projects solely on the basis of their professional judgments. At the same time, serving as an executing agency for UNDP projects and joint projects with other agencies has resulted in substantial income to WHO for overhead, and this has encouraged the expansion of the organization's interest in programs for developing countries. For instance, the 1994–95 WHO budget projects more than $22 million in financing for WHO programs from the other organizations of the UN system.[22]

DISEASE CONTROL

If WHO participation in the development work of the UN system represents a departure from some of the organization's original goals, its current campaign to eliminate poliomyelitis and its earlier efforts to control malaria and eradicate smallpox are much more conventional.

The malaria program reaches almost back to the inception of the organization and is connected with a broader approach to dealing with tropical diseases that includes both research and training. Unexpected factors, such as the emergence of mosquitoes that resist insecticides, have unfortunately left the program far short of its goals.

In contrast, the smallpox virus yielded to a worldwide WHO campaign, and in 1977 the disease was declared eradicated. A continuing WHO immunization program aims to bring six other communicable diseases under control, with the current priority among those six being given to the management of poliomyelitis, more commonly known as "polio." The World Health Organization also has been giving increasing attention to tuberculosis and cholera, both of which have recently shown sharp increases in their virulence and in the number of cases worldwide. Finally, WHO is concerned with worm infection and tropical diseases.

These programs operate through WHO cooperation with national public health services, which on request receive expert assistance and policy advice from the organization's personnel. Some of these programs also involve cooperation with the UN Children's Fund, the UN Development Program, and the World Bank.[23] Using conventional organizational procedures, WHO reviews the progress of these programs, brings together leading experts to establish guidelines for dealing with each disease, and makes recommendations to governments through its deliberative organs. This entire process encourages the development of informal connections among national and international officials, many of whom meet repeatedly in the context of specialist meetings either within or outside of the WHO structure.

The United States generally has given steady support to WHO programs that seek to build the capacity of national public health services to control communicable diseases, especially in the developing world. This support is consistent with the history of international cooperation on public health issues, the skills of the U.S. Public Health Service in this field, and the emphasis of the U.S. government on protecting its population. Communicable-disease programs, especially when they include immunization, involve small per patient costs but substantial aggregate costs for the WHO budget. Consequently, the United States tends to be an obvious target for WHO requests aimed at accumulating the resources required to support these types of programs.

THE GLOBAL AIDS EPIDEMIC

In some respects, the acquired immunodeficiency syndrome (AIDS) fits easily into the framework of international cooperation on public health problems. As part of the broader health problem of sexually

transmitted diseases, AIDS is now a priority concern of the World
Health Organization.

Soon after the rather mysterious emergence of AIDS as a health
problem in the early 1980s,[24] epidemiologists began to assemble data
on the disease's incidence. Based on this information, WHO subsequently forecast a global pandemic. This prediction was bolstered after
biomedical investigation determined that the human immunodeficiency virus (HIV) caused the disease we call AIDS and that neither a vac-
cine nor an effective treatment existed. Therefore, the impact on broad
sections of the global public not only would have specific public health
consequences, but also could raise the kind of fears that were associated with the plagues that affected earlier historical periods. If AIDS was
to be approached on the basis of the best medical knowledge and skills
available to public health administrations, it made sense for governments to turn promptly to the World Health Organization as the international instrument capable of providing a global response and support
to national health services.

It would be fair to say that, in fact, WHO was engaged reasonably
quickly in the global response to the AIDS epidemic. The United States,
which is well equipped with public health and biomedical research
facilities at its Centers for Disease Control (CDC) and its National
Institutes of Health, led the global response to AIDS. Nevertheless, the
response process was far from smooth and uncontroversial.

The controversial elements emerged at the level of U.S. national
politics as well as at the international level. In the United States in particular, AIDS was initially associated with homosexual life-styles and
practices, and only later was the disease linked with heterosexual activities. Significant problems arose in dealing with the AIDS epidemic
because public discussion of sexuality in the United States and in other
countries tends to be inhibited by social and cultural prohibitions. When
it became clear that blood supplies containing HIV could also cause
infection by the disease, blood-supplying organizations only reluctant-
ly reviewed their practices.[25] Later, even when the extent of the epidemic was becoming clear, frequently the response of government
leaders was sheer disbelief and denial.

Officials of the Centers for Disease Control took the first steps in
the early 1980s toward international cooperation. This led to both informal and formal approaches to the World Health Organization, where
senior officials initially reacted with caution. Among their considerations was the question of whether the disease, about which practically
nothing was known, had more significance than other illnesses, such as
malaria or heart disease, that at that time caused more deaths than
AIDS. More importantly, the most effective approach to preventing the

spread of AIDS required changing human sexual behavior, a delicate matter under any circumstance and one which many governments were not eager to approach.

By 1986, however, the WHO Executive Board, Director-General Mahler, and the organization's senior officials were convinced of the need to make the fight against AIDS a priority. The creation of the Global Program on AIDS (GPA) followed, with the appointment of Dr. Jonathan Mann, who had experience with the CDC and the U.S. Public Health Service, as its head, and with the appropriation by the United States of the first large financial contribution to that program. Within two years, practically every government in the world had been contacted by Mann's rapidly assembled staff, and initial preventive programs were put into place. Mann made the protection of human rights part of the preventive agenda for AIDS, arguing that levels of HIV infection could be efficiently determined only if the rights of the infected were guarded. That added a distinctive element to the conventional legislative approach to epidemic control.

AIDS was one aspect of WHO's program activities to which public health specialists in the United States gave special attention. In addition, the economic implications of AIDS concerned the U.S. Agency for International Development, which became an important source of financing for programs in developing countries and which sponsored its own bilateral AIDS programs.

The approach of the GPA under Mann to combating the AIDS epidemic had the enthusiastic support of Mahler and the WHO Executive Board. Mann deliberately sought to create a wide constituency for the GPA, including advocacy organizations whose input had rarely been solicited by WHO in the past. As a result, the Global Program on AIDS seemed poised for effective action. Nevertheless, in the disciplined, managed atmosphere of WHO, a new program cutting across existing administrative units with control over substantial financing unavoidably created internal conflicts, criticism, and rumor. Moreover, according to informed observers, when the new director-general, Hiroshi Nakajima, replaced Mahler in 1988, he brought with him a more intrusive and authoritarian style of management. Over the succeeding months, Mann's grand vision for WHO's response to the AIDS crisis was cut back by the new director-general, who wanted to rein in the GPA and treat AIDS in a more conventional manner as one of several significant global health problems.

Mann abruptly resigned in 1990. The public health and foreign affairs officials of the United States reacted with dismay, even though Nakajima appointed Dr. Michael Merson, an American serving in a senior post at WHO, to replace Mann. These events were unfolding simultaneously with an evolving controversy that brought the U.S.–WHO relationship over AIDS-related issues into the spotlight.

1990 SAN FRANCISCO AIDS CONFERENCE

Even though the United States played a leading role in establishing the Global Program on AIDS, its failure to apply WHO guidelines on the admission of travelers infected with HIV generated a bitter and ongoing controversy in the United States. This controversy emerged during the planning of the sixth International AIDS Conference, which was scheduled to be held in San Francisco in 1990.

As a result of legislation that originated in the U.S. Senate, HIV infection was added to the list of dangerous and contagious diseases that obligated the Immigration and Naturalization Service to exclude people from entering the United States. This legislative reaction to the AIDS epidemic was not confined solely to the United States, despite the fact that a WHO panel of experts had issued a report in 1987 stating that such exclusionary practices would have no effect on the progress of the epidemic.

Attempts by the U.S. government to apply the new regulation and at the same time to relax its implementation so as not to interfere with attendance at the conference resulted in considerable friction, especially between the U.S. government and the nongovernmental organization representatives who intended to go to the San Francisco conference. In the end, largely as the result of efforts by nongovernmental groups, including Red Cross societies and their officials, to mobilize support in the United States and elsewhere, the conference was canceled and held later in Paris.

Although the world's scientists did gather in San Francisco as scheduled, the potentially discriminatory nature of the U.S. exclusion regulation led the organizers of the eighth (1992) International AIDS Conference to move the session from Boston to Amsterdam. As that conference focused more than any previous one on the social and human rights impacts of the AIDS epidemic, its relocation dramatized the failure of the U.S. government to conform fully to a standard of international cooperation that was endorsed by its own medical specialists.

NAKAJIMA'S REELECTION AND THE QUESTION OF LEADERSHIP

The director-general of the World Health Organization is expected by both member states and the organization's staff to take initiatives and to play a leading role in the formulation of international health policy. This particular role was fashioned by a succession of imaginative

and respected chief executives of the organization, and it extends well
beyond the realms of management and routine operations. In addition to
these activities, the director-general is expected to make comprehensive
recommendations regarding national policies and programs that must be
carried out by WHO and member-state governments. Success in this
area requires a solid professional reputation, policymaking skills for formulating recommendations, and the diplomatic poise and ability to gain
support from key individuals, organizations, and governments.

Nakajima's first five-year term of office ran to 1993,[26] but well before
his first term expired, U.S. representatives had begun to criticize the
director-general on professional grounds, and eventually they openly
turned against him. The U.S. representatives complained that Nakajima's
management style was abrupt and dictatorial, and they quarreled with
some of his financial decisions. In addition, they asserted that the for-
ward-looking leadership of earlier regimes had diminished and that staff
morale had slumped. Finally, they viewed Nakajima's travels and statements as directed more often to securing his own reelection than to the
substantive work of the organization. West European officials concurred
with the United States in their negative views of Nakajima's leadership
of WHO. However, Nakajima had strong backing from the Japanese
government, which considered it important that the senior Japanese official within the UN system retain his position.

During his campaign for reelection in 1993, some state representatives accused Nakajima and the Japanese government of buying Third
World votes. Nakajima was reported to have sought the support of Third
World states by promising to deliver favors, and it was alleged that his
individual efforts coincided with a Japanese government campaign using
diplomatic channels. In the end, by 18 votes in favor to 13 opposed,
Nakajima was recommended to the World Health Assembly for reelection. A divided World Health Assembly then elected Nakajima to a second five-year term as the director-general of WHO. It was the first time
that the assembly had not elected a director-general unanimously.

This controversy seriously damaged Nakajima's ability to play an
effective role as WHO's leader. It called into question both his probity
and his professional abilities. Even though he was reelected, Nakajima
now faces a more hostile and constraining relationship with the organization's members than have any of his predecessors.

EXTRANEOUS POLITICS: THE MIDDLE EAST CONFLICT WITHIN WHO

As has been the case elsewhere in the UN system, the Middle East
conflict has served as the basis for injecting extraneous political issues
into debates within WHO's deliberative bodies. During the 1970s, the

governments of the Arab states and their allies around the world attempted by parliamentary maneuvers to isolate Israel throughout the UN system. In the case of the World Health Organization, an Arab-led effort to expel Israel from the organization was consistently thwarted by the strong opposition of the United States, which let it be known that it would withdraw from WHO if Israel were forced out of the organization.

The Arab–Third World coalition had, however, managed to impel the Palestine Liberation Organization (PLO) into formal observer status in the UN General Assembly in the 1980s. Despite the warnings of the United States, Arab governments then decided on a similar campaign for PLO membership in the World Health Assembly. In 1989, this effort appeared to be on the verge of success, but once again the United States made it clear that it would withdraw from the organization if the PLO were admitted. A behind-the-scenes, eleventh-hour deal to have the issue postponed until the next session of the assembly was brokered by Director-General Nakajima. While subsequent changes in world politics have tended to make this particular issue less problematic, similar campaigns may impact the organization's effectiveness in the future.

Such attempts to manipulate the proceedings of UN agencies for political purposes constrain the smooth development and management of those organizations. This sort of tactic, and such difficulties as the questions about leadership that were illustrated by the reelection of Hiroshi Nakajima to the director-generalship of WHO, also call into doubt the voting systems employed by UN institutions that give equal status to all member states, regardless of whether they are large or small, rich or poor, powerful or weak.

U.S. POLICY AND THE WORLD HEALTH ORGANIZATION

The evolution of U.S. policy toward WHO has been dogged by a fundamental question. Should the United States attempt to lead the organization and support its programs, or should it seek to benefit directly from WHO programs while playing a lesser role within the organization? That central question leads to further queries about the respective gains and losses that the United States would incur by adopting a more passive role within the organization. These are significant questions, but because many WHO programs are quite specialized and can thus be considered separately, the most important choices facing the United States involve the selection of which WHO activities it will support from among the broad range of development, prevention, and research operations undertaken by the organization. Each area provides the United States with possibilities for leadership through skill, financing, the provision of personnel, and participation in decisionmaking bodies.

A greater leadership role for the United States within WHO will necessarily involve costs. It will require taking firm positions on divisive issues and sustaining commitments to those positions, the financing of new and more effective health programs, and the piecing together of political support from other member states within the organization's complex system of deliberative bodies. It is likely that a large proportion of the biomedical and public health establishments in the United States would support a stronger U.S. leadership role within the organization. Whether there is support for U.S. leadership on the larger social-policy issues that provide the backdrop to some WHO programs is a related, though much more complex, question. Both of these queries about U.S. leadership within WHO condition, but do not determine, the level of financial support that the U.S. government might provide to the organization.

Similarly, there are substantial costs attached to U.S. passivity within the World Health Organization. If the United States were to play a diminished role, Director-General Nakajima would be freer to pursue his own agenda for the organization. Other member governments would take over the leadership of the organization, and they would no doubt at times promote decisions and policies that would be opposed by some U.S. constituencies.

The ability of the United States to monitor effectively both WHO programs and world health conditions requires active engagement. While it seems unlikely that the state of public health in the United States would be quickly diminished by a passive U.S. role within WHO, U.S. specialists working in the organization would have fewer incentives to maintain contacts with their counterparts in the United States and fewer opportunities to learn from the experiences of other countries on such matters as infant mortality. The United States would no doubt maintain its contributions to bilateral development-assistance programs, but reduced U.S. participation in WHO development projects would make it much more difficult for the United States and other donor governments to contribute to international health programs.

Given the high level of U.S. interest in many of the specialized activities of the World Health Organization, a policy that seeks to enhance the role of U.S. leadership within that agency offers much that is attractive. Most WHO programs are compatible with or complement the national health policy goals of the United States. The organization promotes constructive interaction and cooperation among leading medical and health care specialists. Moreover, WHO is popular among the developing countries. More importantly, however, WHO has the potential for further development, as indicated by its response to the

AIDS crisis, its success in eradicating smallpox, and its plans for eliminating polio. Finally, a greater U.S. leadership role in WHO would provide the opportunity to place a new emphasis on issues involving environmental health and human rights.

The World Health Organization is an institution that is accountable to numerous governments. It would be futile to expect that they would always endorse the views of the United States. The political characteristics of WHO as a multilateral organization therefore require that those hoping to influence its outputs must also participate in its policymaking processes. WHO should not be treated as an instrument by which the United States can make immediate and direct gains, but as one of several means for promoting long-term international cooperation on specific issues involving international health policy.

POLICY DEVELOPMENT

The policy of the United States toward the World Health Organization, like U.S. policy toward all international organizations, is affected by a wide range of diplomatic considerations. For example, the U.S. position on the participation of the Palestine Liberation Organization in WHO bodies was part of the broader U.S. policy toward the PLO and thus unrelated to health issues. In general, however, U.S. policy toward WHO emanates from national biomedical and public health institutions. A typical U.S. delegation to the World Health Assembly is overwhelmingly drawn from these professional communities. And, for more specialized gatherings, there usually are no U.S. representatives from outside of these communities. In the process of considering U.S. policy regarding WHO programs, the influence of the Department of Health and Human Services and its several bureaus and institutes tends to predominate.

The controversies over infant formula, the trade in pharmaceuticals, and AIDS have made it clear that interest in WHO programs among nonspecialists throughout the United States has grown rapidly in recent years. Competent nongovernmental organizations have emerged to serve as watchdogs over the agency, and these NGOs are beginning to contribute to policymaking at the international level. The growth of such links between WHO and broader public health constituencies was anticipated in the organization's constitution, but they now raise questions about U.S. efforts to seek contributions from outside the conventional participant networks. Policy formulation and the development of international health law[27] would certainly benefit from the increased involvement of private groups and public organizations.

The expanded participation of U.S. public groups in the making of international health policy could be rather easily encouraged, and would no doubt pay handsome dividends in terms of U.S. support for WHO and global health care.

FINANCING

The level of the U.S. financial contribution to the World Health Organization can hardly be treated as a major expense by a government that now drafts an annual budget amounting to hundreds of billions of dollars. Nor are the additional voluntary contributions that the United States makes to WHO programs extraordinarily large. It thus makes little sense for congressional committees to spend hours debating the details of these allocations (though of course they tend to do precisely that). Nevertheless, it is obvious that U.S. participation in WHO is haunted by a looming financial shadow.[28]

The contribution of the United States to the World Health Organization should not be treated as a purely financial issue, either by Congress or by the executive branch, but rather as an opportunity to examine the balance and emphasis of programs, the efficiency of WHO's institutional structures, and the ability of the organization to reach the goals that it sets for itself. In addition, financial accountability has never been a prominent issue because WHO typically has had a reputation for being well managed. The accusations of financial mismanagement directed at Nakajima[29] are so unusual in the history of the organization as to suggest that serious problems in this area are quickly detected by the international community.

Were the U.S. government to seek to manipulate WHO policies by withholding its assessed contributions, it would be making a largely futile, as well as decidedly illegal, gesture.[30] The result of such a strategy would be to weaken the organization and call into question the good faith of the United States. And it would frustrate, rather than facilitate, the task of creating and maintaining long-term cooperation with other member states. Withholding financial assessments is a tactic that has hardly worked very well in any institutional setting within the UN system.

Voluntary contributions are another matter altogether. By raising or lowering its voluntary contributions, the donor government has a more direct effect on programs and employment with WHO or any other UN agency. This practice involves the danger of potentially damaging valuable international programs, but nevertheless it certainly sends a clear signal. If the United States intends to play a greater leadership role in WHO, a suitable tactic would be to redistribute parts of its voluntary contributions and even to raise them modestly in return for a stronger voice in selected programs. Done quietly, the tactic of redistributing voluntary funds can be expected to have a decisive effect. A less direct alternative would be for the U.S. government to emphasize bilateral programs that often run parallel to WHO field activities.

POLICY APPLICATION

Policymaking in the World Health Organization requires activating a complex institutional structure that encompasses a variety of political interests emanating from the 184 member governments and their diverse national constituencies. This is not a forum that can easily be dominated by any single member state, but the U.S. government nevertheless can expect a considerable degree of responsiveness from the World Health Organization. In the past, the United States certainly has received this type of responsiveness, even if at times WHO decisions do not entirely accord with U.S. goals. This high level of WHO responsiveness to U.S. objectives is due in part to the technological, organizational, and scientific skills wielded by the United States, in part to its financial contributions to the organization, and in part to the abilities of U.S. officials to organize support from other government representatives and private groups.

The current uneasy relations between the United States and the director-general that it publicly opposed should not mean that the organization has become useless to U.S. policymakers. The United States has every reason to expect high standards of management and a tangible contribution from the WHO staff, which has more professional expertise than can be found within most international agencies. Few complaints about management were heard before the Nakajima regime began, and prior to Nakajima's directorship the organization developed a reputation for sound administration under the leadership of assistant directors-general of U.S. nationality.[31]

Although accountability is not the only desirable quality of an international organization, public institutions certainly attract scrutiny. The U.S. government has demanded a high standard of performance from the current director-general of the World Health Organization. The ability of the United States to monitor the performance of WHO could perhaps be improved if the personnel at the U.S. mission to the United Nations in Geneva always had the requisite analytical skills. In addition, the United States can back up its observations with persuasion within the Geneva Group, the informal consultative body composed of WHO's principal donor governments.

The efforts of the U.S. government to enhance its leadership role within WHO could be supported by several specific approaches aimed at improving decisionmaking processes, including the following:

◆ Broaden and deepen consultations with nongovernmental organizations. This would produce more publicity about WHO policy and about any shortcomings in management. In addition, a public review of policy might be conducted that would involve government agencies, nongovernmental groups, and the U.S. Congress.

◆ Urge more active WHO participation in the international protection of basic human rights.

◆ Emphasize professional standards and goals in the WHO Executive Board and the World Health Assembly, which should help to restrain parliamentary manipulation on extraneous issues.

◆ Seek more cross-disciplinary projects in order to emphasize the social and economic aspects of the organization's goals.[32] In addition, it will be important to ensure that the U.S. mission in Geneva is fully and competently staffed to support these cross-disciplinary initiatives.

◆ Begin early consideration of possible candidates for the post of director-general, and seek professional and nongovernmental support for that individual. At the same time, encourage U.S. nationals of the highest competence to work in WHO.

◆ Use extrabudgetary contributions to shape programs of special relevance to the United States (e.g., the Global Program on AIDS).

◆ Within the UN system more generally, press for the integration of development programs of individual UN agencies, including WHO. While the usual catchword is "coordination," the real point is defining integrated goals so that the talents of the participating agencies can reinforce each other.

The policies of the United States should aim to strengthen those WHO programs that promise to be most effective. The United States should emphasize the long-term goals of the organization and the importance of international cooperation in the field of health care. Most importantly, the United States should take advantage of the organization's stability to ensure that WHO is more than an occasional benefactor in finding solutions to health care problems. And the United States should maintain a strong substantive interest in an international organization that has been described as a "success story" among multilateral institutions.[33]

≈9≈

THE UN COMMISSION ON SUSTAINABLE DEVELOPMENT:
BUILDING THE CAPACITIES FOR CHANGE

KATHRYN G. SESSIONS AND E. ZELL STEEVER*

*T*he United States, which has long been a pioneer in environmental protection at the national level, has had a more mixed record internationally, often guiding and sometimes blocking progress. The new Clinton administration is eager to provide leadership at the United Nations, and it has expressed a keen interest in making the UN Commission on Sustainable Development (CSD) an effective forum for mobilizing global action on a range of environmental concerns. This renewed willingness of the United States to provide international leadership on environmental issues is long overdue, and it has been much welcomed at the United Nations.

Yet the new commission, established as a result of the 1992 Earth Summit, has a mandate not only to protect the environment but also to promote the integration of environment and development, or "sustainable development," reflecting the growing acknowledgment by the international community that environmental and economic concerns must be

* This chapter represents the personal opinions of the authors; it does not necessarily represent the official views of the United Nations Association of the USA, the Department of the Army, the U.S. Army Corps of Engineers, or any other federal agency.

addressed in tandem if they are to be resolved successfully. Thus, if the United States is to play a leading role in the commission, it must do more than reestablish its leadership in the environmental arena, it must also change the way it approaches the relationship between environmental and economic issues. The price of a U.S. failure to alter its own policies will be quite high because the commission cannot succeed without the participation and, in many instances, the leadership of the United States.

At the same time, there could be substantial rewards if the United States plays a strong leadership role within the Commission on Sustainable Development. The creation of sustainable development policies and programs offers tremendous opportunities to bridge the long-standing political differences between the developing and the industrialized countries. Moreover, international debates concerning sustainable development have encouraged governments around the world to support greater public participation in decisionmaking, which reinforces the deeply held U.S. interest in democratization. Most importantly, the sustainable development policies can provide a unifying theme for reforming UN programs that deal with the interrelated problems of poverty, environmental degradation, and population growth. These benefits would complement the growing U.S. emphasis on multilateral efforts to maintain international peace and security.

To be sure, the obstacles confronting the United States in its efforts to reestablish leadership in this area are considerable. In seeking to build a strong commission, the United States must confront its own capacity to reconcile the often opposed goals of economic development and environmental protection, which has important implications for U.S. domestic policy. The United States must also confront the substantial challenge of working with a diverse array of countries to tackle highly interrelated socioeconomic and environmental problems—each quite difficult on its own—as well as the institutional challenges of building and sustaining effective global responses to economic and ecological interdependence.

This chapter presents a short history of the UN Commission on Sustainable Development, an assessment of the challenges and constraints facing the commission, and an overview of options for asserting U.S. leadership in this important new global organization.

HISTORY OF THE COMMISSION

The Commission on Sustainable Development is an innovative response to three apparent failures of the UN system: first, the failure to recognize the importance of protecting the global environment within the institutional structure of the UN system; second, the failure to achieve an international consensus concerning the most effective responses to socioeconomic problems, including underdevelopment and poverty; and third, the failure to develop mechanisms for cross-sectoral decisionmaking. Each of these failures is revealed in the history of the United Nations itself.

THE ROAD TO RIO

The word "environment" does not appear in the UN Charter. This omission reflects a lack of awareness, at the time of the UN's founding, of the intimate relationship between human activities and the health of the planet's ecosystems. Lacking a specific institution for dealing with environmental concerns, these issues first gained the attention of the world body in June 1972 with the UN Conference on the Human Environment, held in Stockholm, Sweden.

The Stockholm conference marked the beginning of international concern about the global environment. It affirmed the importance of preserving the "human environment," and most importantly, it led to the creation of a new multilateral institution, the United Nations Environment Program (UNEP). In addition, at that time many governments followed the example of the United States by creating national environmental protection agencies and enacting environmental legislation. Nevertheless, member states continued to view environmental problems as peripheral to the "real" work of the United Nations, and in the years following the Stockholm conference governments treated environmental programs as discrete and largely irrelevant for social and economic policymaking.

A more central aim of the United Nations, in the eyes of its founders, was the economic and social advancement of all peoples. To achieve this goal, the United States and other member countries have created an array of multilateral institutions over the years that range from the UN Development Program (UNDP) to the World Bank. This institution-building, however, was not accompanied by the provision of consistent policy guidance, due in large part to disagreements among governments over economic priorities, paradigms, and decisionmaking processes. Within the United Nations, long-standing tensions between the East and West—over competing economic and political ideologies—were later reinforced and exacerbated by tensions between the North and South over the mechanisms and forums for making economic decisions. With little basis for consensus among governments, the body established by the UN Charter to coordinate international efforts in the economic and social fields—the Economic and Social Council (ECOSOC)—was never given the support by member states it would have needed to serve as an effective policymaking forum.

Reinforcing this politically driven fragmentation of the UN system was the tendency of member states to create UN bodies that paralleled the sectoral structures of most of the industrialized country governments, reflecting a Western propensity for specialization as the avenue to excellence. If few member governments developed effective mechanisms to integrate social, economic, and environmental policies, international efforts to address the interrelationship of multilateral agencies and programs were virtually nonexistent. In such areas as agriculture, health, and environmental protection, each multilateral organization has its own governing board and mandate, and ECOSOC, the ostensible coordinator, has to this day little power over either the budgets or the policies of UN organizations working in the economic and social fields.

By the late 1980s, the international community had begun to recognize the necessity of adopting new approaches to interrelated socioeconomic and environmental problems. The improvement of East-West relations created space on the international agenda for dealing with quality-of-life issues, many of which had been ignored during the cold war years. With roughly one billion people now living in absolute poverty, the prospect of the world population doubling to more than ten billion within the next thirty or forty years promised to strain already-struggling economies. At the same time, increasing scientific evidence of global environmental degradation—from the loss of biological diversity to the threat of global climate change—spurred the activism of citizens groups in the United States and other industrialized countries. With nearly two decades of work having made seemingly little dent in the problems of underdevelopment and environmental degradation, the international community needed to seek a fresh approach to these concerns.

In 1987, the World Commission on Environment and Development, chaired by Norwegian Prime Minister Gro Harlem Brundtland, urged the General Assembly to take action on the related problems of poverty, environmental degradation, and population growth. The World Commission, which came to be known as the "Brundtland Commission," made a great impact on the international community with its call for major shifts in policy toward more "sustainable development," which it defined as "development that meets the needs of the present without compromising the ability of future generations to meet their own needs."

These events set the stage for the UN Conference on Environment and Development (UNCED), which was held in Rio de Janeiro in June 1992, the twentieth anniversary of the Stockholm conference. The Earth Summit, as it came to be called, was preceded by two and a half years of intensive international negotiations, and it culminated with the largest heads-of-state summit meeting in history.

The Rio Conference

At the Earth Summit, most public attention was focused on two legally binding international conventions that were separately negotiated prior to the conference and were opened for signature at UNCED. These agreements, the Framework Conventions on Climate Change and on the Protection of Biological Diversity, addressed two of the most pressing issues of global environmental concern.

The United States drew considerable criticism for its stance on both framework conventions. In Rio, the United States refused to sign the biodiversity convention over concerns with the provisions on financing and intellectual property rights—making it the lone industrial-state holdout on the treaty. In the case of the climate-change convention, then President George Bush did sign the agreement in Rio, after the United States successfully pressed other governments to drop provisions concerning specific targets and timetables for reducing greenhouse-gas emissions.

The quiet successes of the Rio conference attracted much less publicity from the eight thousand members of the world press who covered the UNCED proceedings. These successes included the adoption by a consensus of the 178 participating governments of an action plan called Agenda 21. Agenda 21 is intended to provide an agenda for action on the integration of environmental and developmental activities and issues into the twenty-first century, and it includes over twenty-four hundred recommendations in over 150 program areas. Agenda 21 is, in effect, a global workplan for integrating protection of the environment with the promotion of sustainable economic development.

The process of negotiating Agenda 21 led to perhaps the greatest success of the Earth Summit, namely a form of "perestroika" or new thinking about environmental and developmental concerns. Although the diplomats and nongovernmental representatives who participated began the UNCED negotiations with their own specific priorities—ranging from climate change to poverty—most of them emerged with a new appreciation of the linkages between these problems and of the need for coordinated action across sectors, borders, and generations. This learning process that began during the conference led to a broad acceptance of "sustainable development" as a new concept for dealing with the interrelationship between socioeconomic and environmental issues.

One factor that contributed to this learning process was the unprecedented involvement of nongovernmental organizations (NGOs) in the Earth Summit. Many of the fourteen hundred NGOs accredited to the UNCED conference worked throughout the preparatory negotiations, contributing draft texts and background information for the official agreements and lobbying government delegates. The United States and some other governments included NGO observers on their official delegations, which served to further deepen the involvement of nongovernmental groups in the negotiating process leading up to the Rio conference. In addition, many NGOs worked "outside" the official UNCED process, organizing coalitions of interested citizens' groups to build public awareness of the UNCED agenda and its goals prior to the conference. And finally, at Rio the NGO community organized the 1992 Global Forum, an independent series of events that was attended by thirty thousand people from around the world.

This extensive citizen participation created a broad network of people concerned about the diverse problems addressed by the United Nations through the UNCED process. The participation of NGOs also enriched the official negotiations by expanding the pool of ideas and perspectives under consideration, encouraging a more holistic approach and thus reinforcing the movement by governments toward sustainable development as a new policy direction.

Despite the considerable achievements of the representatives involved in the UNCED negotiating process, as the talks concluded it was clear that the international community had only begun to explore the potential benefits of the sustainable development framework. It also was clear that responsibility for implementing the formidably broad UNCED agreements would be widely dispersed throughout the UN system. To overcome these problems, the delegates included a recommendation in Agenda 21 that the United Nations create a Commission on Sustainable Development, which they envisioned as a high-level forum for continuing the global dialogue on sustainable development and monitoring progress toward the long-term goals set in Rio de Janeiro.

THE ROAD FROM RIO

Acting on the recommendations of the Rio conference, the 47th UN General Assembly authorized the creation of the Commission on Sustainable Development in December 1992. One month later, in January 1993, ECOSOC formally established the commission, negotiated its rules of procedure, and elected its first member governments, which included the United States.

The primary mandate of the CSD is to review the progress being made in implementing the recommendations of Agenda 21 at both the national and the international levels. In addition, the commission is charged with promoting international discussions of those "urgent and emerging" sustainable development concerns that may not have been adequately addressed at the UNCED conference.

The commission was established as a functional commission of ECOSOC and is composed of fifty-three member states serving three-year terms. States that are not members of the commission may participate in CSD meetings as observers without the right to vote on its decisions and resolutions. The representatives of international organizations, including the international financial institutions, may also participate in CSD meetings as observers. ECOSOC also invited the NGOs accredited to UNCED to apply for accreditation to the ECOSOC roster so that they might participate as observers in CSD sessions. Observer status ultimately was granted to more than five hundred NGOs, which joined other ECOSOC-accredited NGOs as participants in the first CSD meeting.

Exactly one year after the Rio conference, in June 1993, the CSD held its first substantive session at the UN headquarters in New York City. To signal their continuing commitment to sustainable development issues, fifty-six states sent high-level delegations to the session led by either ministers or ambassadors. Also attending the session were the representatives of more than twenty international organizations and some three hundred NGOs, of which more than a third were from the United States. The United States and a number of other governments included NGO representatives on their official delegations.

To tackle the mammoth job of monitoring the implementation of all Agenda 21 recommendations, the commission adopted a three-year workplan to review national and international progress toward implementing those recommendations by 1997. For each of the next three years, the CSD will consider specific "cross-sectoral" issues such as financing and technology for sustainable development, and it will also focus on clusters of "sectoral" issues. In 1994, for example, the sectoral focus will be on the interrelated concerns of health, human settlements, fresh water, hazardous chemicals, and toxic wastes. Each annual session of the commission is to conclude with a ministerial-level meeting, where senior government representatives will have an opportunity to discuss urgent and emerging concerns and give political impetus to the commission's recommendations.

CHALLENGES FACING THE COMMISSION

Despite the broad consensus among UN member states concerning the urgent need to create the Commission on Sustainable Development, the new body was launched before several underlying issues surrounding its work were resolved. This gives the commission's member governments considerable leeway to shape the commission as they reach agreement on its future activities, but it also renders the commission vulnerable to the uncertainties that accompany a lack of direction. Most importantly, however, it provides a unique opportunity for constructive U.S. participation in the commission's activities. In the crucial first years of the commission, U.S. leadership could help build both the political consensus and analytical framework needed to enable the new body to realize its potential.

BUILDING CONSENSUS

Perhaps the most important challenge facing the commission is to nurture the fragile international consensus on sustainable development. The creation of a stronger working consensus regarding the definition and implications of the sustainable development concept will provide new energy and direction to the work of the international community in the areas of environmental protection and economic development, areas which in the past have been persistently divisive.

Since the UNCED conference, both the United States and the United Nations have begun to adopt the sustainable development concept as the basis of a new policymaking framework. Yet these efforts are handicapped by the limited consensus that now exists on the definition of sustainable development. Neither the Rio Declaration nor Agenda 21 provides a succinct definition of this complex concept, nor do they spell out clear norms of behavior in the field of sustainable development. Moreover, the definition of sustainable development employed by the Brundtland Commission, though it is often repeated, was not included in the Rio documents, and it provides little practical guidance for the international community.

At the commission's first session in June 1993, as the member governments began making concrete decisions to put the sustainable development concept into practice, it became apparent that substantial divisions still exist between states concerning the new policy framework. The absence of agreement on a working definition of sustainable development means that the first priority of the United States must be to help create a consensus among countries on the meaning and policy implications of the sustainable development concept.

The differences between the governments of the northern and southern states over the meaning of sustainable development must be bridged for the sustainable development framework to function effectively. Many developing-country governments, which are just now beginning to acknowledge the relevance of environmental concerns for their economic development, view sustainable development with considerable suspicion and fear that it will be used to impose environmental conditionality on a dwindling pool of development assistance. As a result, the "Group of 77" (G–77) developing countries, which now number 129 members, have insisted that the commission serve as a forum for discussing how to finance sustainable development.

Many northern governments, on the other hand, have long been reluctant to use UN bodies for economic policymaking and are less than enthusiastic about having the commission deliberate financial issues. Consequently, northern governments have tended to emphasize the environmental aspects of sustainable development, and they therefore view the commission primarily as an environmental forum.

These differences were in evidence during the 1993 CSD session, as those governments negotiating the establishment of intersessional working groups quarreled over the issues that each working group would address. The strength of the G–77 ultimately prevailed, however, and two working groups were established, with one focusing on issues related to financial resources and the second considering issues of technology transfer, cooperation, and capacity-building. Whether the discussions of the working groups will produce constructive arrangements for greater cooperation in the realm of sustainable development or will simply rehash seemingly irreconcilable differences still remains to be seen.

The "environment vs. economy" controversy that dominates the debate over defining sustainable development serves only to perpetuate a false dichotomy. To be sure, it is increasingly being demonstrated and accepted that the underlying sources of many environmental problems lie in existing economic patterns and policies. There clearly are many situations where environmental and economic goals conflict, as well as many short-term costs associated with making adjustments for environmental reasons. Yet such adjustments may, in the long run, be inevitable given that current economic patterns may not be sustainable, dependent as they are on the limitless consumption of natural resources and externalizing the ecological costs of emissions and wastes. And there are also many opportunities to simultaneously achieve both ecological and economic goals, but these opportunities are routinely missed because of the fragmented policymaking framework that is now employed. Similarly, the North–South debate tends to imply a zero-sum game, when in fact the quality of life of communities around the world is increasingly interdependent.

The United States can play an important role in the search for environmentally sound and mutually beneficial development policies and practices, and it already seems to be moving in that direction. For instance, the recent offer of the U.S. government to work with Colombia in preparing for the CSD intersessional working group on technology was a major step forward because it suggested a new U.S. willingness to open a constructive dialogue and a desire to find win-win situations, rather than settling for the usual rhetorical standoff. The real test will revolve around whether the initial enthusiasm of the Clinton administration for using the commission to promote U.S. environmental technologies proves to be more than a self-serving U.S. sales pitch and is balanced with efforts to meet the concerns of others.

The ability of the United States to play a leadership role in consensus-building on sustainable development is dependent on the United States itself adopting a more integrated approach to solving environmental and developmental concerns. In general, the posture of the United States at the 1993 CSD session was well received, with many member states and NGOs expressing their appreciation for the new U.S. interest in the commission and in creating new international partnerships to deal with environmental and developmental issues. However, the representatives of the United States, including Vice President Albert Gore, continually stressed the problems of environmental degradation and population growth without expressing similar concerns about the problems of poverty and underdevelopment.

The U.S. focus on environmental issues at the United Nations in fact reflects the orientation of the Clinton administration's domestic programs. The President's Council for Sustainable Development, which was established in June 1993 to "advise the President on matters involving sustainable development" and "develop and recommend to the President a national sustainable development action strategy that will foster economic vitality," appears to be focused primarily on integrating environmental protection into U.S. business activities. An outgrowth of the White House Office on Environmental Policy, the membership of the President's Council includes representatives of business and environmental groups, but it does not include significant representation from other relevant constituencies, such as organizations concerned with poverty, finance, economics, and community development. As it stands, the council will need to demonstrate that sustainable development means improving the quality of life for all Americans as much as it means improving the quality of ecosystems.

In order to play an effective leadership role in the commission, the U.S. delegation will need to be careful not to push a solely environmental agenda. Instead, it will need to address the socioeconomic concerns of countries as well, seeking solutions that are friendly both to the environment and to affected communities. When conflicts arise, as they inevitably will, the United States can help lead fair and genuine efforts toward their resolution. This approach is important not only for keeping the developing countries engaged, but also for acknowledging that no country, including the United States, can tackle economic, social, or environmental problems within a vacuum.

A U.S. leadership role can be further enhanced by constantly looking for ways to move the debate on sustainable development forward within the commission. The U.S. delegation therefore should seek to make the commission a forum for addressing the interrelationship of economic and ecological problems in a pragmatic and constructive way, which would solidify and bring meaning to the largely rhetorical commitments to sustainable development that have been made by governments. To accomplish these goals, the commission should help to identify differences of opinion as well as potential areas for agreement, it should serve as a forum for the exchange of information and ideas about how to tackle specific sustainable development projects and problems, and it should seek to gradually build broad-based consensus among governments regarding acceptable norms of behavior in the realm of sustainable development.

Any political consensus regarding sustainable development that emerges within the commission will face another crucial test. That test will revolve around whether the commitments made in the commission by governments are reinforced or offset by their domestic policies and their actions in other international forums. Many of the issues that will be dealt with by the commission have profound implications for domestic policies, raising the likelihood that CSD decisions will be either weak or undermined by domestic institutions. To the extent that national economic policies are affected, the agreements reached by governments within the commission may require subsequent action by national legislative bodies or federal agencies. This requirement adds a potentially damaging constraint to the global consensus-building process, and it reconfirms the need to simultaneously build a consensus on sustainable development at home.

BUILDING A NEW FRAMEWORK

Should UN member states reach a consensus on integrating environmental and economic concerns to create a working sustainable development framework, they will still face considerable analytical and practical challenges in putting that framework into practice. As a framework for guiding policy decisions, the sustainable development concept remains underdeveloped and therefore provides few tools for guiding policies, programs, and projects. While most UNCED participants now acknowledge the linkages between socioeconomic and environmental forces, the understanding of these linkages is extremely limited within the broader policymaking community and among the general public. As a result, important work remains to be done for assessing the nature and implications of these linkages.

When the new sustainable development framework is assembled, implementing the necessary changes will not be easy. Traditional solutions to socioeconomic problems tend to focus on discrete sectoral responses that promote highly specialized policies. Moreover, traditional bureaucratic structures are sectorally oriented, with few mechanisms for cross-sectoral analysis and decisionmaking. The historical lack of training for or experience in such interdisciplinary approaches means that the capacities for adopting the sustainable development framework are inadequate within the UN system and in member governments.

Considerable work will be needed to develop specific policy ideas concerning *how* to promote the sustainable development concept. The Brundtland Commission suggested that "sustainable development is not a fixed state of harmony, but rather a *process of change* [emphasis added] in which the exploitation of resources, the direction of investments, the orientation of technological development, and institutional changes are made consistent with future as well as present needs." The UNCED process reaffirmed this idea because the complex conference, which involved many different actors and dealt with many different yet interrelated issues, helped to generate the belief that sustainable development is a *process* rather than a state of being.

The UNCED conference also produced a number of useful recommendations for improving decisionmaking processes. For example, the Rio Declaration highlights the importance of "process" rights and responsibilities—such as public access to information, public participation in decisionmaking, and the use of environmental-impact assessments—for ensuring that decisions reflect the broadest possible input from society. Agenda 21 recommends mechanisms such as national sustainable-development strategies and full-cost accounting standards that reflect the environmental and social costs and benefits of transactions. Agenda 21 also emphasizes that the quality of policy decisions depends in large part on who is involved in the process. Eight chapters of the action plan recommend ways to strengthen the role of major sectors of society in decisionmaking processes from the level of the local community to the UN system.

The CSD must begin to highlight the ways in which these suggestions for improving decisionmaking can be applied. A good place to start is the CSD's annual reviews of specific issues, which could demonstrate the benefits of integrating input from a wide range of sectors and regions into the policy process.

Critical to this process will be the quality of information and ideas flowing into the commission and its secretariat. The annual CSD reviews will be based in large part on two consolidated reports produced annually by its secretariat, with each focusing on the clusters of issues that are on that year's CSD agenda. One consolidated report, based on reports submitted to the CSD secretariat by national governments, will assess trends in implementing the relevant Agenda 21 recommendations at the national level. The second consolidated report will assess progress at the international level, drawing on contributions from international organizations both inside and outside the UN system.

The United States can do much to ensure that the CSD secretariat has the capacity and the mandate to collect, evaluate, and consolidate information. The secretariat is quite small, and some consideration should therefore be given to seconding experts to it from national governments and international organizations. The United States should further support the secretariat by actively sharing national scientific and technical information.

Another challenge with respect to the collection of information on sustainable development activities is more political. Governments and international organizations tend to submit reports that cast their own efforts in the most favorable light, and some may try to influence the CSD secretariat regarding the content of the consolidated reports. For the reporting process to be useful, a method must be found to reward candid appraisals of the sustainable development problems encountered by states. In this respect, the U.S. reports should help to set a standard of excellence by reporting not only on projects and policies that have succeeded, but also on those that have failed. In addition, the United States can build support among governments for the maintenance of the highest professional standards in the secretariat's work, and the U.S. government should encourage the secretariat to draw on independent as well as official sources in producing its reports.

Another related challenge will be for the commission to fully utilize the expertise of nongovernmental organizations in its work. Sound policy ideas and substantial amounts of information are generated by the NGOs working on sustainable development or specializing in specific areas, as happened in the UNCED process. The work of the CSD secretariat would be greatly facilitated if it could make extensive use of nongovernmental expertise. But many member governments still feel threatened by such NGO participation, particularly when nongovernmental assessments of progress conflict with those of governments. Washington can help set a positive tone for actively engaging nongovernmental organizations in the commission's work by stressing the value of bringing all the relevant information and expertise into the policy process.

In its initial years, the commission will be something of an experiment in expanding the relationship between nongovernmental actors and international organizations. The key to expanding the commission's relations with NGOs is its relatively flexible rules of procedure, which permit that relationship to evolve and develop simultaneously with the sustainable development field itself. Again, U.S. leadership will be needed to maintain the support of governments for the widest possible participation by nongovernmental groups.

The CSD also must stimulate changes in the broader decisionmaking processes of national governments. It has begun this process by encouraging governments to adopt national sustainable development strategies and to coordinate their planning in the environmental and economic spheres, but much more needs to be done. Current U.S. efforts to formulate a national sustainable development strategy should provide a good basis for initiating a dialogue at the next CSD session about reorienting national decisionmaking processes.

The commission also could help stimulate improvements in other decisionmaking processes by, for instance, building consensus on new models of production. Historically, production has been conceived of as a linear process based on the assumption that natural resources, energy, and the environment's ability to absorb wastes are all limitless.[1] In this traditional conception, "externalities" such as environmental degradation do not impose costs on producers in the absence of government-imposed penalties.

A more sustainable approach would be provided by a closed-loop system where the production process is designed so that energy is conserved, wastes are minimized, and by-products are recycled back into the production process. In this system, every effort would be made to use natural-resource inputs as efficiently as possible. Individual production activities might be linked—for example, by colocating interdependent manufacturing processes—so that the waste products of one activity might become the inputs for another activity. The United States should encourage governments to discuss in the CSD their experiences regarding the most effective regulatory and incentive structures for sustainable production processes.

The United States should also work within the commission to support the negotiation of agreements on the introduction of sustainability-impact review procedures—building on the U.S. experience with environmental-impact assessments—for use throughout the UN system. These procedures could require, for example, that all project proposals include a brief written review of:

◆   the extent to which affected communities have been involved in the decisionmaking process;

- the economic, social, and environmental impacts of the proposed action, including any unavoidable adverse impacts of
  the proposed action;

- the sustainability of the proposed action (e.g., plans for efficient use of energy and materials, reliance on environmentally friendly inputs, waste minimization, and recycling of
  residuals); and

- alternatives to the proposed action.

CONSTRAINTS ON THE COMMISSION

Although the Commission on Sustainable Development is a new institution, it has already begun facing important constraints on its effectiveness and ability to achieve the goals set forth in its mandate. In
addition, as the most influential member of the commission, the United
States enters this process with numerous constraints on its own ability
to play a strong leadership role in the area of sustainable development.
Indeed, the financial, institutional, and political obstacles facing the
United Nations parallel those faced by the United States, as the global
organization and the global power attempt to shift course.

FINANCING: WHO WILL PAY FOR THE COMMISSION?

In recent years, the diplomats of the United States have increasingly been placed in the position of making political commitments that
the U.S. government cannot uphold for lack of a commitment of financial resources. Unfortunately, this may prove to be the situation that
also faces U.S. representatives to the CSD seeking to support its work of
building sustainable development.

The governments that participated in the Earth Summit agreed that
the objectives of Agenda 21 would require new financial assistance to
developing countries to assist with the costs of programs that would benefit the global environment and build sustainable development. The
UNCED secretariat estimated that the cost of implementing the Agenda
21 recommendations in developing countries would cost over $600 billion
annually, including $125 billion that the secretariat suggested should be
provided by the international community as grants or concessional loans.
The governments in Rio also agreed that the "costs of inaction could out-
weigh the financial costs of implementing Agenda 21," and that such
"inaction will narrow the choices of future generations."

Financial resources remain essential to meeting the goals of UNCED. In addition, substantial financial support from the developed world for sustainable development projects would grease the wheels of greater North-South consensus. Nevertheless, the industrialized countries have failed to make commitments anywhere near the order of magnitude that the UNCED secretariat estimated would be needed to implement Agenda 21. Furthermore, those pledges that were made by developed states were vague; for example, the European Community pledged three billion European Currency Units (ECUs) toward the implementation of Agenda 21, but its own press releases acknowledged that no information was available about where this money would come from, whether it was new or redirected assistance, or for what specific programs the funds would be used.

In the first year after UNCED, few significant promises were made regarding new financial assistance for implementing Agenda 21. The Rio agreements have been, in effect, caught in the larger economic downturn that has been affecting all development assistance. Economic and, in some cases, political difficulties have led many industrialized countries to freeze or even reduce their aid levels. The levels of assistance from Arab countries have declined, and many of the former communist countries continue to move from the role of donor to recipient states. The announcement by Japan at the 1993 CSD session that it would significantly increase its sustainable development assistance was certainly welcomed. However, the developing countries remain discouraged by the scarcity of financial support for Agenda 21.

The regular UN budget, which now includes financing for the CSD secretariat, remains under a "zero-growth" budgeting policy at the insistence of the United States and other donor countries, meaning that new programs in the area of sustainable development must come at the expense of existing efforts in other areas. The "Capacity 21" program, established by UNDP in response to its new Agenda 21 responsibility for helping build the capacities within poorer countries for environmental protection and sustainable development, has to date been able to mobilize only about $40 million of the targeted $100 million that will be required for its pilot phase.

Preoccupied with the problems of domestic and global recessions, the United States and other donor governments have found it increasingly difficult to maintain domestic support for their current aid levels. This has led many states to emphasize the importance of redirecting financial aid flows toward sustainable development. Complicating this effort, however, is the difficulty of assessing what portion of current flows and programs would appropriately be counted as promoting sustainable development. A recent study by Bread for the World, a U.S.-based citizens group, estimated that only one out of every four dollars spent by the United States in its fiscal year 1994 foreign aid budget was allocated toward efforts consistent with sustainable development and humanitarian goals.

This type of assessment is, of course, intimately linked to debates over the definition of sustainable development. Without greater consensus on the meaning of sustainable development, it will be difficult for the United States or other countries to make significant shifts in their development assistance. Indeed, if U.S. political commitments are to be backed up with the necessary financial resources, the Clinton administration not only must develop a new rationale for U.S. foreign assistance but also must clearly articulate that rationale and "sell" it to Congress and to the American public.

A SYSTEM IN DISARRAY

A second set of constraints facing the commission and those concerned about sustainable development issues is *institutional* in nature. Despite the fact that implementing Agenda 21 should significantly impact many UN programs, agencies, and organs, the new commission has no control over the budgets or governance of any of these bodies. Nor is its parent institution, ECOSOC, capable of exercising effective coordination over the sprawling array of multilateral institutions dealing with economic, social, and environmental concerns.

At this point, the commission will remain dependent on the voluntary cooperation of UNEP, UNDP, the Food and Agriculture Organization, and a host of other UN bodies. The recommendations of the commission, which must be forwarded to ECOSOC and through that institution to the other organizations of the UN system, will carry no authority other than the political strength of the consensus behind them. Yet the extent to which interested governments can strengthen ECOSOC's coordinating role remains to be seen.

One current proposal would give ECOSOC greater control over four operational agencies—the UN Development Program, the UN Children's Fund, the World Food Program, and the UN Population Fund—and thereby strengthen the likelihood that CSD decisions concerning those bodies would be recognized. However, the success of this reform proposal is by no means assured, and it would affect only a small group of the UN organizations that can implement the sustainable development concept.

As discussed by Roger Coate in chapter 3 of this volume, efforts to reform ECOSOC and the UN system predate UNCED by years and are likely to continue well into the future. To be sure, the approaching fiftieth anniversary of the United Nations in 1995 has given new impetus to the reform agenda. Yet the movements seeking to reform the United Nations and to build sustainable development appear to be on distinctly separate tracks, with considerable suspicion between the proponents of each goal. In fact, many advocates of UN reform view the commission's creation and the establishment of the Department for Policy Coordination and Sustainable Development within the UN Secretariat as running against the grain of reformist efforts to streamline the organizational structure of the United Nations.

On the other hand, many of the groups and individuals who participated in the UNCED conference are skeptical about the effectiveness of multilateral institutions and they have little knowledge of or interest in the broader UN reform process. Most NGOs working on environmental and developmental issues, as well as many from the business and industry sectors that are central to sustainable development, perceive the state-oriented UN system as poorly reflective of their interests and inhospitable to their active participation. Even prominent government officials involved in establishing the commission have expressed concern that it will become another empty "talk shop" featuring predictable debates and producing little substantive result.

MOVING INTO THE MAINSTREAM

Left largely untouched by the UNCED process was the critical—and politically difficult—issue of the relationship between the international trade and financial institutions and the goals of sustainable development. The U.S. delegation to UNCED, for example, was under instructions from the Treasury Department to avoid any reference in the Agenda 21 recommendations to the World Bank or the International Monetary Fund, long the targets of criticism from citizens groups for the adverse ecological and social impacts of their lending. Nor was there much reference to the General Agreement on Tariffs and Trade, whose free trade mandate does not address environmental or social concerns, or to the activities of transnational corporations.

It was agreed at the Earth Summit that the international financial institutions would participate actively in the commission, and that the CSD would be a major global forum for reviewing the financing of sustainable development. However, considerable differences remain between states regarding both the appropriate linkages between the commission and the international financial institutions (IFIs), and the extent of discussions of financing that will take place within the commission. Long-standing differences between the North and South over financial decisionmaking mechanisms confront the commission, with the industrialized countries preferring to make financial policy in those forums where voting is weighted by contribution, and with the developing countries insisting on using the one-state, one-vote system of the United Nations.

A first step toward addressing the role of the IFIs in sustainable development was taken at the 1993 CSD session. At that session, senior representatives of UN agencies and the IFIs provided information about their organizations' expertise and areas of work. This incipient dialogue should continue and be expanded in future years. Beyond dialogue, a modest beginning at setting policy directions was made at the 1993 CSD session, with the final document recognizing "the importance of making trade and environment policies mutually supportive and favorable to sustainable development."[2] The commission also urged the financial institutions to increase efforts to integrate sustainable development into their objectives, policies, and programs. The international community could increasingly use the commission to build a political consensus regarding priority areas for sustainable development financing—with the World Bank, the Global Environmental Facility, and other institutions then serving as the actual financing mechanisms.

Without a stronger commitment from the governments of the industrialized countries to pursue the goals of sustainable development within the trade and financial institutions, however, the decisions of the commission on financing will be little more than useless rhetoric.

OPPORTUNITIES FOR U.S. LEADERSHIP

The Commission on Sustainable Development offers the United States a fresh start at promoting international cooperation on the quality-of-life issues that concern all peoples of the world. To take full advantage of this opportunity, the United States must begin at home, as was acknowledged by Vice President Gore at the 1993 CSD session. In years past, the United States has in fact frequently provided leadership through such domestic achievements as the creation of national environmental legislation and the evolution of a very active nongovernmental sector.

The United States is well placed to play the lead role in pioneering sustainable development policies through the development of national mechanisms for decisionmaking that integrate socioeconomic and environmental concerns and that actively involve interested communities and constituencies both inside and outside of government. The Clinton administration has taken some early steps in the right direction. However, much more must be done to shift the United States toward an integrated approach to environmental and economic policymaking.

For the sustainable development concept to gain broad acceptance, furthermore, the Clinton administration's sustainable development proponents will need to reaffirm their concern for quality-of-life issues. The administration also must begin to educate the public about the ways in which sustainable development is in their best interest, as well as highlighting the ways environmental and socioeconomic gains may be mutually supportive; it can do this by demonstrating methods for integrating these factors into the decisionmaking process so as to increase mutual gains and manage the inevitable conflicts. Treating sustainable development as primarily an issue of environmental policy simply will not work.

The President's Council on Sustainable Development, established to help formulate a U.S. sustainable development strategy, is one possible vehicle for this work. The work of the council, however, should be complemented by a clearly identified, high-level mechanism within the federal government with the responsibility for reviewing and coordinating sustainable development work throughout the federal system. This role appears to have been given to the White House Office on Environmental Policy, which is at the appropriate level, but that office has neither the resources nor a broad-enough mandate—being limited to environmental policy alone—to coordinate sustainable development policy as envisioned in Agenda 21.

With relatively minor changes to the National Environmental Policy Act (NEPA), the U.S. Congress could authorize and encourage a national sustainable development policy that would integrate social, economic, and environmental considerations for those activities affecting the quality of the human environment within the United States and abroad. Sections of NEPA already encourage sustainable development, such as Section 101(a), which calls on policymakers to "create and maintain conditions under which man and nature can exist in productive harmony, and fulfill the social, economic, and other requirements of present and future generations of Americans."

Among other options for improving the national sustainable development policies of the United States are: the creation of a National Sustainable Development Commission, which could, for example, conduct public hearings around the country;[3] the formation of national and regional roundtables to bring together the various policymaking sectors to discuss specific sustainable development concerns; and the encouragement of state and local governments to formulate their own Agenda

21 plans with broad public participation.[4] In fact, some communities in the United States have already begun to undertake such efforts, which are critical to building grassroots support and capacities for sustainable development.

Leadership at the national level must be complemented by leadership at the international level. The best place to begin is within the Commission on Sustainable Development, where the United States should lead the effort to build a broader consensus among the member states concerning the sustainable development concept and its implications for policymaking. Early in its term of office, the Clinton administration took steps to place a greater U.S. emphasis on international environmental and population issues. Now the challenge facing the United States is to pursue these global priorities not unilaterally, but rather by working in partnership with others, and to address human as well as environmental needs. The United States must respect the concerns of other states and peoples, work with them to build support for U.S. environmental initiatives, and pair those initiatives with related measures to address the socioeconomic and political concerns of poorer countries. This will take time, patience, and considerable effort.

Perhaps the greatest challenge is for the United States to bring sustainable development policy from the periphery to the centers of global economic policy. A U.S.-led effort to build consensus around a broadly shared conception of sustainable development should provide a basis for many other international policies, including the effort to reform the United Nations. The initiation by the United States of a dialogue on how to incorporate sustainable development into the reform of ECOSOC or the various economic-development organizations could help to overcome the long-standing suspicions among developing countries concerning the underlying goals of the developed countries' efforts to reform the United Nations.

Similarly, the United States should use its influence within other international organizations to ensure their full cooperation with the Commission on Sustainable Development. The United States can also help to reinforce CSD decisions by sending consistent messages through its representatives in other international arenas. This is particularly important with respect to the international financial institutions and will require top-level leadership, as this step would necessitate greater policy coordination between the Departments of State, Treasury, and Commerce than has been the case in the past.

The diplomatic challenge facing the United States is matched by a financial challenge: The U.S. government will be expected to back up its commitment to sustainable development with additional financial resources. Given the country's current budget-deficit problems, as well as a political environment that is unusually hostile to foreign aid expenditures, the Clinton administration will find it difficult to come up with new funding. Furthermore, any available resources are likely to be allocated to countries of long-standing strategic interest, such as the East European states and the former Soviet republics, or to those states with large populations and consequently greater impacts on the global environment, such as China and India.

These financial pressures may lead to a reevaluation of the existing bilateral and multilateral development assistance, trade, and financial policies of the United States based on sustainable development criteria. The Commission on Sustainable Development could provide a very useful forum for international dialogue on these issues, provided that the dialogue is genuine and that expectations remain realistic. By focusing such discussions on specific issue areas—identifying problems, reviewing existing national and international efforts, and forging agreement on what needs to be done—the United States could help the commission avoid rhetorical debates over financial issues. In addition, to allow for a more realistic assessment of UN financial requirements in the new and emerging issue-areas involving sustainable development, this is a propitious time to reexamine the U.S. insistence on a zero-growth budget for the world body.

There is much the United States can do to facilitate constructive partnerships among states in building sustainable development, even in the absence of additional financial commitments. Having led an effort during the UNCED negotiating process to redirect debates from "technology transfer" to "technology cooperation," the United States is now in a position to help build the capacities of the poorer countries and of the global community to undertake the integration of environmental and developmental problems through a variety of information-sharing partnerships.

For example, the United States should work within the CSD working group on technology cooperation to craft an agreement creating regional information clearinghouses and research networks, as recommended in Agenda 21, and to facilitate the greater sharing of information in the realm of environmentally sound technologies. The United States should also keep the promise it made at the Earth Summit to share publicly available sustainable development technologies, using the commission to illustrate the utility of various technologies for solving specific problems.

A wide range of options exists for promoting change with relatively low public investment—from information exchanges, to fellowships and training programs, to efforts to ensure that U.S. foreign assistance meets domestic environmental standards and supports the participation of affected communities in decisionmaking. And given that a substantial amount of U.S. development financing comes from the private sector, the United States could foster a dialogue within the commission concerning the means for assuring appropriate standards for development projects.

With support and leadership from the United States, the Commission on Sustainable Development offers great potential to the international community. It could serve to build bridges between the countries of the North and South, as well as the East and West. It could increase both public and government awareness of the common stakes shared by all countries in protecting the global environment and promoting sustainable development, as well as in developing cooperative problem-solving approaches to quality-of-life concerns. It could give some direction to the disparate parts of the UN system working on environmental and economic concerns through the building of a policy consensus and the exchange of information. The commission also could legitimize the increased participation of nongovernmental actors in the UN system, while at the same time preserving the essential decision-making prerogatives of governments.

The active engagement of the United States and Americans is critical. The United States must not fail to take advantage of the opportunity that now presents itself to build the global capacity for coping with complex environmental and socioeconomic problems—and in so doing, to leave a better legacy for future generations.

PART III

THE UNITED STATES AND THE UNITED NATIONS

≈10≈

U.S. POLICY TOWARD
THE UNITED NATIONS

JAMES F. LEONARD

*T*he range and visibility of the issues being dealt with at the United Nations have so expanded in recent years that there is a temptation among UN enthusiasts to equate U.S. foreign policy with U.S. policy toward the United Nations. This would be a serious error, as mistaken in its way as was the older dismissive attitude of much of the U.S. foreign affairs community toward UN activities. Some issues should be managed collectively, through the United Nations, as is frequently the case in the security field. Other issues cannot be effectively handled in UN forums (trade problems are a good example), and it would not be wise for the United States to try to do so.

Where might the new U.S. administration find a reasonable balance? This essay will offer some possible guidelines for five major areas of importance to the United States. The only general advice that makes sense is: Don't generalize! Any "ideological" tilt either for or against using the United Nations will distort and confuse the U.S. effort to achieve its goals. Principled pragmatism will be our best counsel.

One can illustrate this point with examples from the economic area, where UN institutions have a limited role, and from the security area, where the end of the cold war and the rise of regional conflicts have put the Security Council in the headlines on a daily basis.

The UN Charter gives the Economic and Social Council (ECOSOC) a mandate in its field as broad as that of the Security Council. ECOSOC, however, lacks the power to make its decisions mandatory; like actions of the General Assembly, they may be called "decisions" but in fact are recommendations. Intense dissatisfaction with the work of ECOSOC has generated repeated attempts at reform, including the enlargement of the council from its original 18 members to the present 54, and efforts by developing countries to move important issues outside of its framework, most notably by establishing the UN Conference on Trade and Development (UNCTAD). However, these cures have generally been worse than the disease.

Should the United States have another go at a major reform of ECOSOC and related bodies? Reform is always an appealing battle cry, but the new administration would be well advised to pass on this one. The obstacles to really basic reform both in developed and developing countries are just too great. If others want to make the effort, the United States should of course participate in a positive and accommodating spirit, but it would not be wise to invest our political capital in this cause.

On the other hand, a modest reform of ECOSOC seems close to being adopted. The United States backed this reform proposal and helped to shape it. We should now do our best to make it work, particularly its objective of enhancing cooperation among the main UN development agencies. The reform should also improve the orderliness and relevance of ECOSOC proceedings. If it generally goes well, we should consider how it might be broadened to additional areas. Meanwhile, we should seek to continue strengthening the best of the governing councils, especially that of the UN Development Program (UNDP).

The situation in the security area is quite different. The UN Charter *does* give the Security Council all the powers it needs, as well as the vitally important six vetoes (the five permanent members plus the collective veto that any seven members possess through their ability to withhold the votes needed to pass a decision). What the Security Council needs is a better apparatus for wise, informed, and effective decisionmaking, and the commitment of major powers to ensure that the United Nations has the money and forces needed to enforce its decisions. It is possible, though not certain, that a political consensus is now developing in favor of remedying these shortcomings along the lines discussed in the final section of this essay and by Barry Blechman in chapter 4 of this book. A decision by the Clinton administration to lead this particular reform effort is more than desirable; the new administration would be irresponsible not to offer as much leadership as the international community will accept. The administration appears to agree, and while its first moves may seem to many to be cautious and limited, that is surely better than "vaulting ambition, which overleaps itself and falls."

THE PROBLEM OF RESOURCES

Any mention of leadership immediately raises the question of resources: first and foremost, money. The availability of resources other than money can also be important, such as the time, involvement, and willingness of high officials to make the efforts needed to encourage nongovernmental institutions and governments to support the work of the United Nations. Nevertheless, money is the most convincing evidence of a country's commitment—especially a wealthy country. Other governments will not believe that the United States is serious about our leadership role or our specific objectives if we plead that the world's richest and strongest country "cannot afford" to support the United Nations.

The prompt and full payment of our assessed contributions to the United Nations and other agencies may not need further debate. Withholding those contributions was always illegal and harmful to our own interests. Moreover, since the later years of the Reagan administration, through President Bush's four years in office and into the Clinton administration, the principle of full payment has been accepted by the U.S. government. A reasonable schedule for liquidating our arrearages is also being met, and one must pray that a current congressional challenge to this schedule will be overcome.

The United States now needs to put its weight behind two objectives: first, the acceptance of the Ford Foundation (Ogata-Volcker) report on financial reform;[1] and second, the replacement of the "zero-growth" principle with a pragmatic willingness to expand UN budgets where increases are justified, just as we have been—and should remain—determined to cut them when they are not justified.

As called for in the Ford report, the United States should lead the other major contributors to the UN budget in supporting the quarterly payment of dues with interest charges when payments are unavoidably late. The report proposes a number of other financial reforms of real utility, many of which were discussed by Ronald Spiers in chapter 2 of this book.

A willingness to support even small increases in UN budgets will be politically difficult, given the continuing U.S. budget deficit, but it is essential. A general "principle of parsimony" is more than defensible, it is vital. But it is also vital to look at the budget of each UN organization on its own merits, case by case. For example, as discussed by Thomas Graham in chapter 5, the IAEA budget will have to expand substantially to cover that agency's new responsibilities in the former Soviet Union, even though desirable downward adjustments should be made in its safeguard expenditures in developed countries of low proliferation risk.

Voluntary contributions present a more difficult challenge to the Clinton administration. The extreme budgetary constraints that are so painful today, both domestically and in the international programs of the United States, will not be lifted in the next year or two, and perhaps not even in this decade. Yet the problems of the world will not go on vacation while we are getting our national revenues and expenditures into balance. This fact has been recognized in both the Bush and Clinton budgets, which have called for a continued substantial level—some $22 billion annually—of allocations to international activities in the so-called 150 account. What has not been clearly recognized is the need to restructure that account.

Despite the end of the cold war, large sums of aid continue to go into "defense support" and "security assistance" to Israel and Egypt and to what formerly were "base-rights countries." The aid to Israel and Egypt is justified as encouraging the vitally important peace process. The military component of this aid is particularly quixotic. Israel requires U.S. defense assistance because the Arab armies are modernizing, but the largest (and least threatening) Arab army—the Egyptian—is modernizing with U.S. aid money, and the wealthy Arab states of the Gulf are modernizing because the United States has refused to lead any serious international efforts to limit arms transfers in the Middle East. The recent stunning breakthrough in the peace process now should trigger a reexamination of this situation.

Other assistance programs to developing countries that are far from being the poorest of the poor are being reduced, although they persevere largely on the momentum generated during the cold war period. Some of this aid always was economic assistance disguised as military support, particularly in Africa, but many current cases lack any military or economic justification and simply reflect the political difficulty of terminating handouts to old friends. Somewhere in the grand total of the $22 billion allocated to the 150 account, or in the Defense Department's $270 billion, or in the CIA's $27 billion, it should be possible to find one or two billion that could be shifted to the really effective UN programs that deserve our support. Yet sadly, at this moment it appears likely that the most pro-United Nations and pro-development U.S. administration in many years will find itself compelled by budgetary pressures to make a major cut in its funding for one of the best-run and most important of all UN agencies, the UN Development Program.

If the Clinton administration has no alternative but to accept a cut in its 1994 fiscal year budget for UN activities, perhaps it could secure commitments from congressional leaders for a two- or three-year program of steady, substantial increases for the best-run, most effective UN agencies, particularly UNDP and UNICEF, which are currently directed by highly respected Americans.

What level of voluntary contributions can other donor states reasonably expect from the United States? What should we normally be prepared to offer as our share? The answer will naturally vary substantially from case to case, but a figure somewhere in the range between 20 percent and 30 percent seems reasonable. When judged by the standard UN formula that apportions assessed contributions on the basis of national income, the "fair share" of the United States would be as high as 35 percent. Yet a figure that high is not realistic in domestic political terms. If a U.S. administration proposed a figure that high, it would probably encounter serious problems in Congress and badly needed programs could be crippled or delayed.

The general rule for programs that we favor should thus be that the United States will furnish around 25 percent of whatever budget commands a consensus in the donor community, which for voluntary programs often comprises no more than ten significant contributor states. There will be cases when we might provide more support, for example in controlling nuclear proliferation, a problem that obviously affects U.S. security. And there no doubt will be many programs that we are less committed to and are willing to support only in a more limited way. The support of the United States for economic, social, and political development must be looked at comprehensively; the UN portion of U.S. development aid will often be only a fraction of the total U.S. contribution.

If the United States is to return to its proper position as *a* (if not *the*) leading supporter of UN voluntary programs, it should enlist the other major donor states in a determined effort to ensure that these programs are better integrated with each other. Coordination has always been a serious weakness of the United Nations, though it must be recognized that the same weakness is found in national governments, as Roger Coate points out in chapter 3 of this book. Member governments are guilty of failing to coordinate the activities of their own agencies, who then export their quarrels into UN forums. How the United Nations might achieve better coordination—or better "integration"—among its many organizations and programs is discussed below.

THE UN AGENDA

The United States must have its own agenda if it is to use the United Nations in the pursuit of national purposes. And, of course, the United States must expect that each of the other member states will have its own agenda designed to serve its national purposes.

Our concern here is with what is attempted and sometimes achieved through the work of the entire UN system, including the specialized agencies. In this chapter, the work of the international financial institutions (or the "IFIs"), especially the World Bank and the International Monetary Fund, is touched on only in passing. The rest of the extremely broad spectrum of activities of the UN family of institutions could be sliced up in any number of different ways. I have selected five clusters of issues for more detailed comment: the global economy, the global environment, humanitarian assistance, human rights, and international security.

Assigning priority among these five would not be a helpful exercise. Even in a centralized, pyramidal bureaucracy like the United States, different issues are routinely managed by various branches or teams, and each issue has "top priority" until the very last stages of the decision-making process. From the U.S. perspective, however, there is no doubt about which of these five clusters should receive the most concentrated and sustained attention from the president and the secretary of state: the issue of international security. In fact, this is already the case.

Difficult and painful crises, such as the former Yugoslavia, are constantly forcing themselves onto the foreign policy agenda of the United States. This state of affairs is not likely to change in the next few years. Moreover, the intensity of these crises makes it difficult for senior U.S. officials to reflect seriously on the long-range aspects of the issues that occupy much of their time. As a result, decisions concerning urgent matters are made in an ad hoc manner, and those decisions can crystallize into precedents and guidelines applicable to future contingencies without there having been an opportunity to think through the long-term implications of those decisions. This same unavoidable "adhockery" is being duplicated within the governments of the other major member states of the United Nations. Tragically, the old bipolar world dissolved into multiple crises before anyone had time to rethink how world order could be maintained or even what that expression might mean.

For the other developed countries of the United Nations, issues of peace and security should also be at the top of their agendas. Most of these countries are closer than the United States to areas of crisis or potential crisis, and as a result, they are more likely to be affected by refugee flows, terrorism, and the other consequences of such crises.

The developing countries may have a somewhat different perspective on issues involving international security. They have long maintained economic development as their first priority. Today, however, the developing states are increasingly conscious of how fragile peace and social order can be, and they are well aware of the widespread repercussions of a breakdown in that peace and order. Therefore, the support of the developing states for a more effective international security system can be expected. Nevertheless, to enlist the full cooperation of the developing world in *our* security agenda, it will be necessary to convince them that the United States is serious about *their* development agenda. And, of course, in the long run *their* development is greatly in *our* interest.

The mutual interest of all countries in economic development has emerged even more clearly with the collapse of the communist bloc. The rescue of the "redeveloping" economies of Central and Eastern Europe is clearly understood in the United States and Western Europe to be a matter of vital concern. Moreover, the plight of the former communist states has reminded the "developed" countries that they must be careful not to neglect renewing their own infrastructures and thus bring on stagnation. Finally, it is important to note that the state of the U.S. economy would be rather worse were it not for the dynamism of several Asian economies that until quite recently were important consumers of development assistance. It would be hard to find a better example of how foreign aid can work in the national interest of the United States.

THE GLOBAL ECONOMY

If one scans the entire field of international issues, it is clear that economic matters predominate. Security issues are more prominent, more acute, and arguably more important, but far more people and institutions are directly affected by economic issues. This is particularly true if the private sector is taken into account. The UN Charter recognized this in establishing the Economic and Social Council as a "principal organ" of the United Nations, though without the mandatory authority that Chapter VII gives to the Security Council.

Yet it is only in the development area that the United Nations today has an important economic function, and even there the World Bank and the related international financial institutions play the leading role. The UN Development Program is of great importance, but its resources are limited compared with the bilateral programs of the major donor states, and even those are limited compared with the role of the private sector in international investment, technology transfer, etc.

It would not be an appropriate use of the State Department's limited human and political resources for that agency to encourage other federal agencies and major governments to take more seriously the macroeconomic debates in ECOSOC and the General Assembly's Second Committee. The skeptical and often hostile attitudes toward ECOSOC in finance ministries, central banks, and other government circles are too deep seated and too well founded to be overcome in present or foreseeable circumstances.

The available energies and resources should instead be directed at improving the effectiveness of UN activities in the development area. Such an outcome is desired by the debaters within ECOSOC and the General Assembly, and it is the objective of the limited reform of ECOSOC's work that was almost approved at the last (47th) General Assembly and is under consideration in the present Assembly.

If this modest reform is finally adopted and works out well, it will both organize ECOSOC proceedings in a more orderly way and improve coordination among the congeries of agencies that deal with the diverse aspects of development. The difficulty that the Assembly has experienced in agreeing on this mini-reform is a reminder of how unlikely it would be to achieve a truly basic reform of ECOSOC under present circumstances. On the other hand, schemes for reducing and interlocking the memberships of the governing boards of these institutions have also been proposed, and these proposals may have merit. A much simpler, even primitive, approach holds more promise of near-term results. That approach would focus on a steady strengthening of the coordinating role of the UN Development Program, endowing that agency with control over a growing sum of money for allocation among the other UN agencies working in the development field. This should enable UNDP to exert influence over independent agencies of the UN system by granting or withholding funds to supplement their regular budgets. Such an arrangement would not subvert the "sovereignty" of the "dukes" who head these agencies, or of their governing boards, but it would encourage greater cooperation for the sake of the marginal, though useful, resources that cooperation would generate.

The UN Development Program can also assist the under secretary-general for humanitarian affairs as the Department of Humanitarian Affairs (DHA) develops plans for improving the coordination of disaster relief, especially in the field and at the development end of the relief-rehabilitation-development continuum. At least at the present stage and perhaps over the long run, UNDP should be able to perform some functions better than DHA. Such tasks would include preparing for the next crisis at the national level and training the local personnel who are far more cost-effective than imported experts. In addition, this is an area where the outstanding capabilities of the U.S. Agency for International Development should be helpful to both DHA and UNDP.

Diffuseness has been an undesirable characteristic of UN development efforts for years. The U.S. should encourage UNDP to focus its efforts, and those of other agencies to the extent that it can influence them, on a short list of objectives that could actually be attained in a relatively short time span. Some of UNICEF's programs, such as childhood inoculations, are good models: they have succeeded to an astonishing degree. Like WHO's eradication of smallpox, these successes do a great deal to improve the UN's somewhat dubious image.

The horrifying costs of putting what are at best bandages on the wounds of armed conflict should remind us that development assistance is by far the most cost-effective form of preventive diplomacy. Somalia today illustrates this point. The military effort there is costing ten times more than the relief and rehabilitation program, and the latter is far from fully funded.

Southern Africa offers a more encouraging example. A major international effort has averted the worst effects of the terrible drought there. If the effort had failed, one can hardly doubt that the endemic conflicts in the region would have become far more unmanageable. Needless to say, this success, led by the United Nations, has not been on the front pages.

A possible way to enhance the role and effectiveness of the United Nations in development relates to the "Group of Seven" (G–7) countries. If there is any such thing as a steering committee for the global economy, itself a very arguable point, then the G–7 is it. But this group totally lacks any voice that represents the interests and the viewpoints of the developing world—which is, after all, most of the human race.

The G–7 has led an effort to provide assistance to the former Soviet republics. A logical follow-up to this opening toward Moscow would be for the G–7 to devote a portion of its meetings to discussing development with a limited number of high-level representatives from the largest developing countries, such as China, India, Brazil, and Indonesia, as well as from the "Group of Seventy-Seven" (G–77), the IFIs, and the United Nations. If the UN representative were the director-general of UNDP, then that official's influence within the UN development system would automatically be enhanced by the interaction in the G–7 forum.

Over the long run, it seems natural to undertake some truly radical restructuring aimed at giving the United Nations a larger role in steering the world economy. It would, however, have to develop in an unforced way that actually contributes to sustainable development, not as a kind of appeasement of the G–77 by the G–7. It may be that a steady, deliberate enhancement of the representative character of the G–7 will achieve this specific goal. If, some years from now, a generally satisfactory institution has crystallized out of that process, the restructuring of the United Nations and the rewriting of Chapters IX and X of the UN Charter would then be appropriate and useful.

A radical reform of the Economic and Social Council may be far over the horizon—as is, regrettably, a reform of the General Assembly. On the other hand, the modest proposal made by Ronald Spiers in chapter 2 for spreading out the General Assembly's work throughout the year may be realizable, and the attempt should certainly be made. Spiers's proposals for reforming the Secretariat, and particularly its economic and social departments, should be strongly pressed by the United States.

THE GLOBAL ENVIRONMENT

In fostering the growth of the international institutions that will help to protect the long-run habitability of the earth, the United Nations has had the advantage of writing on a nearly clean slate. Prior to the UN Conference on the Human Environment, which was held in Stockholm in 1972, there were really no international institutions dedicated to environmental concerns, and the main institution that the Stockholm conference generated—the UN Environment Program—has been primarily occupied since then in identifying urgent problems and pushing initial measures for alleviating those problems. The recently established UN Commission on Sustainable Development (CSD) must now confront the enormous agenda laid out at the UN Conference on the Environment and Development, which was held in Rio de Janeiro in 1992, as well as the implications of that agenda for further institution-building at the global level.

Since the new Commission on Sustainable Development is a UN body facing a relatively open playing field, it would be natural for additional institutions to be created under the aegis of the United Nations. A number of farsighted people have suggested that future generations may owe more to UN work on sustainable development than to anything else the United Nations will be doing in the next century.

The work of the Commission on Sustainable Development offers an enormous opportunity to the U.S. government. The United States can make a substantial contribution, at extremely low cost, by putting the most capable Americans available to work designing the architecture of the future system of international environmental institutions.

The best minds of other countries, especially in the developing world, must also be involved, but it is in the United States that one can most readily assemble a critical mass of highly qualified people (including the citizens of other countries) to address almost any question. Once sensible proposals have been formulated, the energies and capabilities of the U.S. government are uniquely suited to promoting and modifying them as necessary to get worldwide support.

The task of designing the architecture or institutional structures of the international system can rarely be done "in-house"—in the State Department or even jointly with all the relevant federal agencies. The pressures of day-to-day work on senior officials are simply too great. Fortunately, an enormous array of institutes, foundations, think tanks, and academic centers has emerged in the United States and needs only modest encouragement from the U.S. government to plunge into these tasks. The opportunity—and responsibility—of the Clinton administration lies in activating these volunteers and guiding their efforts toward those areas of work where their contributions can be most effective.

The United Nations has even fewer capabilities than the U.S. government for performing this sort of long-range planning in-house. Yet, as the new U.S. administration gets its own thinking geared up, a continuing relationship with the United Nations and other elements of the international community will be important. The secretary-general has said that he envisions the United Nations University (UNU) becoming the organization's "think tank" for sustainable development. If the United States utilizes UNU as a major component in the planning and research that it will be doing, this suggestion of the secretary-general could be translated into reality.

In the wide-ranging worldwide discussions preceding the Rio conference, there was a natural but probably wrongheaded tendency to begin designing the new international environmental architecture from the top down. A number of thoughtful people have for some years now suggested replacing the Trusteeship Council, which no longer has any real duties, with an Environmental Council, which would be established as a "principal organ" of the United Nations like the Security Council or ECOSOC. This concept may have merit, but like almost all changes to the UN Charter, it should be very deliberately and prudently studied. There should be a much broader consensus than exists today regarding the basement and lower floors of this new building before the tower is designed.

One vital issue on which there is as yet no convergence of views relates to the powers that might be provided to the United Nations for dealing with environmental problems. If the member governments are not yet disposed to relinquish significant elements of their sovereignty regarding environmental problems, then any new body would simply be another ECOSOC. There is no need to bother revising the UN Charter to produce yet another "talk shop."

At the other pole, governments must be—and are—very cautious in granting the United Nations or other international institutions the power to enforce norms. Norms must be established, of course, and that work is well under way through such instruments as the Montreal Protocol on Substances that Deplete the Ozone Layer. In addition, the compliance of states with norms must be ensured, but this is not a simple matter. Rigid compliance machinery will simply lead some states to disregard their commitments, and both the norms and the enforcement process will be discredited. Resolving problems through "conciliation commissions" or technical working groups is a much more effective means of encouraging state compliance with international norms.

The U.S. tradition on this perennial problem is instructive. We have combined—sometimes in alternating phases, sometimes at the same moment—an expansive "liberal" philosophy of urging that strong powers be conferred on international institutions, and a cramped "conservative" philosophy reflected in a determination to "not let foreigners tell us what to do." We are not unique in this respect; one can see the same impulses at work in France, for example, as it leads the way toward the further integration of the European Community. This almost universal dichotomy within national cultures creates special problems when a country is in a position of leadership, as the United States unavoidably finds itself. We appear hypocritical, urging other states to surrender bits and pieces of their sovereignty while we hide behind the Constitution or the Congress even as our sheer size and power protect the sovereignty of the United States against any serious incursions.

It is essential that the policymakers of the United States be conscious of these contradictory trends in U.S. policy toward international institutions. We should neither ask more of others than we ourselves are willing to give, nor offer more than the Congress and public opinion will allow us to deliver. The problem of enforcing environmental norms will have far less importance in practice than in the abstract. Almost all environmental disputes will be settled or managed through negotiations rather than through legalistic adjudication by third parties. For this reason, it will not be a fatal flaw to allow considerable flexibility in the compliance procedures built into the international environmental structure that is being designed.

In more down-to-earth matters, the Commission on Sustainable Development is already beginning to produce some benefits. At its initial meeting in June 1993, the high level of attendance was heartening and the United States reestablished the international leadership role that environmentalists here and abroad have been longing to see reaffirmed. Moreover, the CSD has begun to find ways, even at this early stage, to ensure that development institutions take proper account of environmental concerns. The nomination of a highly respected environmentalist, Gustave Speth, as director of the UN Development Program suggests that that organization will need little prodding from the CSD. In addition, the CSD's initial interactions with the World Bank and the other IFIs seem to have gone well. There will have to be quiet, steady pressure from the U.S. government, working together with other donor governments, to ensure that the Rio messages get through to all the parts of the UN development system. Getting the messages down into national decisionmaking and action by local groups is the most difficult and most important step in the whole process. Here again, the UNDP, with its emphasis on "the field," will play a key role.

HUMANITARIAN ASSISTANCE

In the history of the last century or two, there is a short list of accomplishments that one could point to as evidence that humanity has progressed morally, that we are "better" or less evil today than our ancestors were ten, twenty, or even one hundred generations in the past. One might cite as examples the prohibition—though not yet the elimination—of slavery and torture. The effort to provide assistance to people in deep distress—whether as a result of wars, floods, earthquakes, droughts, or famines—certainly belongs on that short list. One observer of this trend describes how, as a young man in Calcutta during World War II, he witnessed a famine that took hundreds of thousands of Indian lives while the warehouses bulged with "untouchable" stocks of grain. This tragedy occurred because at that time there was not a sufficiently strong moral imperative that could compel the authorities to open the warehouse doors.

Such a moral imperative is widely felt today, but the world has not yet mobilized sufficient resources to cope with disasters. As Gil Loescher points out in chapter 7, the High Commissioner for Refugees and other UN agencies, the Red Cross, and private voluntary organizations (PVOs) are all permanently "behind the wave" struggling to deal with multiple crises and well aware that the next disaster will hit before the existing crises have passed. As a result, these organizations have great difficulty setting aside the time and money needed to become better organized for dealing with future disasters, to say nothing of accumulating the stocks of food, equipment, and trained personnel that will be required to address the next contingency.

The current situation in the area of humanitarian assistance is made to order for a U.S. initiative. The record of the United States on payments for our assessed UN contributions may be shameful, but our record on voluntary humanitarian assistance is a source of legitimate pride. The numerous PVOs based in the United States lead the field, which testifies to the fact that "foreign aid" is not unpopular among the people as long as it is given freely.

In thinking through what the United States can do in the field of humanitarian assistance, two basic elements seem indisputable: First, the only feasible place to establish a focal point for effective planning and coordination is within the United Nations; and, second, the only way that such a focal point can be developed is with the support and leadership of the United States. Our dedicated Nordic and Swiss friends as well as other players in this field have been giving us excellent advice on how to proceed, but they do not have enough influence to make it happen by themselves.

The United Nations, the U.S. Agency for International Development, and other private and governmental actors are currently supporting a promising research effort that is comprehensively examining humanitarian activity.[2] As this study and others also under way are completed, the U.S. government should give serious consideration to their recommendations with the objective of putting together the required intergovernmental consensus for action at the United Nations.

Meanwhile, the creation of the Department of Humanitarian Affairs, headed by Under Secretary-General Jan Eliasson, was an excellent first step. While the department's mandate as defined by General Assembly Resolution 46/182 is admirably broad, Eliasson has moved carefully but energetically to develop the department's coordinating role and to activate the prescribed interagency machinery.

The department remains gravely short of resources, both money and personnel. Most of all, however, DHA needs the strong support of the major governments within both the North and the South to overcome resistance to the mandate that the General Assembly gave the department. Such resistance sometimes has a valid basis, but it often comes from UN agencies that simply do not like being "coordinated"; from private voluntary organizations, some of whom see no reason to pay attention to any UN official; and, most seriously, from governments, a few of whom continue to cherish their "sovereign right" to mistreat their citizens.

The General Assembly has given the Department of Humanitarian Affairs what should prove in the long run to be a most effective instrument for improving coordination within the UN system—the Central Emergency Revolving Fund. The $50 million figure established for the fund's budget is pitifully inadequate in a world where the leading relief agency (the UN High Commissioner for Refugees) is operating in 1993 on a budget of approximately $1.5 billion while still falling woefully short of meeting its funding needs. Nevertheless, the principle behind the new fund's coordinating activities has been established, and the size of the fund should be substantially enlarged as world economic conditions improve and as—one may hope—the present surge in the number of major crises diminishes, even if only briefly.

While we should praise this progress toward effective coordination of humanitarian relief efforts, it is essential to keep in mind that "coordination can be a mixed blessing."[3] The styles and the codes of both governmental and nongovernmental actors in the humanitarian field vary widely. For instance, the International Committee of the Red Cross operates very differently from Médecins Sans Frontières, but the world would be a worse place if either organization did not exist. It is annoying to governments and to the United Nations to have organizations out in the field that refuse to coordinate their activities, and sometimes ignorant and unqualified PVO representatives do real harm. On balance, however, the PVOs are a priceless asset. If governments can find ways to direct even more humanitarian assistance through PVOs without compromising the independence of those organizations, that course should certainly be taken.

The real challenge facing the UN in this field, however, is much more basic than "coordination." The challenge is to develop an integrated structure—what Gil Loescher in chapter 7 calls a "multidimensional response"—embracing institutions, principles, guidelines, rules, laws, and agreed roles and missions that encompass political and economic as well as humanitarian factors, and that extend from early warning, preventive diplomacy, and the control of conflict to relief, rehabilitation, and the resumption of development. No single document can serve as a "master plan" for this structure, nor will the structure ever be really finished. DHA should be the midwife of this seemingly impossible but essential process, and strong, steady U.S. support will be vital if anything that could be called a success is to emerge from the years of effort that will be required.

The ghastly situation in Angola today underlines how far we are from solutions to the dilemmas created when political and humanitarian factors collide. The poison that politics can introduce is a stark contrast to the relative success of drought relief in other areas of Southern Africa, even including Mozambique. Some very basic attitudes will have to change if a new paradigm for humanitarian activity is to develop.

None of this can happen without adequate funding. Gil Loescher has rightly called for a larger share of UNHCR's budget to come through assessed contributions, and the same applies elsewhere. Agencies like UNICEF and UNDP are carrying out what have now clearly become "normal" functions, and the predictable portions of such budgets should be predictably available to their managers.

The United States should examine what could be done through the United Nations to give more protection to PVO representatives in the field, and for that matter, to the members of the media as well. Several years ago the General Assembly, alarmed by terrorist attacks on diplomats, reacted by declaring that those terrorists who attacked international diplomats would be pursued wherever they hide around the world. Extraordinary courage has been shown by aid personnel and reporters in Bosnia, Somalia, and elsewhere, and quite a few have been murdered. The General Assembly should not only pay them tribute, as it does to the military personnel who fall in the service of the international community, but it should also serve notice to these murderers that they are war criminals whose arrest and trial will remain on the UN agenda as long as they are alive.

As the resources and capacities of the Department of Humanitarian Affairs grow, it should move to meet the long-term need for training and research in the field of humanitarian relief. The interim report of the research project cited above (and in note 2) contains a penetrating and balanced discussion of enhancing professionalism, and it is clear that the concept of a single research and training institute would not be an appropriate instrument for achieving this objective. A loose network of training institutions might, however, be quite valuable. The United Nations University is capable of fostering such networks, and if the concept has merit, the United States and the United Nations should jointly commission a study of its feasibility. It might be noted that there is a similar need for training and research in the enormously expanding field of peacekeeping.

HUMAN RIGHTS

In chapter 6 of this book, Morris Abram recounted the leadership that was demonstrated in June 1993 by the United States at the World Conference on Human Rights in Vienna. At that conference, the United

States helped to repel a serious challenge to universality in the human rights field. Abram also emphasized the need to firmly establish the role of a High Commissioner for Human Rights. As he notes, the creation of this position may be a step in the wrong direction. On the other hand, the commissioner could prove to be a high-level defender of human rights, and his appointment could lead to other reforms, including those that Abram rightly calls for.

To assess this possibility, we must first return to some basic points. The principal offenders against human rights are governments, and thus an intergovernmental commission of instructed representatives is fundamentally flawed as an instrument for dealing with the abuse of human rights. When the UN Commission on Human Rights was initially established, the subcommission of "experts" was created as a gesture toward correcting this flaw, but it was an empty gesture. The United States, like the other member states, gave its representatives on the subcommission little leeway to act on their own, leaving the private organizations as the most steadfast defenders of basic freedoms.

The times have now changed. With the end of the cold war, the U.S. no longer has any shred of justification for going easy on "friendly" dictators. A majority of the world's governments have moved *toward* if not *to* democracy, and they now include in their vocabulary something more than mere dishonest lip service to international human rights standards. As Abram observes, shame—the principal sanction the international community has, or will have anytime soon, against states who abuse human rights—is at times surprisingly effective, though not always. Moreover, shame works to bring even regimes that are themselves somewhat repressive into alignment behind condemnations of governments that are truly outrageous. Since it is possible to now get such condemnations even from the General Assembly, one wonders whether there is any useful purpose still being served by the Commission on Human Rights and its subcommission.

The establishment of a High Commissioner for Human Rights could still be utilized by the United States to precipitate a broad and no doubt extended review of the entire UN human rights structure. Such a review should of course take account of the possibilities opened up by the recent U.S. accession to the two key human rights covenants, which have their own machinery. In the course of such a review, ways should be sought to enhance the status of private human rights groups. They are just as valuable in this field as the PVOs in the relief field.

Now that the position of High Commissioner for Human Rights has been created, the United States should insist on stringent arrangements to insulate that office and the Center for Human Rights from governmental pressures. The basic statute establishing the new office should reiterate the prohibition contained in Article 100 of the Charter against seeking or receiving "instructions from any government. . . ." An annual public ceremony featuring the administration of an oath to this same effect would also be a healthy reminder to all concerned. In addition, a commission comprised of either three or five persons, where each commissioner would have the right to reach and publish his or her own conclusions on particular cases, would clearly be preferable to having a single individual serve as the high commissioner.

The horrors perpetrated in the former Yugoslavia bring forward another important element of any international human rights reform: the need for machinery to deal with war crimes. Just as the experiences of World War II, and especially the Holocaust, brought a burst of institution-building in this as well as other fields, it seems likely that current circumstances may produce a similar opportunity for creative and more than marginal improvements in the existing human rights structures.

The profound and justified indignation that Muslim governments, among others, feel about what the Muslims in Bosnia have been suffering may provide a political basis for enlisting them as partners in the reworking of the UN human rights institutions. This will be particularly true if the recent astonishing breakthrough in the Middle East peace process can now produce a fundamental change in the situation of the Palestinians in the occupied territories. It is time for the United States and other governments to begin reflecting on these attractive possibilities. There should be no haste. International institutions are built to last for decades, and once constructed they are not easily tinkered with. The accomplishments of the 1940s were significant, and if we are going to improve on them, we should set our objectives very high indeed.

INTERNATIONAL SECURITY

The primary and fundamental charge that the international community gave to the United Nations in the UN Charter is "to maintain international peace and security." The primacy of this task is reflected in the famous opening words of the preamble: "determined to save succeeding generations from the scourge of war. . . ." The charge is reiterated in the first paragraph of Article 1 and reflected in the popular lament, "If it can't make peace, what good is it?" The centrality of the peacemaking responsibility of the United Nations is further underlined by the unique authority that the UN Charter confers on the Security

Council in Chapter VII: the authority to mandate, to command, and in effect to order member governments to comply with its decisions. The "decisions" of the General Assembly and of lesser UN bodies are in reality recommendations, but in receiving membership in the organization, each member of the United Nations has agreed to accept as mandatory the decisions of the Security Council concerning "what measures shall be taken in accordance with Articles 41 and 42, to maintain or restore international peace and security."[4]

Within the United Nations, one member, the United States, bears a special responsibility in matters of war and peace. The United States was the most powerful member of the United Nations at its founding in 1945, and it remains so almost half a century later. Moreover, the power of the United States is not merely based on military strength; it remains preeminent, though not predominant, in the full range of economic, scientific, and technological fields. Most importantly, the United States has a unique political capacity to organize international action toward specific objectives. For U.S. policymakers to recognize this reality is not arrogance; on the contrary, to avoid this fact is to evade the responsibilities that accompany power. We must not forget that a failure to lead is merely another form of leadership. It says to other countries that this task is not worth the candle, or that it is not aimed at a worthy or an attainable objective.

The United States thus cannot shirk the burden of leading the effort that is already under way to build a new and better "world order" in the security field. It is easy to mock the grandiloquent echoes of Hitlerian arrogance in that phrase, but that will not make the problem of conflict go away. There are too many wars and rumors of wars—too much disorder in the world—for Washington to allow itself to say to other governments or to regional organizations, "You take care of that one," or even worse, "That one is hopeless." The leaders of the United States and, with its backing, the United Nations must face the challenges that history presents to them. There will certainly be failures, but there must be no failure to try.

This does not mean that the United States must do everything itself, only that it must try to ensure that what can be done is done. Today, and no doubt increasingly in the future, as other powers and regional groups gain in strength, they will be able and they should be willing to carry a growing share of the security burden. There may well be situations that neither the United States nor the whole international community acting together can do any more than palliate. Perhaps, as many experts argue, the collapse of what was the state of Yugoslavia has been such a case (though I would not agree). Worse disasters may

certainly arise in the future. Yet, even so, the United States has a duty
to lead the effort to mitigate these disasters, and now—at this moment
in history—it must lead the effort to build new capacities within the
United Nations and within regional organizations to forestall such
eventualities.

When it becomes necessary to deploy UN forces, either for peacekeeping or peace-enforcement, the United States should, in general, be
prepared to contribute troops. Sometimes, when regional states are
ready to carry most of the burden, the United States might provide
only a token contingent, or perhaps nothing but money. More often,
U.S. forces should be the backbone of an operation. Whatever the
numbers, the United States must not arrogate to itself an exceptional
status. We should be as willing as others to see our forces under a
commander of another nationality, insisting of course that the commander be competent. And we should not adopt the offensive notion
that our forces should not get mud on their boots, confining our contribution to naval, air, or logistic units. It is repugnant and even racist
to argue that UN forces should come from countries where wages are
low and "life is cheap."

It is not terribly difficult to compile a rather staggering list of the
deficiencies of the existing UN system. Ambassador Madeleine
Albright, the permanent representative of the United States to the
United Nations, presented a frank but by no means exhaustive compi-
lation of these deficiencies in two speeches she delivered in June 1993.
Even earlier, Secretary-General Boutros Boutros-Ghali had issued his
Agenda for Peace report and had begun efforts—within the limited means
available to him—to correct a number of problems. As Albright pointed out, these deficiencies developed as a result of the fact that "for forty
years, the Soviet Union, our [U.S.] government, and many other governments often saw the United Nations as a sideshow, an elaborate
debating society, to be tolerated but not taken seriously." Her evaluation
is, if anything, an understatement.

If the United States is now again ready to lead, however cautious-
ly, where should it focus its efforts? If I can use the human body as a
metaphor, I would say that the UN Charter gave the United Nations a
sound, strong skeleton, but that forty years of the cold war kept that
skeleton from developing as it should have. The body of the United
Nations must have muscle if it is to maintain international peace and
security, and in chapter 4 of this book Barry Blechman has examined
how this might be accomplished. The balance of this chapter will suggest how the United States could further develop the rather rudimen-
tary brain—or, more prosaically, the decisionmaking machinery—of

the United Nations so that it can effectively manage the greatly expanded muscle which has been hastily improvised to deal with a cascade of new international crises.

There does not seem to be any dissent from the proposition that increased capacities for "early warning" and "preventive diplomacy" would enable the United Nations to prevent some crises from escalating to a critical phase. Yet there is considerable reluctance to acknowledge that the UN staff must be improved and enlarged if the secretary-general and the Security Council are to receive timely warnings and dispatch diplomats or military observers on preventive missions. The secretary-general and his handful of grossly overburdened principal assistants cannot manage multibillion-dollar peacekeeping operations and simultaneously oversee the resolution of an increasing number of global conflicts. Yet the decade-long mantra of "zero real growth" continues to be heard from the United States and the other major financial contributors to the United Nations.

No one doubts that the Secretariat budget contains large numbers of low-priority or "deadwood" items from which resources could be transferred to more pressing needs. In particular, unessential positions should be eliminated to provide the resources that will be needed to create more important positions within key departments and organizations. Such a change has taken place in the International Labor Organization under the pressures of the "zero real growth" budget. But the secretary-general and his under secretary-general for administration and management cannot simply shuffle UN positions by fiat. They must have the strong support of the principal contributors and, at the very least, the acquiescence of other member states. Instead, UN officials face active resistance from governments that look on Secretariat positions as national property, regardless of whether the position performs a worthwhile function or not.

The "establishments" in many poorer countries, as well as in wealthy states, understandably value the privilege of filling positions in the United Nations with their own citizens, but this particular form of "development assistance" is hardly helping those countries. Rather, it is aid to the richest of the poor, or even to the rich among the rich. In blunter terms, it is a form of corruption. This practice damages the United Nations and greatly hampers the efforts of U.S. administrations to secure the funds that pay 25 percent of the salaries of those same UN officials.

The current secretary-general began his term of office with praiseworthy reductions in the upper levels of the Secretariat's staff. The Clinton administration should maintain pressure on the secretary-general to redistribute existing midlevel positions to the overstressed offices that are doing truly important work. While that is being done, the United States should endorse modest increases in the overall Secretariat budget to meet the organization's most pressing needs, such as training peacekeeping forces. If, in consequence, the increased capacities of the United Nations to undertake preventive diplomacy or preventive deployment avert even one crisis like Yugoslavia, it will have been one of the most cost-effective investments that the United States has ever made in an international institution.

Like preventive diplomacy, Security Council reform is on everyone's lips. However, discussions of "reform" should not begin and end with "enlargement." The United States is rightly supporting the enlargement of the Security Council to accommodate permanent membership for Japan and Germany, but this will not come quickly. Nor will enlargement, when it comes, automatically make the council more effective and efficient, particularly since a package of additional members is likely to prove necessary to satisfy the growing demands for geographic balance and for the inclusion of regional powers such as India, the second-largest country in the world in terms of population.

During the years that will be required for the necessary consensus to emerge on enlarging the Security Council, the United States should lead the council to reform and strengthen its practices and procedures in ways that do not require charter amendment. The council has, for example, complete freedom to revise its rules of procedure (Article 30) and to "establish such subsidiary organs as it deems necessary . . ." (Article 29). These tools provide the council with the means to increase its effectiveness even without changing its composition, and they should be utilized.

Acting under Article 29 of the UN Charter, the Security Council should reorganize its structure of committees, which perhaps would better be termed working groups. These are now composed only of states that are members of the council. Nonmembers should be drawn into the reorganized committee framework. Committees should be created for examining sanctions, military enforcement measures, and identifying and training military forces. The recommendations made by Barry Blechman in this book regarding the Military Staff Committee (MSC) should be accepted, and then a Security Council committee should be created to oversee the work of the MSC and its staff. Finally, if the Security Council is to play a larger role in the areas of disarmament and nonproliferation, as many diplomats and experts are now urging, it would be appropriate to create a committee to oversee the council's activities in those areas.

An expanded committee structure would make it possible to increase the involvement of countries such as Germany, Japan, India, and Brazil in the work of the Security Council. An important responsibility of the council president should be to brief committee members who are not council members when there are private meetings of the council. This would alleviate the ridiculous situation where ambassadors are obliged to hover outside the council chamber to learn about the results of the council's important private meetings.

As governments put forward their candidacies for participation in an expanded committee structure, there will be an opportunity to give new life to the "quality control" that the drafters of the UN Charter wrote into Article 23. That article says that the nonpermanent members of the Security Council should be selected with "due regard being specially paid, in the first instance to the contribution of Members of the United Nations to the maintenance of international peace and security and to the other purposes of the Organization. . . ." This criterion has been badly neglected in favor of the other criterion laid down in Article 23, that of "equitable geographical distribution."

One standard for measuring a government's contribution to international peace and security—though certainly not the only one—should be the willingness and ability to contribute to the military forces for peacekeeping and peace enforcement that the Security Council and the UN must at times organize. The knowledge that even a small contingent, say one-thousand soldiers, of its own citizens could be put at risk by a particular council action should lead each government to be cautious and restrained in passing resolutions that involve the possible use of force.

The new Clinton administration has quickly recognized the many serious shortcomings of the United Nations in the peacekeeping field. As a result, the U.S. administration has persuaded the Security Council to ask the secretary-general for reform proposals on a number of specific problems. The inability of the United Nations to engage in long-range planning has not, however, appeared on the list of reforms that the United States is pushing. At this point, the United States and the council are understandably focused on short-range operational problems, but someone should be planning five to ten years ahead.

The function of long-term planning can rarely be performed by personnel who also have ongoing operational responsibilities. The United Nations does not have a "think tank" at present that can fill this gap. The UN University in Tokyo might be charged with the task, but the "thinkers" should not be far from the action in New York. Moreover, UNU's modest budget is now fully committed. If, however, the United

States were to provide some leadership on this issue, funding could probably be raised to set up a small planning group at a university in New York City, close enough and yet not too close to the Secretariat and the Security Council.

The problem of financial resources is even more central in the security field than in other areas of UN activity. In this book, several contributors have urged the expansion of contingency funds as a way of fostering greater coordination among development agencies and thus more-effective UN responses to disasters or conflicts. In the security area, the need for a contingency fund has been so obvious that one is actually being established. As with the other funds, it is clear that only a fraction of the financing that is needed can at this moment be contemplated. We should, however, at least initiate an honest debate on what kind of contingency fund the international community should create. What criteria should be developed for "sizing" the fund? What procedures would be appropriate for its management and for the release of funds when a contingency arises? And how should income from the fund be apportioned between preparing for contingencies and plowing income back into enlarging the fund?

It is not possible here to attempt even initial answers to these questions. In the area of UN financing, the first priorities for U.S. policy must be to implement the reforms of the Ogata-Volcker report and to liquidate U.S. arrearages to both the regular and peacekeeping accounts. There is one financial reform that should be added to the Ogata-Volcker list, and that is the merging of peacekeeping budgets into a single account *and* into the regular budget of the United Nations. The separation of the accounts for different peacekeeping operations serves no purpose other than to maximize the likelihood that a government—or, most often, a U.S. congressman—will find a pretext for "sending the United Nations a message" by cutting or delaying an appropriation.

Peacekeeping is a fundamental responsibility of the United Nations. The United States therefore should pay its share of this UN activity through a single legislative decision along with its "regular" dues. There will, of course, be unpredictable contingencies and a need for "supplemental" appropriations to meet them. Just as Gil Loescher in chapter 7 has proposed with respect to humanitarian assistance and the UN High Commissioner for Refugees, the core costs of UN peacekeeping operations are predictable within limits and governments should be assessed for these expenses along with their regular dues. When this is done, the special scale for peacekeeping should be eliminated, as recommended by Barry Blechman in chapter 4, and the costs allocated in the normal way.

A high priority must be given to drawing lessons from the successes and failures of the peacekeeping operations in Namibia, Angola, Somalia, Bosnia, Cambodia, and elsewhere over the past several years. There are painful dilemmas to be faced, for example, regarding relief work in situations where military action is under way. Out of this reflection on the recent experiences of the United Nations, which should be carried out within governments and by private think tanks around the world, there will emerge a new consensus on what the United Nations must be ready to do in emergencies and on how that action is to be financed. The fiftieth anniversary of the United Nations in 1995 may be too soon to look for anything more than a preliminary consensus on these matters, but because target dates can sometimes be useful, I would suggest the turn of the century as appropriate. Meanwhile, additional experiences will accumulate, and these should provide a better indication than we have today of where the United Nations should be heading.

THE ISSUE OF LEADERSHIP

Leadership is the one challenge the United States cannot evade. As I said earlier, a failure to lead is also a kind of leadership, especially in the area of international collective security. The United States is the world's preeminent military power and is so omnipresent around the globe, in part as a legacy from our long struggle with the Soviet threat, that when we choose not to lead it is equivalent to asserting that a collective response from the international community is not in order or is simply not possible.

This is true even with regard to regional disputes. It is obviously desirable to deal with as many problems as possible at the regional level. It is often forgotten, however, that the countries and peoples of a region have long histories of relations with each other, and human nature being what it is, those histories are generally filled with bitter memories. Consequently, two states in conflict will very often prefer to have third-party mediators come from outside their region. The United Nations thus has a substantial advantage over regional organizations when it comes to mediating local conflicts.

Does the United States have to lead on every issue, whether great or small, that confronts the United Nations? Obviously not. The United States has no monopoly on wisdom, imagination, or capable leaders to innovatively manage international undertakings. Nevertheless, we should distinguish between those instances where the United States can simply remain involved and those where it will be obliged to play a prominent leadership role. For example, the United States was at the center of the recent negotiation that produced the UN peace plan for Cambodia, but when it came to implementing the plan, the United States wisely stayed in the background. We have, after all, our own rather fresh memories of involvement in that unhappy country.

The most accurate response to the question of whether the United States should lead when issues are dealt with through the United Nations is that the United States must at least be substantively and positively involved. It need not be high-profile involvement, though that is sometimes essential, but the United States cannot seem uninterested or unconcerned. In a very real sense, a U.S. abstention on a major issue before the United Nations is a vote of no. While abstaining or voting no (either literally or figuratively) does not, of course, mean that nothing will happen, it does generally mean that we will have little influence over the outcome. This is one of the reasons that the U.S. decision not to sign the Law of the Sea Treaty and the decision to withdraw from UNESCO were contrary to U.S. interests. When the United States decides to cede its role in a UN activity that still goes forward, we not only forgo important opportunities to contribute to positive developments, we also diminish our ability to prevent harmful decisions. A walkout by the United States may at times be the only way to make a vitally important point, but it is extremely difficult to justify a prolonged U.S. absence from an important and almost universal global institution.

The United States will on occasion have to choose between leading through the United Nations, multilaterally, or leading through unilateral action. The preference should always be for acting with others, usually through the United Nations, but the possibility of acting alone, or with others outside of the United Nations, will always be there as a last resort. It is hard to imagine the United States or almost any other government accepting the obligations of a United Nations that did not have an Article 51. But contingencies calling for unilateral action are increasingly unlikely and exceptional. The charge that working wherever possible through the United Nations means subjecting U.S. independence and sovereignty to someone's paralyzing veto is simply nonsense, and pernicious nonsense to boot.

U.S. policymakers should seek opportunities to exert leadership in the United Nations for positive reasons and not merely to limit damage. The United States possesses a significant share of the human resources that the world has available for dealing with international problems. This reservoir of talent—in the State Department and other federal agencies, as well as in the nongovernmental, business, media, and academic communities—represents a substantial portion of the world's total pool of such expertise. The ranks of capable people are expanding in Europe, Japan, and throughout the developing world, but for historical reasons—including the relative absence of private foundations that can finance books such as this volume—these other national talent pools are somewhat more limited than in the United States. If one examines the global pool of scientific skills, for instance—the pool from which will have to come the solutions to the world's environmental problems—the relative weight of the United States in these areas is even more impressive. It would simply be wrong for the United States not to mobilize these resources as fully as possible in the common interest.

Leadership is thus much more than placing oneself at the head of a parade or delivering a stirring speech. It requires a sustained, government-wide effort to develop solutions and to nurse those solutions, without arrogance or coercion, through the tortuous process of gaining support for them from the entire international community. The final result of U.S. involvement may often look quite different from our initial proposals, but without a strong U.S. effort the problem may simply not be addressed. This was true, for instance, in the creation of the United Nations itself, as well as in the founding of the World Bank and the International Monetary Fund, in the negotiation of the Universal Declaration of Human Rights and the Atoms for Peace and nuclear nonproliferation treaties, and in great achievements outside the United Nations such as the Marshall Plan and the North Atlantic Treaty Organization. The world has changed a great deal over the past decades, but on the matter of leadership it has hardly changed at all.

APPENDIX

The UNITED NATIONS
At a Glance

I. GENERAL ASSEMBLY

By the opening of the 48th Session of the General Assembly in September 1993, the United Nations had 184 members. In an unprecedented move in September 1992, the General Assembly decided that the new Federal Republic of Yugoslavia—Serbia and Montenegro—could not continue the membership of the former Yugoslavia, and it barred that country from participating in Assembly deliberations. Although Yugoslavia is denied voting rights in the Assembly, where each state has one vote, it is counted among the 184 members.

The Assembly controls the U.N.'s finances, makes nonbinding recommendations on a variety of issues, and oversees and elects some members of other U.N. organs. By tradition it meets in plenary session from the third Tuesday in September through mid-December, but with the growth of its agenda in recent years it has tended to remain in session, meeting as necessary, until the following September. The Assembly can also meet in emergency session to address an immediate threat to international peace and security—as it has done on nine occasions (most recently in January 1982)—and in special sessions—as it has done on 18 occasions (most recently in April 1990 on International Economic Cooperation).

Diagram labels: TRUSTEESHIP COUNCIL · SECURITY COUNCIL · ECONOMIC AND SOCIAL COUNCIL · GENERAL ASSEMBLY · SECRETARIAT · INTERNATIONAL COURT OF JUSTICE

Major Committees of the General Assembly

President of the 48th General Assembly.....................................H.E. Mr. Samuel R. Insanally (Guyana)

Committees	Chairpersons
First Committee (Disarmament and International Security)	H.E. Dr. Adolf Ritter von Wagner (Germany)
Second Committee (Economic and Financial)	H.E. Mr. René Valéry Mongbé (Benin)
Third Committee (Social, Humanitarian, and Cultural)	H.E. Mr. Eduard Kukan (Slovak Republic)
Fourth Committee (Special Political and Decolonization)	H.E. Dr. Stanley Kalpagé (Sri Lanka)
Fifth Committee (Administrative and Budgetary)	H.E. Mr. Rabah Hadid (Algeria)
Sixth Committee (Legal)	Mrs. Maria del Luján Flores (Uruguay)

Housekeeping Committees make recommendations on the adoption of the agenda, the allocation of items, and the organization of work. Some housekeeping committees (all but the last consisting of government representatives):
1. General Committee
2. Credentials Committee
3. Committee on Relations with the Host Country
4. Committee on Conferences
5. Committee for Programme and Coordination
6. Committee on Contributions

A variety of other bodies (most consisting of experts who serve in their own capacity):
1. Board of Auditors
2. International Civil Service Commission
3. Joint Inspection Unit
4. Panel of External Auditors of the United Nations, the Specialized Agencies, and the International Atomic Energy Agency
5. Administrative Tribunal
6. United Nations Joint Staff Pension Board
7. United Nations Staff Pension Committee
8. Investments Committee
9. Advisory Committee on Administrative and Budgetary Questions

Special Committees That Report on Special Issues

There are some 75 such subsidiary organs, among them:
1. Special Committee on the Situation with regard to the Implementation of the Declaration on the Granting of Independence to Colonial Countries and Peoples
2. Committee on the Exercise of the Inalienable Rights of the Palestinian People
3. Special Committee against Apartheid
4. Committee on the Peaceful Uses of Outer Space
5. Special Committee on Peacekeeping Operations
6. United Nations Scientific Committee on the Effects of Atomic Radiation
7. Ad Hoc Committee on the Indian Ocean

Commissions

Three major commissions report to the General Assembly:

1. *International Law Commission*, established in 1947 to promote the development and codification of international law. The Commission, which is made up of 25 experts elected by the Assembly for five-year terms, meets every year in Geneva to prepare drafts on topics of its own choosing and on topics referred to it by the Assembly and by the Economic and Social Council.

2. *United Nations Commission on International Trade Law*, established in 1966 to promote the harmonization of international trade law and to draft international trade conventions. The 36-country body also provides developing countries with training and assistance in international trade law.

3. *Disarmament Commission*, a deliberative body established by the General Assembly in 1952. Reporting annually to the Assembly, it makes recommendations on various problems in the field of disarmament to be submitted as recommendations to the Assembly and, through it, to the negotiating body—the Conference of the Committee on Disarmament.

Other Organizations Created by and Reporting to the General Assembly:

■ Office of the United Nations Disaster Relief Coordinator (UNDRO)—clearinghouse for information on relief needs and assistance, and mobilizer and coordinator of emergency assistance.

■ Office of the United Nations High Commissioner for Refugees (UNHCR)—extends international protection and material assistance to refugees and negotiates with governments to resettle or repatriate refugees.

■ United Nations Centre for Human Settlements (Habitat)—deals with the housing problems of the urban and rural poor in developing countries, providing technical assistance and training, organizing meetings, and disseminating information.

■ United Nations Children's Fund (UNICEF)—provides technical and financial assistance to developing countries for programs benefiting children and also provides emergency relief to mothers and children. It is financed by voluntary contributions.

■ United Nations Conference on Trade and Development (UNCTAD)—works to establish agreements on commodity stabilization and to codify principles of international trade that are conducive to development.

■ United Nations Fund for Women (UNIFEM)—an autonomous agency associated with the U.N. Development Programme that supports projects benefiting women in developing countries. It is financed by voluntary contributions.

■ United Nations Development Programme (UNDP)—coordinates the development work of all U.N. and related agencies. The world's largest multilateral technical assistance program (UNDP currently supports more than 6,000 projects around the world), it is financed by voluntary contributions.

■ United Nations Environment Programme (UNEP)—monitors environmental conditions, implements environmental projects, develops recommended standards, promotes technical assistance and training, and supports the development of alternative energy sources. The U.N. system's principal body in the environment field.

■ United Nations Population Fund (UNFPA)—helps countries to gather demographic information and to plan population projects. UNFPA is financed by the voluntary contributions of governments and its policies set by a Governing Council.

■ United Nations Institute for Training and Research (UNITAR)—an autonomous organization within the U.N. that provides training to government and U.N. officials and conducts research on a variety of international issues.

■ United Nations Relief and Works Agency for Palestine Refugees in the Near East (UNRWA)—provides education, health, and relief services to Palestinian refugees.

■ United Nations University (UNU)—an autonomous academic institution chartered by the General Assembly. It has a worldwide network of associated institutions, research units, individual scholars, and UNU fellows, coordinated through the UNU center in Tokyo, but no faculty or degree students.

- United Nations International Research and Training Institute for the Advancement of Women (INSTRAW)—an autonomous, voluntarily funded body that conducts research, training, and information activities to integrate women in development.

- World Food Council (WFC)—a 36 nation body that meets annually at the ministerial level to review major issues affecting the world food situation.

- World Food Programme (WFP)—jointly sponsored by the U.N. and the Food and Agriculture Organization, supplies both emergency food relief and food aid to support development projects.

II. SECURITY COUNCIL

The Security Council has primary responsibility within the U.N. system for maintaining international peace and security. It may determine the existence of any threat to international peace, make recommendations or take enforcement measures to resolve the problem, and establish U.N. peacekeeping forces. The Security Council has 15 members: five permanent members designated by the U.N. Charter and 10 nonpermanent members nominated by informal regional caucuses and elected for two-year terms; five are elected each year. Decisions on substantive matters require nine votes; a negative vote by any permanent member is sufficient to defeat the motion. Security Council resolutions are binding on all U.N. member states.

Permanent Members	Term Ending Dec. 31, 1994	Term Ending Dec. 31, 1995
China	Brazil	Argentina
France	Djibouti	Czech Republic
Russian Federation*	New Zealand	Nigeria
United Kingdom	Pakistan	Oman
United States	Spain	Rwanda

*Inherited the permanent seat of the Soviet Union in 1991.

III. ECONOMIC AND SOCIAL COUNCIL (ECOSOC)

Under the authority of the General Assembly, ECOSOC coordinates the economic and social work of the U.N. and its large family of specialized and affiliated institutions. ECOSOC meets once a year, alternating between New York and Geneva, for a four-to-five-week plenary session. The 54 members of ECOSOC are elected by the General Assembly for three-year terms; 18 are elected each year.

Term Expires Dec. 31, 1994

Angola	Brazil	Madagascar
Australia	Colombia	Philippines
Bangladesh	Ethiopia	Poland
Belarus	India	Suriname
Belgium	Italy	Swaziland
Benin	Kuwait	United States

Term Expires Dec. 31, 1995		Term Expires Dec. 31, 1996	
Bahamas	Nigeria	Bulgaria	Ireland
Bhutan	Norway	Chile	Japan
Canada	Republic of	Costa Rica	Pakistan
China	Korea (South)	Egypt	Paraguay
Cuba	Romania	France	Portugal
Denmark	Russian Federation	Germany	Senegal
Gabon	Sri Lanka	Ghana	Tanzania
Libya	Ukraine	Greece	Venezuela
Mexico	United Kingdom	Indonesia	Zimbabwe
	Zaire		

IV. TRUSTEESHIP COUNCIL

The five members of the Trusteeship Council—China, France, Russia, the U.K., and the U.S.—are also the five permanent members of the Security Council. At birth, the Trusteeship Council had more members and administered 11 trust territories, but as the latter achieved independence or joined neighboring independent countries, the membership of the Council was reduced. In 1991 the Security Council (which has final say on "strategic territories") voted to end trusteeship over three of four island groups belonging to the 11th territory: the U.S.-administered Trust Territory of the Pacific Islands. Trusteeship over the fourth island group, Palau—the U.N.'s last trust territory—was in process of termination by late 1993.

V. INTERNATIONAL COURT OF JUSTICE (WORLD COURT)

The International Court of Justice hears cases referred to it by the states involved and provides advisory opinions to the General Assembly and the Security Council at their request. It is made up of 15 members, who are elected by an absolute majority of both the Security Council and the General Assembly for nine-year terms; five judges are elected every three years.

Term Expires Feb. 5, 1997

Roberto Ago (Italy)	Mohamed Shahabuddeen (Guyana)
Mohammed Bedjaoui (Algeria)	
Stephen M. Schwebel (United States)	Nikolai Konstantinovich Tarassov (Russian Federation)

Term Expires Feb. 5, 2000

Andres Aguilar Mawdsley (Venezuela)	Christopher Gregory Weeramantry (Sri Lanka)
Gilbert Guillaume (France)	Raymond Rangeva (Madagascar)
Robert Jennings (United Kingdom)	

Term Expires Feb. 5, 2003

Carl-August Fleischhauer (Germany)	Abdul G. Koroma (Sierra Leone)
Geza Herczegh (Hungary)	Shigeru Oda (Japan)
	Jiuyong Shi (China)

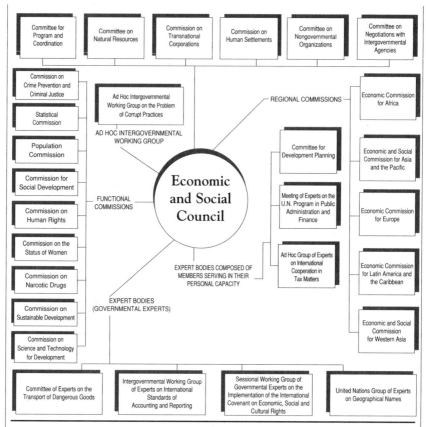

VI. SECRETARIAT

The Secretariat administers the programs and policies established by the other U.N. organs. It is headed by the Secretary-General (currently Boutros Boutros-Ghali of Egypt), who is elected by the General Assembly upon the recommendation of the Security Council for a five-year term. The Secretary-General is authorized by the U.N. Charter to bring to the attention of the Security Council any matter that he believes may threaten international peace and security (Article 99) and may use his good offices to attempt to resolve international disputes.

An international civil service staff of some 14,000, drawn from 150 nations, carries out the day-to-day activities delegated to the Secretary-General. This number includes not only the men and women who work at U.N. Headquarters in New York and in offices in Geneva, Vienna, and elsewhere, but also the technical experts and economic advisors who oversee economic and peacekeeping projects in the field. (Not included are the staff members of the U.N. Development Programme, the U.N. High Commissioner for Refugees, and the U.N.

Children's Fund—an additional 17,000 worldwide.) Article 100 of the Charter calls upon the Secretary-General and the staff to maintain their independence from governmental or other authority external to the Organization, and it calls upon member states to recognize and respect "the exclusively international character of the responsibilities of the Secretary-General and the staff."

The efficiency of the Secretariat has been undermined by an increase over time in the number of related and often overlapping departments and offices as well as the number of high-level officials who report directly to the Secretary-General. In February 1992, Secretary-General Boutros-Ghali began the process of restructuring the Secretariat with the elimination of 14 high-level posts and the consolidation of a dozen departments. During a second phase, begun in late 1992, the Secretary-General created three departments in the economic and social area and "redeployed activities" among U.N. headquarters in New York and Europe.

VII. SPECIALIZED AGENCIES

The specialized agencies are autonomous intergovernmental organizations related to the U.N. by special agreements. They report annually to the Economic and Social Council.

■ **Food and Agriculture Organization of the United Nations (FAO)** works to increase food production, raise rural standards of living, and help countries cope with emergency food situations.

Jacques Diouf (Senegal), Director-General
Via delle Terme de Caracalla 00100 Rome, Italy

Washington, D.C., Office:
1001 22nd Street, N.W., Suite 300
Washington, D.C. 20437
New York Liaison Office:
Suite DC1-1125
One United Nations Plaza
New York, N.Y. 10017

■ **International Civil Aviation Organization (ICAO)** works to facilitate and promote safe international air transportation by setting binding international standards and by recommending efficient practices. ICAO regulations govern international flights.

Dr. Philippe Rochat (Switzerland), Secretary-General
1000 Sherbrooke Street West
Montreal, Quebec
PQ H3A 2R2
Canada

■ **International Fund for Agricultural Development (IFAD)** lends money on concessional terms for agricultural development projects, primarily to increase food production for the poorest rural populations.

Fawzi Hamad Al-Sultan (Kuwait), President and Chairman of the Executive Board
Via Del Serafico 107
00142 Rome, Italy

New York Liaison Office
Room S-2955
United Nations
New York, N.Y. 10017

■ **International Labour Organisation (ILO)** formulates international labor standards and provides technical assistance training to governments.

Michel Hansenne (Belgium), DirectorGeneral
4 Route des Morillons
CH-1211 Geneva 22, Switzerland

Washington, D.C., Office:
1828 L Street, Suite 801
Washington, D.C. 20036

■ **International Maritime Organization (IMO)** promotes international cooperation on technical matters related to shipping and provides a forum to discuss and adopt conventions and recommendations on such matters as safety at sea and pollution control.

William A. O'Neil (Canada), Secretary-General
4 Albert Embankment
London, SEI 7SR, England

■ **International Monetary Fund (IMF)** provides technical assistance and financing to countries that are experiencing balance of payments difficulties.

Michel Camdessus (France), Managing Director
700 19th Street, N.W.
Washington, D.C. 20431

■ **International Telecommunication Union (ITU)** promotes international cooperation

in telecommunications, allocates the radio-frequency spectrum, and collects and disseminates telecommunications information for its members.

Pekka J. Tarjanne (Finland), Secretary-General
Place des Nations
CH-1211 Geneva 20, Switzerland

■ **United Nations Educational, Scientific and Cultural Organization (UNESCO)** pursues international intellectual cooperation in education, science, culture, and communications and promotes development by means of social, cultural, and economic projects.

Federico Zaragoza Mayor (Spain), Director-General
UNESCO House
7, place de Fontenoy
75007 Paris, France

New York Liaison Office:
Two United Nations Plaza
Room DC2-0900
New York, N.Y. 10017

■ **United Nations Industrial Development Organization (UNIDO)**—to date, the only U.N. organ ever to be converted into an independent, specialized agency—serves as intermediary between developing and developed countries in the field of industry and as a forum for contacts, consultations, and negotiations to aid the growth of industrialization.

Mauricio de Maria y Campos (Mexico), Director-General
P.O. Box 300
Vienna International Centre
A-1400 Vienna, Austria

New York Liaison Office:
Room DC2-1116
Two United Nations Plaza
New York, N.Y. 10017

■ **Universal Postal Union (UPU)** sets international postal standards and provides technical assistance to developing countries.

Adwaldo Cardoso Botto de Barros (Egypt), Director-General
Union Postale Universelle
Weltpoststrasse 4
Berne, Switzerland

■ **The World Bank** is actually three institutions: the **International Bank for Reconstruction and Development (IBRD)**; the **International Finance Corporation (IFC)**; and the **International Development Association (IDA)**. IBRD lends funds to governments (or to private enterprises, if the government guarantees repayment), usually for specific, productive projects. IFC lends to private corporations without government guarantees. IDA provides interest-free "credits" to the world's poorest countries for a period of 50 years, with a ten-year grace period.

Lewis T. Preston (United States), President
1818 H Street, N.W.
Washington, D.C. 20433

New York Liaison Office:
809 U.N. Plaza, 9th Floor
New York, N.Y. 10017

■ **World Health Organization (WHO)** conducts immunization campaigns, promotes and coordinates research, and provides technical assistance to countries that are improving their health systems. It is currently coordinating a major effort to control and cure acquired immune deficiency syndrome— AIDS.

Dr. Hiroshi Nakajima (Japan), Director-General
20 Avenue Appia
1211 Geneva 27,
Switzerland

Pan-American Health Organization/WHO Regional Office for the Americas:
5255 23rd Street, N.W.
Washington, D.C. 20036

■**World Intellectual Property Organization (WIPO)** promotes the protection of intellectual property (e.g., patents and copyrights). It encourages adherence to relevant treaties, provides legal and technical assistance to developing countries, encourages technology transfers, and administers the International Union for the Protection of Industrial Property and the International Union for the Protection of Literary and Artistic Works.

Dr. Arpad Bogsch (United States), Director-General
34 Chemin des Colombettes
CH-1211 Geneva 20,
Switzerland

New York Liaison Office:
Room DC2-0560
Two United Nations Plaza
New York, N.Y. 10017

■**World Meteorological Organization (WMO)** promotes the exchange and standardization of meteorological information

through its World Weather Watch and conducts research and training programs.

G.O.P. Obasi (Nigeria), Secretary-General
Case postale No. 2300
1211 Geneva 2,
Switzerland
[Headquarters: 41 Avenue Giuseppe-Motta]

Other Autonomous Affiliated Organizations

■**General Agreement on Tariffs and Trade (GATT)** is a multilateral regime that sets out norms and rules for international trade and provides a forum for their further elaboration.

Peter Sutherland (Ireland), Director-General
Centre William Rappard
154, rue de Lausanne
CH-1211 Geneva 21,
Switzerland

■**International Atomic Energy Agency (IAEA)** was established under U.N. auspices but is autonomous and not formally a specialized agency. It promotes the peaceful uses of nuclear energy; establishes standards for nuclear safety and environmental protection; and, by agreement with parties to the Non-Proliferation Treaty, carries out inspections to safeguard against diversion of nuclear materials to military uses.

Dr. Hans Blix (Sweden), Director-General
Vienna International Centre
P.O. Box 100
A-1400 Vienna, Austria

U.N. MEMBER STATES *(as of September 21, 1993)*

Membership in the United Nations has nearly quadrupled since the Organization's founding in 1945. There were 51 original member states; today there are 184 members, representing the majority of the world's nations.

Afghanistan, Republic of
Albania, Republic of
Algeria
Andorra, Principality of
Angola, People's Republic of
Antigua and Barbuda
Argentina
Armenia
Australia
Austria
Azerbaijan (Azerbaijani Republic)
Bahamas, Commonwealth of the
Bahrain, State of
Bangladesh, People's Republic of
Barbados
Belarus, Republic of
Belgium
Belize
Benin, Republic of
Bhutan, Kingdom of
Bolivia
Bosnia and Herzegovina
Botswana
Brazil
Brunei Darussalam
Bulgaria, Republic of
Burkina Faso (formerly Upper Volta)
Burundi, Republic of
Cambodia, Kingdom of
Cameroon, Republic of
Canada
Cape Verde, Republic of
Central African Republic
Chad, Republic of
Chile
China, People's Republic of
Colombia
Comoros, Federal Islamic Republic of the
Congo, Republic of
Costa Rica
Côte d'Ivoire
Croatia
Cuba
Cyprus
Czech Republic
Denmark
Djibouti, Republic of
Dominica, Commonwealth of
Dominican Republic
Ecuador

Egypt, Arab Republic of
El Salvador
Equatorial Guinea
Eritrea
Estonia, Republic of
Ethiopia
Fiji, Republic of
Finland
France
Gabon (Gabonese Republic)
Gambia
Georgia
Germany
Ghana
Greece
Grenada
Guatemala
Guinea, Republic of
Guinea-Bissau, Republic of
Guyana, Republic of
Haiti
Honduras
Hungary, Republic of
Iceland
India
Indonesia, Republic of
Iran, Islamic Republic of
Iraq
Ireland
Israel
Italy
Jamaica
Japan
Jordan, Hashemite Kingdom of
Kazakhstan, Republic of
Kenya, Republic of
Korea, Democratic People's Republic of (North Korea)
Korea, Republic of (South Korea)
Kuwait, State of
Kyrgyz Republic
Lao People's Democratic Republic
Latvia, Republic of
Lebanon
Lesotho, Kingdom of
Liberia, Republic of
Libyan Arab Jamahiriya
Liechtenstein, Principality of
Lithuania, Republic of
Luxembourg
Macedonia, Former Yugoslav Republic of
Madagascar, Democratic Republic of
Malawi, Republic of
Malaysia
Maldives, Republic of
Mali, Republic of
Malta
Marshall Islands, Republic of the
Mauritania, Islamic Republic of

Mauritius
Mexico
Micronesia, Federated States of
Moldova, Republic of
Monaco
Mongolia (Mongolian People's Republic)
Morocco, Kingdom of
Mozambique, Republic of
Myanmar, Union of (formerly Burma)
Namibia, Republic of
Nepal, Kingdom of
Netherlands, Kingdom of the
New Zealand
Nicaragua
Niger
Nigeria
Norway
Oman
Pakistan
Panama
Papua New Guinea
Paraguay
Peru
Philippines, Republic of the
Poland, Republic of
Portugal
Qatar, State of
Romania
Russian Federation
Rwanda (Rwandese Republic)
Saint Kitts and Nevis
Saint Lucia
Saint Vincent and the Grenadines
Samoa, Independent State of Western
San Marino, Republic of
Sao Tome and Principe
Saudi Arabia
Senegal, Republic of
Seychelles, Republic of
Sierra Leone, Republic of
Singapore, Republic of
Slovak Republic
Slovenia, Republic of
Solomon Islands
Somalia (Somali Democratic Republic)
South Africa
Spain
Sri Lanka, Democratic Socialist Republic of
Sudan, Republic of
Suriname, Republic of
Swaziland, Kingdom of
Sweden
Syrian Arab Republic
Tajikistan, Republic of
Tanzania, United Republic of
Thailand
Togo
Trinidad and Tobago, Republic of

Tunisia
Turkey
Turkmenistan
Uganda, Republic of
Ukraine
United Arab Emirates
United Kingdom of Great Britain and Northern Ireland
United States of America
Uruguay
Uzbekistan, Republic of
Vanuatu, Republic of
Venezuela
Viet Nam, Socialist Republic of
Yemen, Republic of
Yugoslavia
Zaire, Republic of
Zambia, Republic of
Zimbabwe, Republic of

The following maintain Permanent Observer Missions to the U.N.:
Holy See
Switzerland (Swiss Confederation)

Prepared as a public information service by the United Nations Association of the United States of America (UNA-USA), an independent, nonpartisan, nationwide membership organization. Through its programs of research and education, UNA-USA seeks to strengthen public knowledge about the United Nations, to increase the effectiveness of international organizations, and to promote constructive U.S. policies on matters of global concern.

This report was prepared with the assistance of Kristin Willey.

Additional copies available from the Publications Department, UNA-USA. Single copies, $1.00; 50 copies, $25; and 100 copies, $40. Postage included on prepaid orders.

United Nations Association of the United States of America

485 Fifth Avenue, New York, N.Y. 10017 (212) 697-3232 FAX (212) 682-9185

Washington Office:
1010 Vermont Avenue, N.W., Suite 904,
Washington, D.C. 20005
(202) 347-5004
FAX (202) 628-5945

12/93

NOTES

CHAPTER 1

1. Final Report of the United States Commission on Improving the Effectiveness of the United Nations, *Defining Purpose: The U.N. and the Health of Nations* (Washington, D.C.: U.S. Government Printing Office, September 1993).

2. *Defining Purpose: The U.N. and the Health of Nations*, p. 18. The recent report of the Independent Advisory Group on UN Financing employs fiscal year figures for the cost of UN peacekeeping operations. Their numbers are $819 million for 1991–92 and $3.8 billion for 1992–93. In addition, they note that UN peacekeeping expenses for calendar year 1992 were $1.4 billion. *Financing an Effective United Nations*: A Report of the Independent Advisory Group on U.N. Financing (New York: Ford Foundation, 1993), p. 29.

3. Paul Lewis, "U.S. Plans Policy on Peacekeeping," *New York Times* (November 18, 1993).

4. *Financing an Effective United Nations*, pp. 1–2.

5. This figure includes the regular UN budget, peacekeeping, and voluntary contributions to the United Nations, as well as to UNICEF, UNDP, and the UNFPA, but it does not include the budgets of the specialized agencies or the funds provided to those organizations by other UN institutions. These figures are taken from *Financing an Effective United Nations*.

6. *Financing an Effective United Nations*, Table III, pp. 32–33.

7. *Financing an Effective United Nations*, p. 4.

8. Richard Thornburgh, Unpublished Report to the Secretary-General (New York: United Nations, March 1993).

CHAPTER 2

1. See also the author's op-ed pieces in the *New York Times*, March 13, 1992, and the *Washington Post*, May 19, 1992.

2. *The United Nations in Development: Reform Issues in the Economic and Social Fields, a Nordic Perspective* (Stockholm: GOTAB, 1991).

3. *An Agenda for Peace* (New York: United Nations, 1992), p. 26.

4. Ibid., p. 30.

5. Ibid.

6. Ibid., p. 31.

7. Unpublished Report to the Secretary-General (New York: United Nations, March 1993), p. 18.

8. These figures are taken from UN Document ST/ADMSER.B/420, "Status of Contributions as of 31 October 1993" (November 8, 1993).

9. *Financing an Effective United Nations: A Report of the Independent Advisory Group on U.N. Financing* (New York: Ford Foundation, 1993).

10. See, for instance, the author's "Time to Get Right with the U.N.," *Washington Post*, May 19, 1992, p. A19.

CHAPTER 3

1. Inis Claude argued this point in his insightful study of collective security. Inis Claude, *Swords into Plowshares*, fourth edition (New York: Random House, 1984), chapter 12.

2. Boutros-Ghali, *An Agenda for Peace* (New York: United Nations, 1992).

3. For a thorough and up-to-date review of reform attempts in the social and economic field, see: J. Martin Rochester, *Waiting for the Millennium: The United Nations and the Future of World Order* (Columbia: University of South Carolina Press, 1993), pages 129–151 and 162–191; and Gene M. Lyons, "Competing Visions: Proposals for U.N. Reform," in C.F. Alger, G.M. Lyons, and J. Trent, eds., *The United Nations and the Policies of Member States* (Tokyo: United Nations Press, 1994), in press.

4. A Study of the Capacity of the United Nations Development System (Geneva: United Nations, 1969) document DP/5.

5. Joint Inspection Unit, *Concluding Report of the Implementation of General Assembly Resolution 32/197 Concerning the Restructuring of the Economic and Social Sectors of the United Nations System*. UN Document JUI/REP/89/7 (1989).

6. The United Nations Association of the United States of America, *A Successor Vision: The United Nations of Tomorrow*, Final Panel Report (New York: UNA–USA, September 1987); David Steele, *The Reform of the United Nations* (London: Croom Helm, 1987); Nordic UN Project, *The United Nations and Development: Reform Issues in the Economic and Social Fields*, Final Report (Stockholm, 1991); J. Martin Rochester, *Waiting for the Millenium*; and, Max Jakobson, *The United Nations in the 1990s: A Second Chance?* (New York: UNITAR, 1993).

7. Ibid.

8. *Financing an Effective United Nations: A Report of the Independent Advisory Group on U.N. Financing* (New York: Ford Foundation, 1993).

9. J. Martin Rochester, *Waiting for the Millennium*, pp. 212–213.

10. UNA–USA, op. cit., and Rochester, op. cit.

11. Maurice Bertrand, *Planning, Programming, Budgeting, and Evaluation in the United Nations System*, (New York: United Nations Association of the USA, March 1987).

12. Oran Young, "Political Leadership and Regime Formation: On the Development of Institutions in International Society," *International Organization* 45 (Summer 1991), pp. 281–308.

CHAPTER 4

1. Missions begun after the end of the cold war include El Salvador ('91), Western Sahara ('91), Angola ('91), Kuwait ('91), the former Yugoslavia ('92), Cambodia ('92), Mozambique ('92), Somalia ('92), Rwanda ('93), Georgia ('93), Haiti ('93), and Liberia ('93); in addition, the United Nations has sent good offices missions to South Africa and Tajikistan. The figures are from *Blue Helmets: A Review of U.N. Peacekeeping* (New York: UN Department of Information, August 1990) and "Summary of Contributions to Peace-keeping Operations by Countries as of July 1993," UN Document.

2. *Financing an Effective United Nations: A Report of the Independent Advisory Group on U.N. Financing* (New York: Ford Foundation, 1993), pp. 17–24. The group of eleven government and private financiers and businessmen was cochaired by Shijuro Ogata and Paul Volcker. The group also recommended abolishing the special peacekeeping assessment formula.

3. Mitterrand's proposal can be seen in "Address by François Mitterrand, President of the French Republic, Before the United Nations Security Council Summit" (French Embassy release, January 31, 1992); Boutros-Ghali's report is *An Agenda for Peace* (New York: United Nations, 1992); Urquhart's proposal appeared in the *New York Review of Books,* June 10, 1993, pp. 3–4.

4. Charter of the United Nations, Article 47, paragraphs 1 and 2.

5. "Address by President Bush to the United Nations," *New York Times,* September 22, 1992, p. A1.

6. *Washington Post,* June 18, 1993, p. A1, and August 5, 1993, p. A1.

7. See, for example, Jeffrey Laurenti, *American Public Opinion and the United Nations, 1992: Evolving Perceptions of a Changing World* (UNA–USA Occasional Papers, 1992); and Alan F. Kay et al., "Global Uncertainties," *Americans Talk Issues,* Survey no. 21 (Americans Talk Issues Foundation, May 1993).

CHAPTER 5

1. For this reason, the IAEA statute contains a number of ambiguities. See Paul C. Szasz, *The Law and Practices of the IAEA* (Vienna: International Atomic Energy Agency, 1970).

2. David Fischer, "Innovations in IAEA Safeguards to Meet the Challenges of the 1990s," in David Fischer, Ben Sanders, Lawrence Scheinman, and George Bunn, eds., *A New Nuclear Triad: The Non-Proliferation of Nuclear Weapons, International Verification, and the International Atomic Energy Agency* (Southampton, England: Program for Promoting Nuclear Non-Proliferation, 1992); Lawrence Scheinman, *The International Atomic Energy Agency and World Nuclear Order* (Washington, D.C.: Resources for the Future, 1987), p. 37.

3. The assertion that any deviation from the principles of nondiscrimination and trust will destroy the IAEA safeguards system was made by an IAEA official quoted in Mark Hibbs, "Gulf War Will Shift IAEA Safeguards Priorities— By How Much," *Nucleonics Week* 33, no. 8 (February 20, 1992).

4. Fischer, op. cit.

5. For a discussion of the negotiations over the resolution on "strengthening the agency's main mission" at the 1991 and 1992 general conferences, see Scheinman, op. cit., p. 46; "IAEA Developments," *Program for Promoting Nuclear Non-Proliferation Newsbrief*, no. 15 (Autumn 1991), pp. 4–5; and "IAEA Developments," *Program for Promoting Nuclear Non-Proliferation Newsbrief*, no. 19 (Autumn 1992), pp. 5–6.

6. The 1994 regular budget has allocated $65 million for safeguards out of a total of $190 million.

7. There has been a tenfold increase in spending on technical assistance since the mid-1970s: in 1976, $5.4 million; 1979, $8.5 million; 1981, $13 million; 1985, $26 million; 1991, $49 million; and in 1993, $56 million. Scheinman, op. cit., p. 247; and "IAEA Technical Assistance in 1991," *IAEA Bulletin* 34, no. 3, p. 42.

8. One significant quantity (SQ) is defined as 25 kgs of U–235 in highly enriched uranium, 75 kgs of U–235 in low-enriched uranium, and 8 kgs of plutonium.

9. From 1985 to 1991, the number of inspectors at the IAEA increased from 131 to 154 (Hibbs, op. cit.).

10. Fischer, op. cit.

11. Scheinman, op. cit., p. 232.

12. For a discussion of the Safeguards Implementation Reports, which were begun in 1977, see ibid., pp. 238–39.

13. Scheinman, op. cit., 1992; Lawrence Scheinman, "Lessons from Iraq," *Arms Control Today* 23, no. 3 (April 1993), p. 4; and "IAEA Developments," *Program for Promoting Nuclear Non-Proliferation Newsbrief*, no. 16 (Winter 1991/92), p. 5.

14. One expert has written that prior to 1992, IAEA management specifically excluded the possibility of making special inspections at previously undeclared sites. See Ben Sanders, "IAEA Safeguards: A Short Historical Background," in David Fischer, Ben Sanders, Lawrence Scheinman, and George Bunn, eds., *A New Nuclear Triad: The Non-Proliferation of Nuclear Weapons, International Verification, and the International Atomic Energy Agency* (Southampton, England: Program for Promoting Nuclear Non-Proliferation, 1992), p. 10.

15. This view differs from that of another expert, David Kay, "The IAEA— How Can It Be Strengthened?" (Paper presented at the Woodrow Wilson Center conference entitled "Nuclear Proliferation in the 1990s: Challenges and Opportunities," December 1–2, 1992.)

16. For a discussion of the changing needs for intelligence and its relationship to the IAEA, see Anthony Fainberg, *Strengthening IAEA Safeguards: Lessons from Iraq* (Stanford, Calif.: Stanford University Center for International Security and Arms Control, 1993).

17. R. Jeffrey Smith, "N. Korea and the Bomb: High-Tech Hide-and-Seek," *Washington Post*, April 27, 1993, p. 1.

18. For a discussion of the strengths and weaknesses of the INFCIRC 66 and INFCIRC 153 safeguards system, see Sanders, op. cit.

19. Leonard S. Spector, *Nuclear Proliferation Today* (New York: Vintage, 1984), pp. 21, 342–44.

20. David Fischer and Paul Szasz, *Safeguarding the Atom* (London: SIPRI, 1985), pp. 38–39.

21. Ibid., pp. 36–37.

22. For a contrary view, see Gary Milhollin, "The Iraqi Bomb," *New Yorker*, February 1, 1993, pp. 47–56; Jay C. Davis and David C. Kay, "Iraq's Secret Nuclear Weapons Program," *Physics Today*, July 1992, pp. 21–27; Kay, op. cit.

23. "Companies Delivered Machines for Iraqi Nuclear Program," *Der Spiegel*, February 8, 1993, p. 16. For a listing of key accomplishments by the IAEA, see Leslie Thorne, "IAEA Nuclear Inspections in Iraq," *IAEA Bulletin* 34, no. 1; and *The Arms Control Reporter*, Section 453.b.

24. IAEA GC/OR/351.

25. Rolf Ekeus, *The Iraq Experience and Multilateral Approaches to Controlling Nuclear Proliferation* (Livermore, Calif.: Center for Security and Technology Studies, Lawrence Livermore National Laboratory, 1993); Maj. Gen. Robert W. Parker, "Trust but Verify," *Defense 93*, no. 1, pp. 6–13.

26. After the DPRK signed the NPT in 1985, the IAEA sent the North Koreans the wrong safeguards agreement, allowing the DPRK to stretch out negotiations over the agreement by an additional eighteen months. Leonard S. Spector, *Nuclear Ambitions* (Boulder, Colo: Westview Press, 1990), p. 129.

27. Smith, op. cit.

28. David Albright, "North Korea Drops Out," *Bulletin of the Atomic Scientists* 49, no. 4 (May 1993), pp. 9–11.

29. John Redick, "Nuclear Confidence-Building in Latin America," in *Verification Report 1993: Yearbook on Arms Control and Environmental Agreements* (London: VERTIC, 1993).

30. Steve Coll and Paul Taylor, "Tracking S. Africa's Elusive A–Program," *Washington Post*, March 18, 1993, p. 1.

31. Gamini Seneviratne, "South African Admission Doesn't Mar African Nonproliferation Talks," *Nucleonics Week* 34, no. 16, p. 15. J. W. DeVillies, Roger Jardine, Mitchell Reiss, "Why South Africa Gave Up the Bomb," *Foreign Affairs* November/December 1993 pp. 98–109.

32. "Algeria: Research Reactor Safeguarded," *IAEA Bulletin* 34, no. 1, p. 51; INFCIRC/401.

33. "Syria: Safeguards Agreement Signed," *IAEA Bulletin* 34, no. 1, p. 51.

34. Betsy Perabo, "A Chronology of Iran's Nuclear Program" (Monterey Institute of International Studies, Monteray, Calif., 1992, Mimeographed); Michael J. Inacker, "Federal Intelligence Service: Iran Deceives International Atomic Energy Organization and Works at Atom Bomb," *Welt Am Sonntag*, December 6, 1992, p. 26; David White, "Iran May Soon Have N–Weapons," *Financial Times*, March 9, 1993, p. 4.

35. Scheinman, op. cit., pp. 3–6; Mark Hibbs, "IAEA Explores Iran's Intentions, Minus Evidence of Weapons Drive," *Nucleonics Week* 33, no. 7 (February 13, 1992), p. 12; Mark Hibbs, "IAEA Inspectors to Revisit Iran; 'Nothing on the ground' U.S. Says," *Nucleonics Week* 33, no. 34 (August 20, 1992), p. 7; Claude van England, "Iran Defends Its Pursuit of Nuclear Technology," *Christian Science Monitor*, February 18, 1993, p. 7.

36. Director-General Sigvard Eklund's address to the 29th Session of the UN General Assembly (reproduced in the *IAEA Bulletin*) stated: "This concern [over

nuclear proliferation] was accentuated by the addition of another country to the number of countries possessing nuclear explosives."

37. Ann MacLachlan, "Romania Produced Unsafeguarded Pu, Blix Tells IAEA Board of Governors," *Nuclear Fuel* 17, no. 13 (June 22, 1992), p. 16.

38. H. Grumm, "IAEA Safeguards—Where Do We Stand Today?" *IAEA Bulletin* 21, no. 4 (August 1979), pp. 32–39.

39. This section draws on the writings of experts on the IAEA including Lawrence Scheinman, Ben Sanders, David Fischer, Myron Kratzer, Nelson Sievering, Alan Labowitz, Harold Benglesdorf, Roger Kirk, and William Dircks.

40. For an evaluation of nonproliferation policies that should be adopted toward these dozen problem countries, see Thomas W. Graham and Alden F. Mullins, Jr., "Arms Control, Military Strategy, and Nuclear Proliferation," in David Goldfischer and Thomas W. Graham, eds., *Nuclear Deterrence and Global Security in Transition* (Boulder, Colo.: Westview Press, 1992), pp. 157–70.

41. Thomas W. Graham, "Public Opinion and U.S. Foreign Policy Decision-Making," in David Deese, ed., *The Politics of American Foreign Policy* (New York: St. Martin's Press, 1993).

42. This review covered the *New York Times*, the *Wall Street Journal*, the *Washington Post*, the *Los Angeles Times*, and the *Christian Science Monitor*.

43. Stanley M. Nealey, Barbara D. Melber, and William L. Rankin, *Public Opinion and Nuclear Energy* (Lexington, Mass.: Lexington Books, 1983).

44. J. P. Charpentier and L. L. Bennett, "Nuclear Power Programs in Developing Countries: Costs and Financing," *IAEA Bulletin* 27, no. 4 (Winter 1985), pp. 52–55.

45. One reviewer expressed skepticism that moving a budget line into the Defense Department would produce any real change except with respect to jurisdiction for the budget in the U.S. Congress. Although this may well be the case, this author nevertheless believes that the policy debate concerning the IAEA budget should be framed in the United States as a national security issue, not as a nuclear energy or international organization issue. If this can be done without moving the budget into the Defense Department, so be it.

46. *Financing an Effective United Nations: A Report of the Independent Advisory Group on U.N. Financing* (New York: Ford Foundation, 1993).

Chapter 7

1. For an elaboration of the links between refugee movements and national, regional, and international security, see Gil Loescher, *Refugee Movements and International Security*, Adelphi Paper 268 (London; Riverside, N.J.: Brassey's, for the International Institute for Strategic Studies, 1992); and Myron Weiner, "Security, Stability, and International Migration," *International Security* 17, no. 3 (Winter 1992/93), pp. 91–126.

2. For a recent treatment of intervention in defense of human rights, see Nigel Rodley, ed., *To Loose the Bands of Wickedness: International Intervention in Defense of Human Rights* (London: Brassey's, 1992).

3. Adam Roberts, "The United Nations and International Security," *Survival* 35, no. 2 (Summer 1993), pp.3–30.

4. For a more detailed history of UNHCR's development and policies, see Gil Loescher, *Beyond Charity: International Cooperation and the Global Refugee Problem* (New York: Oxford University Press, 1993).

5. For a more detailed discussion of both short-term and long-term policies for dealing with the global refugee problem, see ibid.

6. For a further discussion of these points, see Doris Meissner, "Managing Migrations," *Foreign Policy*, Winter 1992, pp. 66–83.

7. United Nations, Economic and Social Council, *Draft Report of the United Nations High Commissioner for Refugees* (E/1992/May 1992), p. 56.

8. Ibid.

9. This strategy is outlined in the first UNHCR biennial report, *The State of the World's Refugees: The Challenge of Protection* (New York: Viking-Penguin, 1993). See also Office of the United Nations High Commissioner for Refugees, Inter-Office Memorandum No. 78/92, *The Report of the UNHCR Working Group on International Protection* (Geneva: UNHCR, July 31, 1992).

10. Author's interviews with ICRC staff in Geneva, April 1993.

11. For general background, see Leon Gordenker, *Refugees in International Politics* (New York: Columbia University Press, 1987).

12. Up to 1992, the Office for Research and the Collection of Information (ORCI) had primary responsibility for early warning. Its functions have been divided between the Political and the Humanitarian Affairs Departments, but no one office has been given responsibility for early warning. For background, see the UN Joint Inspection Unit report (A/45/649 and the secretary-general's comments in Add. 1), 1990; and B. G. Ramcharan, *The International Law and Practice of Early Warning and Preventive Diplomacy: The Emerging Global Watch* (Dordrecht: Martinus Nijhoff, 1991).

13. The need for effective early warning has been called for by numerous analysts. See, for example, Leon Gordenker, "Early Warning of Refugee Incidents," in Gil Loescher and Laila Monahan, eds., *Refugees and International Relations* (Oxford: Clarendon Press, 1989), pp. 355–72; and K. Rupesinghe and M. Kuroda, eds., *Early Warning and Conflict Resolution* (New York: St. Martin's Press, 1992).

14. Following discussions at the February 1993 Inter-Agency Standing Committee of the Department of Humanitarian Affairs (DHA), an interagency consultation mechanism for reviewing early warning information of refugee flows and other mass population displacements was established under the aegis of DHA.

15. See Roberta Cohen, *Introducing Refugee Issues into the United Nations Human Rights Agenda* (Washington, D.C.: Refugee Policy Group, 1990); and *United Nations Human Rights Bodies: An Agenda for Humanitarian Action* (Washington, D.C.: Refugee Policy Group, 1992).

16. Francis Deng, *Comprehensive Study on the Human Rights Issues Related to Internally Displaced Persons* (Geneva: United Nations, 1993).

17. UN General Assembly Resolution 46/59, December 1991. The Security Council has recently emphasized the importance of humanitarian concerns in conflict situations and recommended that the humanitarian dimension be incorporated into the planning and dispatching of fact-finding missions.

18. For a good general background to many of the problems, see Kevin M. Cahill, M.D., ed., *A Framework for Survival: Health, Human Rights, and Humanitarian Assistance in Conflicts and Disasters* (New York: Basic Books and the Council on Foreign Relations, 1993); and Larry Minear, Thomas Weiss, and Kurt Campbell, *Humanitarianism and War: Learning the Lessons from Recent Armed Conflicts*, Occasional Paper 8 (Providence, R.I.: Watson Institute for International Studies, Brown University, 1991).

19. See Krister Eduards, Gunnar Rosen, and Robert Rossborough, *Responding to Emergencies: The Role of the UN in Emergencies and Ad Hoc Operations* (Stockholm: The Nordic UN Project, September 1990); and Erskine Childers and Brian Urquhart, *Strengthening International Response to Humanitarian Emergencies* (New York: Ford Foundation, 1991).

20. For a useful background, see Jan Eliasson, "The World Response to Humanitarian Emergencies," in Cahill, ed., op. cit., pp.308–18; and Jacques Cuenod, "Coordinating United Nations Humanitarian Assistance," *RPG Focus* (Washington, D.C.: Refugee Policy Group, June 1993).

21. UN General Assembly Resolution A/Res/46–182, December 19, 1991.

22. See Anthony Lake and contributors, *After the Wars: Reconstruction in Afghanistan, Indochina, Central America, Southern Africa, and the Horn of Africa* (New Brunswick, N.J.: Transaction Publishers, 1991), pp. 23–26.

23. See, for example, Alan Dowty, *Closed Borders: The Contemporary Assault on Freedom of Movement* (New Haven, Conn.: Yale University Press, 1987); Aristide Zolberg, Astri Suhrke, and Sergio Aguayo, *Escape from Violence: Conflict and the Refugee Crisis in the Developing World* (New York: Oxford University Press, 1989); and Peter Koehn, *Refugees from Revolution: U.S. Policy and Third World Migration* (Boulder, Colo.: Westview Press, 1991).

24. For further elaboration on several of these points, see Astri Suhrke, *Towards a Comprehensive Refugee Policy: Conflict and Refugees in the Post-Cold War World* (Geneva: ILO–UNHCR, May 1992).

CHAPTER 8

1. WHO Constitution, *U.S. Treaties and Other International Acts, Series 1808.*

2. J. C. Snyder, "Public Health in the USA," in John Walton, Paul B. Brown, and Ronald Bradley Scott, eds., *The Oxford Companion to Medicine*, vol. 2 (New York: Oxford University Press, 1986), pp. 1171–79; Karen A. Mingst, "The United States and the World Health Organization," in Margaret P. Karns and Karen A. Mingst, *The United States and Multilateral Institutions* (London and New York: Routledge, 1990), pp. 205–9.

3. Allyn Lise Taylor, "Making the World Health Organization Work: A Legal Framework for Universal Access to the Conditions for Health," *American Journal of Law & Medicine* 18, no. 4 (1992), p. 336; Johan Galtung, "A Typology of United Nations Organisations," in David Pitt and Thomas Weiss, eds., *The Nature of United Nations Bureaucracies* (London: Croom Helm, 1986), pp. 72–73.

4. Taylor, op. cit., p. 343. See also pp. 325–31 for a discussion of legal aspects of the WHO "health for all" program that is treated below.

5. Kelley Lee and Gill Walt, "What role of WHO in the 1990s," *Health Policy and Planning* 7, no. 4 (1992), p. 389.

6. The director-general reports to the World Health Assembly and to the United Nations. These reports are titled "The Work of WHO, 1980–81 [etc.]: Biennial Report of the Director-General to the World Health Assembly and to the United Nations." The normative comments in the reports are entirely a matter of the director-general's discretion; thus they provide insight into the director-general's understanding of his organizational role.

7. Ibid., passim; Lee and Walt, op. cit., p. 389.

8. WHO, "The Work of WHO, 1980–81," p. xv.

9. WHO Document EB/87/1991/REC/2, p. 19.

10. United States Government, Report by the President to Congress for the Year 1991, *United States Participation in the United Nations* (Washington, D.C.: Government Printing Office, 1992), p. 224. (Hereafter cited as *President's Report.*)

11. Harold K. Jacobson, "WHO: Medicine, Regionalism, and Managed Politics," in Robert W. Cox and Harold K. Jacobson, *The Anatomy of Influence* (New Haven and London: Yale University Press, 1974), p. 215. The painstaking research that underlies Jacobson's article has not been replicated by other scholars, nor is there an extensive body of scholarly writing about the World Health Organization. Consequently, the estimate made here relies on fragmentary data and personal impressions. Moreover, in view of the importance of biomedical and public health professionals in the management of WHO, Jacobson's reliance on a model of international organization that gives primary importance to states as actors might well have to be modified. His work does, however, point to "subsystem" factors as important in understanding WHO.

12. Ibid., pp. 177–78.

13. WHO Document PB/94–95, "Proposed Programme Budget for the Financial Period 1994–95." These proposals were published in 1992 for use at the 1993 World Health Assembly, where they were the basis of the final decisions. WHO's forward planning is exceptional among the international agencies.

14. Ibid., p. A1.

15. Ibid., p. x.

16. Lawrence K. Altman, "U.S. Quizzes W.H.O. on Abortion Pill," *New York Times*, April 7, 1991, p. 8.

17. Mingst, op. cit., p. 216. I am also indebted to Professor Mingst's article for insights and information used in the rest of this section.

18. WHO Constitution, Article 2.

19. For a brief description of this system and its development, see Peter R. Baehr and Leon Gordenker, *The United Nations in the 1990s* (New York: St. Martin's Press, 1992), Chapter 7.

20. World Bank, *World Development Report 1993: Investing in Health* (Washington, D.C.: World Bank, 1993), pp. 165–66.

21. For a more extended discussion of these and related issues regarding the UN system, see Douglas Williams, *The Specialized Agencies and the United Nations: The System in Crisis* (London: C. Hurst, 1987).

22. WHO Document PB/94–95, op. cit., p. A1. The income from UNDP is sharply down, partly as a result of the new treatment of overhead costs. The World Bank group is not treated for this purpose as part of the UN system.

23. The World Bank asserts that major problems exist with national health services and recommends far-reaching reorganization (World Bank, op. cit., pp. 3–4).

24. The early work on AIDS is authoritatively sketched in Mirko D. Grmek, *History of AIDS: Emergence and Origin of a Modern Pandemic* (Princeton, N.J.: Princeton University Press, 1990).

25. A journalistic treatment that highlights the sharpness of the controversy is Randy Shilts, *And the Band Played On* (New York: Penguin, 1987). CDC has reported that 3 percent of all AIDS cases in the United States are attributable to blood products (*AIDS Weekly Surveillance Report*, June 6, 1988).

26. For details, see a well-informed series of articles by Lawrence K. Altman in the *New York Times*: "U.S. Moves to Replace Japanese Head of W.H.O.," December 20, 1992, p. 1; "U.S. Set Back in Vote on W.H.O. Chief," January 21, 1993, p. 8; and "Embattled Japanese Doctor Retains W.H.O. Post," May 6, 1993, p. 5.

27. Taylor, op. cit., pp. 336–38.

28. The *President's Report*, op. cit., devotes twelve paragraphs to financial and budgetary issues (pp. 258–60), in contrast to three paragraphs for AIDS and one short paragraph each for cholera and tuberculosis. (pp. 256–57).

29. Frances Williams, "WHO Vote Unlikely to Calm Criticism," *Financial Times*, March 30, 1993.

30. Taylor, op. cit., p. 340 and footnote 259.

31. The official in charge of this bureau is no longer a U.S. national. The senior American, according to the *President's Report*, op. cit., p. 254, is the assistant director-general for communicable diseases.

32. Cf. Paul Streeten, "The United Nations: Unhappy Family," in Pitt and Weiss, eds., op. cit., pp. 189–90.

33. Williams, op. cit., p. 34.

CHAPTER 9

1. See, for example, Don V. Roberts, *Transactions* 18, no. 1/GEN (November 1991).

2. "Initial financial commitments, financial flows and arrangements to give effect to the decisions of the United Nations Conference on Environment and Development from all available funding sources and mechanisms," E/CN.17/1993/L.5/Rev.1, June 23, 1993, paragraph 3.

3. In the House of Representatives, Representative John Porter (R–Ill.) has introduced legislation that would create a "Rio Commission," made up of eight members of Congress and three executive-branch officials, to monitor U.S. and international progress toward the goals established at UNCED.

4. A joint House–Senate resolution, House Joint Resolution 166, urging many of these steps, was introduced in the 103d Congress by Representative Nancy Pelosi (D–Calif.) and Senator Claiborne Pell (D–R.I.).

CHAPTER 10

1. *Financinag an Effective United Nations: A Report of the Independent Advisory Group on U.N. Financing* (New York: Ford Foundation, 1993).

2. The Humanitarianism and War project is a joint undertaking of the Thomas J. Watson Institute for International Studies at Brown University, which is located in Providence, Rhode Island, and the Refugee Policy Group, which is based in Washington, D.C. The project codirectors are Thomas G. Weiss and Larry Minear. An interim report on this three-year study, written by Minear, can be found in Kevin M. Cahill, M.D., ed., *A Framework for Survival: Health, Human Rights, and Humanitarian Assistance in Conflicts and Disasters* (New York: Basic Books and The Council on Foreign Relations, 1993). By all accounts, valuable work, which I have not been able to survey, is also being done by the Disaster Management team at Intertect in Dallas; the Development Studies Association of the United Kingdom and Ireland; Queen Elizabeth House at Oxford; the UN Research Institute for Social Development in Geneva; and the underfunded Central Evaluation Unit at UNHCR.

3. Larry Minear makes this same point in his essay "Making the Humanitarian System Work Better," in Cahill, ed., op. cit. pp. 234–56.

4. This phrase is found in Article 39 of the UN Charter.

INDEX

ABOUT THE AUTHORS

MORRIS B. ABRAM was the United States permanent representative to the United Nations and other international organizations in Geneva from 1989 to 1993. Ambassador Abram's long-standing involvement with human and civil rights began as a member of the U.S. prosecution team at the International Military Tribunal at Nuremburg (1946). As a practicing attorney, he argued the landmark "one-man, one-vote" voting rights case before the U.S. Supreme Court. He was president of Brandeis University from 1968 to 1970. In addition, he was co-chairman, planning session, the White House Conference on Civil Rights (1965); vice-chairman, U.S. Commission on Civil Rights (1984–86); and chairman, the National Conference on Soviet Jewry (1983–88). Ambassador Abram is currently the chairman of United Nations Watch, a Geneva-based organization that promotes the balanced, fair, and honest application of the charter principles of the United Nations within the Secretariat and other UN bodies, agencies, and commissions.

BARRY M. BLECHMAN is chairman of the Henry L. Stimson Center, a nonprofit research organization in Washington, D.C., which he founded with Michael Krepon in 1989. In 1977, he was appointed assistant director of the U.S. Arms Control and Disarmament Agency. He has published many works on defense issues, including the widely respected study of politico-military operations, *Force Without War*, as well as *U.S. Security in the Twenty-first Century*; *Silent Partner: West Germany and Arms Control*; and, most recently, the Twentieth Century Fund study *The Politics of National Defense*. He has taught at The Johns Hopkins University, Georgetown University, and the University of Michigan.

ROGER A. COATE is associate professor of international organization at the University of South Carolina. He is president of the International Organization Section of the International Studies Association, and is the editor of the Academic Council on the United Nations System's new journal, *Global Governance: A Review of Multilateralism and International*

Organizations. He was the United Nations Fellow in the United Nations' Centre for Human Rights in Geneva in 1990. He was a staff member of the U.S. Secretary of State's Monitoring Panel on UNESCO during the United States' withdrawal from that organization in 1984. Among his recent publications are *The Challenge of Relevance: The United Nations in a Changing World Environment* (with Donald Puchala); *Unilateralism, Ideology and United States Foreign Policy: The U.S. in and out of UNESCO;* and *The Power of Human Needs in World Society* (with Jerel Rosati).

LEON GORDENKER is professor emeritus of politics at Princeton University and senior research political scientist at Princeton's Center of International Studies. He has observed and studied international organization since the end of World War II and was among the first Americans to join the UN Secretariat, where he worked for eight years. In addition to his work at Princeton, he has taught at other universities in the United States, Africa, and Europe. Among his publications are *The United Nations in the 1990s* (with P. R. Baehr); *The Challenging Role of the UN Secretary-General* (with Benjamin Rivlin); *Soldiers, Peacekeepers and Disasters* (with Thomas G. Weiss); *Refugees in World Politics; International Aid and National Decisions; The United Nations in International Politics;* and *The UN Secretary-General and the Maintenance of Peace.*

THOMAS W. GRAHAM is senior program adviser for international security at the Rockefeller Foundation in New York City. Mr. Graham received his Ph.D. from the Massachusetts Institute of Technology in 1983. He has worked on nuclear nonproliferation for many years, including at the U.S. Arms Control and Disarmament Agency (1977– 81) and as a consultant to the Lawrence Livermore National Laboratory (1981–present). He is the coeditor, with David Goldfischer, of *Nuclear Deterrence and Global Security in Transition,* as well as the author of numerous articles.

JAMES F. LEONARD is executive director of the Washington Council on Non-Proliferation. He was deputy chief of mission at the U.S. Mission to the United Nations from 1977 to 1979, and deputy special negotiator for the Middle East peace negotiations from 1979 to 1981. He also is a former president of the United Nations Association of the USA. Ambassador Leonard served in the Arms Control and Disarmament Agency as assistant director and ambassador on the U.S. Delegation to the Geneva Disarmament Committee from 1969 to 1973. He spent more than twenty years as a foreign service officer, serving overseas in Damascus, Moscow, Paris, and Taipei.

GIL LOESCHER is professor of international relations at the University of Notre Dame. He also is a member of the advisory board to the UN High Commissioner for Refugees' biennial report, *The State of the World's Refugees*. During 1991, he was research associate at The International Institute for Strategic Studies in London, where he wrote *Refugee Movements and International Security* (Adelphi Paper #268). He is the coauthor and coeditor of several publications, including *Calculated Kindness: Refugees and America's Half Open Door, 1945 to the Present*; *Refugees and International Relations*; and, most recently, the Twentieth Century Fund book *Beyond Charity: International Cooperation and the Global Refugee Crisis*. He is currently working on a book on internally displaced peoples and international intervention in the post–cold war era.

KATHRYN G. SESSIONS is senior policy analyst in the Washington office of the United Nations Association of the USA, a leading center of policy research and public outreach on the United Nations and multilateral issues. At UNA-USA, Ms. Sessions monitors policy developments in Washington, does research and writing for the association, and works to promote UNA-USA's perspectives and ideas within the policymaking community. She represented UNA-USA at the 1992 United Nations Conference on Environment and Development in Rio de Janeiro, and she served as an official observer on the U.S. delegation to the UNCED negotiations. She was a nongovernmental representative on the U.S. delegation to the June 1993 meeting of the UN Commission on Sustainable Development.

RONALD I. SPIERS was under secretary-general of the United Nations for political affairs from 1989 to 1992. In that position, he was the senior American in the United Nations. Previously, Mr. Spiers served in a wide variety of assignments in the United States Foreign Service from 1954 until his retirement in 1989. He was assistant secretary of state for politico-military affairs from 1969 to 1973 and assistant secretary of state for intelligence and research from 1980 to 1981. He was under secretary of state for management from 1983 to 1989. He served overseas as American minister in London, as the first American ambassador to the Bahamas, and as the U.S. ambassador to both Turkey and Pakistan. He was awarded the personal rank of career ambassador by President Reagan in 1984.

E. ZELL STEEVER works in the Office of Strategic Initiatives of the United States Army Corps of Engineers, where he is responsible for developing environmental and sustainable development policy. He previously served as a senior policy adviser to the United States UNCED Coordination Center, the U.S. State Department, and as a member of the U.S. delegation to the 1992 UN Conference on Environment and Development in Rio de Janeiro as well as to its preparatory meetings. At the Rio conference, he was the U.S. negotiator and issue coordinator for several chapters of Agenda 21. Prior to joining the Corps of Engineers, he worked in the U.S. Environmental Protection Agency's Office of Research and Development and on water and wetlands policy issues for the President's Council on Environmental Quality.